# DEVELOPING
# EXPERTISE AS
# A SENCo

## LEADING INCLUSIVE PRACTICE

To order our books please go to our website www.criticalpublishing.com or contact our distributor Ingram Publisher Services, telephone 01752 202301 or email IPSUK.orders@ingramcontent.com. Details of bulk order discounts can be found at www.criticalpublishing.com/delivery-information.

Our titles are also available in electronic format: for individual use via our website and for libraries and other institutions from all the major ebook platforms.

CRITICAL
PUBLISHING

# DEVELOPING YOUR EXPERTISE AS A SENCo

## LEADING INCLUSIVE PRACTICE

Edited by Helen Knowler, Hazel Richards
and Stephanie Brewster

First published in 2023 by Critical Publishing Ltd

British Library Cataloguing in Publication Data
A CIP record for this book is available from the British Library

ISBN: 978-1-915080-86-8

This book is also available in the following e-book formats:

EPUB ISBN: 978-1-915080-87-5
Adobe e-book ISBN: 978-1-915080-88-2

Text design by Greensplash
Cover design by Out of House Limited
Project management by Newgen Publishing UK


Critical Publishing
3 Connaught Road
St Albans
AL3 5RX

www.criticalpublishing.com

Printed on FSC accredited paper

# Contents

*Dedications*                                                    vii

*About the book editors*                                        viii

*About the authors*                                              ix

*Acknowledgements*                                               xi

Introduction                                                      1

**Part 1   Examining the SENCo role**

**1**   The role of the SENCo: an essential or an extra?          9
        *Pauline Brewin and Helen Knowler*

**2**   SENCo professional identity and development              21
        *Hazel Richards*

**3**   Pedagogy, inclusion and the SENCo's role                 35
        *Tunde Rozsahegyi and Mike Lambert*

**4**   The SENCo as advocate: speaking up and speaking out      47
        *Kitty Huthwaite and Laura Howieson*

**5**   SENCos engaging with theory                              59
        *Liz Done*

**Part 2   The SENCo at work**

**6**   The SENCo role across ages and settings                  73
        *Hazel Richards, Selena Hall, Jennifer Wells and Zoe Stuart*

**7**   Working with children and young people experiencing additional challenges   91
        *Catherine Lamond*

**8**   Working with parents                                               105
       *Peter Harwood and Zoe Stuart*

**9**   Working with other professionals                                   119
       *Stephanie Brewster*

**10**  Critical reflection in professional practice                       133
       *Hazel Richards and Alicja Legarska*

**11**  SENCos using data to support inclusive practice                    147
       *Laura Howieson, Kitty Huthwaite and Helen Knowler*

**12**  Improving outcomes through evidence-based practice and
       practitioner enquiry                                               159
       *Stephanie Brewster*

       Conclusion                                                          173

       *Acronym list*                                                      179

       *Index*                                                             181

# Dedications

*To my academic sisters for inspiration, love and care – Tasnim, Sarah and Sana. And Jeff for all your support.*

Helen

*For Ian and Isla – you have so often been my catalyst and I am so proud of the adults you continue to become – despite the odds.*

Hazel

*To those who strive relentlessly for better education for all children and young people around the world.*

Stephanie

# About the book editors

**Helen Knowler** is a qualified teacher who has worked in the field of social, emotional and mental health needs for over three decades. Following completion of her master's degree she became a lecturer in higher education and has worked at the Universities of Plymouth, Bristol, Exeter and Wolverhampton. She now leads the Eugenics Legacy Education Project at University College London. Helen's expertise relates to educational exclusion and specifically illegal and hidden exclusion. She is deeply committed to social justice both in her teaching and in research practice and enjoys collaboration with teachers, parents and families, education leaders and supporting organisations that help to prevent permanent exclusion from school.

**Hazel Richards** is an HCPC registered speech and language therapist. She worked in the NHS with children with complex needs for over 20 years, in mainstream and specialist settings and in CAMHS. Her doctoral studies investigated SENCo perceptions of EHC plan implementation, after which she worked as a senior lecturer for the Department for Children and Families, University of Worcester, the special educational needs, disability, and inclusion studies course at the University of Wolverhampton, and now as a senior lecturer in speech and language therapy at Birmingham City University. She wrote and led a NASENCo module entitled *'Improving SEN outcomes through evidence-based practice'* and is passionate about advocating for, supporting, and empowering the agency of SENCos.

**Stephanie Brewster** started out as a speech and language therapist and spent 15 years working in various health and education settings with both children and adults with significant communication needs. A key part of this was supporting pre-registration students on placement and contributing to continuing professional development within the profession. After completing her doctorate Stephanie worked in higher education, engaged in teaching, research and scholarship around disability and diversity. She is currently a senior lecturer at the University of Wolverhampton, in the Special Educational Needs, Disability and Inclusion Studies department, working predominantly with postgraduate learners. She has been involved with the National Award for SENCos for a number of years, and is actively involved in supporting our disabled university students.

# About the authors

**Pauline Brewin** started her teaching career in 1996 in London and has since taught in primary education across different schools, taking on various roles. She has led English provision across the primary phase, worked alongside SENCos supporting inclusion and special educational needs provision, delivered CPD and has been an active part of leadership teams throughout her career.

**Liz Done** is a Visiting Fellow at the University of Exeter and now supervises doctoral students in the University of Plymouth's Institute of Education, specialising in inclusion and post-structuralist theory. She supported a NASENCo programme for several years after returning from Sudan, where she was a professor of health psychology. Liz has published widely on inclusion-related issues and is editor of a collected works on exclusionary pressures in education internationally.

**Selena Hall** is a lecturer within higher education and shares her academic and practice-based experiences surrounding early childhood studies. Selena continues to engage with professionals in the early childhood sector to collaborate, research and present on contemporary themes and topics in this exhilarating subject area. Overall, this then allows the opportunity to support and contribute to students' academic, professional and personal growth, which is a key motivation.

**Peter Harwood** is a senior lecturer in education and inclusion studies at the University of Wolverhampton with many years' experience as a teacher, leader, senior manager and commissioner. He was Head of Special Educational Needs with responsibility for statutory assessment and commissioning in two West Midlands local authorities.

**Laura Howieson** is an experienced inclusion lead, SENCo and pastoral lead and has worked in a variety of settings. Currently working in an all-through multi-academy trust, her passion is to embed truly inclusive practice into every classroom. Previously, as a specialist leader in education for inclusion, she worked with schools to use contextual knowledge about pupils to think holistically and support their learning effectively.

**Kitty Huthwaite** works as an associate tutor and course co-ordinator on Exeter University's SENCo Award and as a consultant specialist teacher with a particular interest in autism and barriers to literacy. Kitty's previous research involved identifying ways to help children to develop collaborative skills while working on Lego models and to transfer these to the context of science experiments in school. She is currently involved in advising on and monitoring special needs courses that develop the knowledge and understanding of prisoners who work as peer mentors.

**Mike Lambert** is a writer, researcher and the author of numerous books. After varied work as a teacher and project leader in the UK and elsewhere, he was principal lecturer in education at the University of Wolverhampton, England. He has a particular interest in the teaching of students with disabilities and has worked internationally for voluntary organisations in this field. His PhD thesis for the University of Warwick was a grounded-theory examination of pedagogy for gifted students.

**Catherine Lamond** is a senior lecturer in special education needs, disability and inclusion studies within the School of Education at the University of Wolverhampton, teaching in the areas of reflective practice, inclusion and specific learning difficulties. She taught in primary schools in England and Ireland, developing a particular interest in supporting children with additional needs. Her research interests focus on children and young people in care, and aspirations for care-leavers.

**Alicja Legarska** is Head of English as an additional language (EAL) at a secondary school, an EAL advisory teacher and Chair of the EAL Academic Community Group. As a professional, she is passionate about developing teaching and learning, training and strategies when working with EAL learners. Having completed the National Award, Alicja is a qualified aspiring SENCo looking to develop teaching and learning to support inclusion within secondary schools.

**Tunde Rozsahegyi** is a senior lecturer in special educational needs, disability and inclusion studies at the University of Wolverhampton. Previously, she trained and worked as a 'conductor' – a specialist educator of disabled children and adults through conductive education in Hungary, then played a key role in establishing the National Institute for Conductive Education in Birmingham, UK. Tunde has a strong interest in inclusive early education and support for children with additional development needs and has written a range of material on this topic.

**Zoe Stuart** is a senior lecturer in postgraduate taught provision (SEND) at the University of Wolverhampton and leads SEND education across secondary initial teacher training. She qualified as a secondary science teacher in 2009 and has worked in mainstream as well as special education settings as both a classroom teacher and as a middle leader.

**Jennifer Wells** is currently programme leader for the MA Education programme at the University of Wolverhampton and has had a long and varied career teaching English and literacy in a range of contexts including to young adults with special educational needs. She was Head of English at a large further education college before moving to a role as a teacher educator and programme leader for a foundation degree in children and young people with teaching assistant/early years/SEND pathways.

# Acknowledgements

We are indebted to the many people who gave generously of their time and expertise to produce this book. First, we would like to acknowledge the contribution of all the authors who delivered timely and well-researched chapters. Their professionalism and willingness to meet deadlines and respond to the comments of the reviewers made editing this book a pleasure.

Particular thanks go to the SENCos, students and colleagues who provided the case studies.

We would also like to acknowledge the generosity of Johanna Fitzgerald for permission to use the Conceptual Model of the SENCo Role, which emerged from research with SENCos and school leaders in the Irish context (see Figure 1.1, Chapter 1).

Our thanks also go to our respective institutions: the Department of Speech and Language Therapy, Faculty of Health, Education and Life Sciences, Birmingham City University (Hazel); the Arena Centre for Research-based Education at University College London (Helen); and the Department for Special Educational Needs, Disability and Inclusion Studies at the University of Wolverhampton (Stephanie).

Thanks also go to our respective families and friends, who have provided much needed moral support, understanding and encouragement throughout.

We would like to thank Julia Morris and Lily Harrison at Critical Publishing who have provided unfailingly wise and responsive guidance, and also colleagues in the field who reviewed the book at various stages of development.

Finally, we would like to thank the children and young people and their families who continue to inspire us with their determination, resilience and wonderful uniqueness.

# Introduction

Unlike roles related to general leadership of teaching and learning in schools, the Special Educational Needs Co-ordinator (SENCo) role and its intended scope is outlined in the Special Educational Needs and Disability (SEND) Code of Practice (DfE and DoH, 2015). This might lead us to assume that the remit of the role is uncontentious. However, as many authors such as Curran (2019), Dobson (2023) and Richards (2022) have shown, how and why SENCos do their work is varied and often highly context specific. Many aspects of a SENCo's practice will be led by the size of their school, the prevalence of SEND, staff experience and engagement and the school's ethos. This variability means that it can be hard to ascertain how to best prepare SENCos for their day-to-day work and strategy, and the role flexibility that has developed since its inception in 1994 has meant that a 'one-size-fits-all' model of the role is almost impossible (if not undesirable) to establish. As Esposito and Carroll (2019) outline, additional training and qualifications are an essential dimension of ensuring high-quality provision so that all children identified as having SEND are supported to achieve and thrive in their setting. This prompts critical questions related to SENCo professional identity and the ways that SENCos come to develop expertise in their role in the day-to-day aspects of their work and when engaged in strategic leadership and change management.

The flexibility of the role, while problematic in some senses, offers a tremendous opportunity for teaching professionals to lead on areas of expertise that are relevant to their own context. It means that there are many opportunities for creative involvement in learning within the SENCo role, and for those of us interested in SENCo learning, professional development is an engaging dimension of their work. This book has been developed to support SENCos and those in related roles who are actively engaged in professional learning, at whatever stage of their career. This could relate to a formal qualification that is mandatory or qualifications pursued for personal goals or for school-based professional learning programmes. The book aims to connect concepts of learning with professional identity and expertise. In doing so, it supports the raising of the professional status of the SENCo and argues that it is crucial that SENCos are given time to focus on their own learning and leadership as they work to ensure that their professional credibility is developed ethically and with well-being in mind.

The book aims to develop SENCos' learning, critical thinking and interrogation skills. It is an edited text in which each chapter critiques current theories of SEND, inclusive education, legislation, policy and research, and offers tangible examples of how these critiques transfer into professional practice. The book is a collaboration by a multidisciplinary team, which has allowed us to embrace sociological, ecological, educational and post-modern perspectives on SENCos' work. This will encourage new lines of thinking about what counts as 'quality' when leading on SEND provision and offer space to think about alternative possibilities when (as often happens) we reach professional cul-de- sacs in our approaches to intervention and support.

Specifically, this book will support SENCos to:

- develop their skills of critical reflection, research literacy, engagement with data and awareness of ethical issues;

- develop their knowledge and skills so that they can craft their professional identities as advocates for children and young people with SEND;

- galvanise change in their own context, including having difficult and respectful conversations about SEND provision and the outcomes for learners;

- actively develop leadership skills that enable SENCos to identify barriers to participation and engagement and to make decisions that support ethical and reflective school improvement.

The book is divided into two parts to structure learning around core dimensions of professional learning for SENCos. Part 1 stimulates reflection around the SENCo role itself because understanding professional identity and how this relates to confidence and credibility within the role is vital if SENCos are to engage and thrive with the leadership dimensions now required and outlined in the SEND Code of Practice (DfE and DoH, 2015). Part 2 emphasises key skills required to do the SENCo role successfully. Through developing their own toolbox – sources of information, people to ask – SENCos become better equipped to respond to new situations. But in our experience of supporting SENCos, we often hear them expressing feelings of challenge or inadequacy because they do not feel 'expert enough'. We think this is the wrong way to think about the role, and instead this book supports the idea that a SENCo working with diverse groups of children, young people and adults will develop ease and familiarity with uncertainty – and it is this ability that is important to nurture and explore.

Our intention is that the book becomes a guide at any stage of the reader's career. It can be read as a whole – our chapter structure offers a logical route through the exploration of key issues we argue are essential for SENCos' learning. The book can also be read chapter by chapter. A single chapter can be a catalyst for prompting further learning if the content is new or unfamiliar or relates to a recent concern in context. An individual chapter can also be read as a reflective guide to support SENCos to think about aspects of their work that might benefit from further learning and/or qualifications. Specific chapters could be used in the design of continuing professional development (CPD) with colleagues and engagement with parents, for example, reading chapters together and organising discussion activities about the issues raised. This can help to support cohesion around understandings of language, process and quality – and provide an important opportunity for the school community to ask questions about school ethos and approaches to SEND provision. We use a range of pedagogical tools in each chapter; they offer a rich source of activities for learning and support our aim for the text to be both engaging and accessible. The chapters follow a broadly common structure and contain features indicated by icons, starting with a chapter map identifying the main themes in a graphic way.

**Table 0.1** *Icon chart*

| | |
|---|---|
| ⊚ | **Chapter objectives** clearly lay out what you will learn from the chapter. |
| 🏁 | **Starting points** prompt reflection on your current knowledge. |
| ⊙ | **Critical questions** at various points stimulate consideration on your own values, beliefs and practices. |
| 🎐 | **Case studies** demonstrate how ideas, theories and issues play out in the 'real world'. |
| 🎏 | **Implications for the SENCo role, identity and practice**: discussion of key issues. |
| 📝 | **Chapter summary** |
| 📖 | **Further reading** details texts and resources to progress your knowledge. |
| 📚 | **References** provide details of the texts cited in the chapter |

In the first chapter of the book, Pauline Brewin and Helen Knowler explore the development of the SENCo role, asking critical questions about the status of the SENCo in contemporary settings. The authors debate the requirement for 'all teachers to be teachers of SEND' and the tension that this statement engenders – if a SENCo is ultimately effective, do they remove the requirement for their role? This links into Hazel Richards' exploration of professional identity in Chapter 2. Hazel unpacks the challenges that SENCos face as they are learning in the role and offers tangible tools for reflection, suggesting how they can thrive and enjoy well-being in their role. In Chapter 3, Tunde Rozsahegyi and Mike Lambert examine an often underexplored aspect of SENCos' work – that of expertise in inclusive pedagogy. They invite serious consideration of the link between pedagogy and outcomes for learners as an opportunity for SENCos to reframe their role from administrators towards experts in inclusive teaching and learning. Developing the reframing of the SENCo, in Chapter 4 Kitty Huthwaite and Laura Howieson explore the challenges of having difficult conversations. They consider how SENCos can develop advocacy leadership (Anderson, 2009) as part of their everyday work, so that relationships and interventions are rooted in social justice frameworks – something we would argue aligns with wider calls for the development of inclusive schools. Finally in this part of the book, in Chapter 5 Liz Done explores SENCo engagement with theory. Liz persuasively argues that appreciation of theory can empower practitioners to fulfil their role in advocating for the rights of children and young people with disabilities and additional needs to equitable educational opportunities.

Part 2 begins with an important consideration of the scope of the SENCo role across age phases and settings in Chapter 6. Hazel Richards, Selena Hall, Jennifer Wells and Zoe Stuart consider the distinctive concerns associated with specific contexts and argue for greater recognition of these different dimensions in the SENCo role. They argue that while there is some core specificity around the SENCo role, there are also differences that need to be considered when thinking about training, induction, learning and development. In Chapter 7, Catherine Lamond models a critical theoretical approach to thinking about adverse childhood experiences (ACEs) and the implications for the SENCo leading on provision. She highlights the importance of considering SEND within the context of intersectionality and offers some practical examples of the ways settings can develop a trauma-informed approach to SEND provision. Working with parents and carers (the theme of Chapter 8) is universally agreed as a vital dimension of a SENCo's work and yet many SENCos have little time to reflect deeply on this strand of their work. Peter Harwood and Zoe Stuart explore the gap between policy rhetoric and context practicalities when working with parents and carers and offer resources that support person-centred authentic engagement with parents and carers to avoid the 'battle' metaphor that is often described in the research literature. In Chapter 9, Stephanie Brewster outlines key critiques of models of professional collaboration. This prompts important reflection on the ways that SENCos see themselves as leaders within teams within and beyond their school settings. Next, in Chapter 10, Hazel Richards and Alicja Legarska focus on the importance of critical reflection for professional learning and development. They offer critical incident analysis (Tripp, 1998) as a tool for SENCos that can be used to support their own learning and ways of evidencing the efficacy of interventions in their setting. In Chapter 11, Laura Howieson, Kitty Huthwaite and Helen Knowler outline key skills in the understanding and use of data as part of the SENCo role. Schools are extremely data-rich, and using data ethically to benefit pupils and their parents, carers and families requires critical reflection and dialogue. They argue that strong data literacy skills are vital to advocate for the best possible outcomes for learners. Finally, in Chapter 12, Stephanie Brewster explores the role of evidence-informed practice, drawing together threads from Chapters 6–11. She argues that an orientation towards practitioner enquiry, reflection and criticality can enhance the development of inclusive practices in schools and cements our view that the SENCo is a learner. This is significant because this disposition, we would argue, offers a productive and creative engagement with the challenges and barriers that SENCos experience in their daily work.

We hope that this book offers useful ideas, new inspiration and some tools to stimulate challenging conversations and transform practice. Our intention is to promote the professional credibility and status of SENCos amid the choppy waters of SEND policymaking in England. By embracing development and learning, we hope that SENCos experience change positively in their settings. We recognise the commitment and dedication that SENCos bring to their work, and we hope that this book becomes a useful resource as they face new tensions and dilemmas.

# References ⧫

Anderson, G (2009) *Advocacy Leadership: Towards a Post-Reform Agenda in Education*. New York: Routledge.

Curran, H (2019) 'The SEND Code of Practice Has Given Me Clout': A Phenomenological Study Illustrating How SENCos Managed the Introduction of the SEND Reforms. *British Journal of Special Education*, 46(1): 76–93.

Department for Education (DfE) and Department of Health (DoH) (2015) *Special Educational Needs and Disability Code of Practice: 0 to 25 Years.* [online] Available at: https://assets.publishing. service.gov.uk/government/uploads/system/uploads/attachment_data/file/398815/SEND_ Code_of_Practice_January_2015.pdf (accessed 8 June 2023).

Dobson, G (2023) The 2022 SEND Green Paper and the SENCo: More Evidence on Demographics, Qualifications, and Leadership Status. *British Journal of Special Education*, 50(2): 219–37.

Esposito, R and Carroll, C (2019) Special Educational Needs Coordinators' Practice in England 40 Years on from the Warnock Report. *Frontiers in Education*, 4: Article 75.

Richards, H (2022) 'It Was Tough Making Sure It Happened': SENCo Experience of the Reality and Risk of Education and Health Care Implementation. *Educational Review.* https://doi.org/10.1080/ 00131911.2022.2033703

Tripp, D (1998) Critical Incidents in Action Inquiry. In Shacklock, G and Smyth, J (eds) *Being Reflexive in Critical Educational and Social Research* (pp 36–49). Social Research and Educational Studies Series, 18. London: Routledge Falmer.

# Part 1 Examining the SENCo role

# 1 The role of the SENCo: an essential or an extra?

**PAULINE BREWIN AND HELEN KNOWLER**

The SENCo as advocate: beyond compliance

The historical development of the role of the SENCo

Reflecting on the role of the SENCo

The SENCo as leader

SENCo role possibilities

The SENCo role in practice

# Chapter objectives 🎯

This chapter explores the role of the Special Educational Needs Co-ordinator (SENCo). The chapter:

* tracks the historical development of the SENCo role;

* explores varied interpretations of the role, and how these constrain SENCos to go beyond compliance;

* reflects on the need for the SENCo role, balancing this with the expectation that every teacher is a teacher of special educational needs and disability (DfE and DoH, 2015; DfE, 2022b);

* considers ways the SENCo can work as an advocate through their leadership.

## STARTING POINTS 🏁

» Why did you – or do you – want to become a SENCo?

» What qualities do you think make a 'good' SENCo?

» What is the value of continuing professional learning for SENCos?

» What inspires you about the people you work with and what excites you about galvanising change in your setting?

# Introduction

The role of the SENCo has been recognised by many researchers as pivotal in developing inclusive practice within educational settings (Glazzard et al, 2019; DfE 2021). This chapter offers a review of the SENCo role and explores the current political and legislative contexts. We develop the arguments of Hallet and Hallet (2017), who suggest that SENCos should be working beyond compliance in relation to the SEND Code of Practice (CoP) (DfE and DoH, 2015) if they are to be 'levers' for inclusive practice in their settings. We suggest that inclusive leadership is a vital dimension of the SENCo role and reflect on the tensions and dilemmas of the role in practice, illustrating it through a case study example.

# Historical development of the role

Since the landmark Warnock Report (1978), perceptions of SEND in schools have evolved considerably, with a significant move towards including all children within mainstream settings, embracing the philosophy of inclusive education (Szwed, 2007; Tissot, 2013). The Education Act 1993 and the subsequent Special Educational Needs Code of Practice (DfE, 1994) recognised and outlined the statutory obligation of schools and the purpose of the SENCo as responsible for co-ordinating provision for pupils with special educational needs

(SEN). The Teacher Training Agency (1998) produced a set of National Standards for SENCos, which identified four key aspects of SEN provision requiring co-ordination:

- *Strategic direction and development of SEN provision in the school.*
- *Teaching and learning.*
- *Leading and managing staff.*
- *Efficient and effective deployment of staff and resources.*

(Layton, 2005, p 54)

These are aimed to support the development and progression of inclusion within schools. Further legislation and two subsequent iterations of the CoP (DfES, 2001; DfE and DoH, 2015) have further strengthened the role of the SENCo, which has developed over time from support for learners and developing pedagogy towards a role that is multifaceted and includes strategic leadership, administrative management and advocacy for effective provision and inclusion (Ekins, 2015; Cowne et al, 2019; Middleton and Kay, 2021). The 'all-encompassing' (Ekins, 2015) role of the SENCo is defined and outlined in the current CoP (2015) as: '*maintaining the day-to-day responsibility for the operation of SEN policy and co-ordination of specific provision made to support individual pupils with SEN, including those who have EHC plans*' (DfE and DoH, 2015, 6.88). In addition, specific key responsibilities are identified (see Table 1.1).

**Table 1.1** *Key SENCo roles and responsibilities*

| |
|---|
| A. Overseeing of day-to-day enactment of the school's SEND policy. |
| B. Co-ordinating assessment and support for children with SEND. |
| C. Liaising with the designated teacher for looked after pupils with SEND. |
| D. Advising on the graduated approach to SEND support. |
| E. Advising on the deployment of the school's delegated budget to meet resources needed to support pupils effectively. |
| F. Liaising with the parents/carers of pupils with SEND. |
| G. Liaising with the multi-professional team. |
| H. Being a key contact with external agencies, especially the local authority and its support services. |
| I. Liaising with potential next providers of education to ensure pupils with SEND and their parents/carers are fully informed about options and a smooth transition is planned. |
| J. Working with the headteacher and school governors to ensure the school meets its responsibilities regarding reasonable adjustments and access arrangements, as per the Equality Act 2010. |
| K. Ensuring the setting's record-keeping of pupils with SEND is up to date. |

(Adapted from SEND CoP (DfE and DoH, 2015, 6.90, pp 108–9))

However, the Green Paper on SEND (DfE, 2022b) identified persisting challenges relating to outcomes, navigating the SEND system and poor efficacy, suggesting that improving SEND expertise across the workforce is required.

---

### Critical questions (?)

» How are you currently able to enact the roles and responsibilities identified in the SEND CoP in your setting?

» In your setting, to what extent is every teacher a teacher of SEND?

» What factors would enhance your daily practice and support for children and young people with SEND?

---

# The SENCo role in practice

With such a wide range of responsibility, accountability and high expectations associated with the role, research has acknowledged the growing complexity and multifaceted nature of the SENCo position (Smith and Broomhead, 2019; Curran and Boddison, 2021). Complexity is further influenced by other factors such as school demographics (including location, size and number of pupils with SEND), additional roles and responsibilities held, and the cultural values and beliefs within the educational setting (Cowne et al, 2019; Middleton and Kay, 2021). Indeed, many SENCos have teaching commitments, including a class teaching role (Ekins, 2015; Fitzgerald and Radford, 2020; DfE, 2021) so it is perhaps unsurprising that research has widely reported issues relating to workload, time and status (Glazzard et al, 2019; Smith and Broomhead, 2019).

Research suggests that perceptions of the importance and position of the SENCo within many schools appear to be that it is a basic statutory role, rather than being strategic, highly valued within school leadership teams, well supported and professionally developed (Morewood, 2012; Tissot, 2013). We would argue that such a scenario creates ongoing obstacles for SENCos wanting to adopt a leadership, rather than managerial, approach. Hindrances such as incorrect assumptions about inclusion, SEND provision and pupils with diverse needs, and systemic barriers around policy and structures were, in Norwich's (2013) opinion, perhaps more driven by the standards and performance agenda than an inclusive one, although the Green Paper (DfE, 2022b) states that the government is just as ambitious for children and young people with SEND as for every other child. However, in reality, much of the work is invisible and misunderstood (Fitzgerald and Radford, 2020), with many SENCos reporting feelings of isolation, reduced professional support, and feelings of responsibility for pupils and parents beyond the operational (Curran, 2019), alongside a lack of formal recognition and status, and an absence of clarity and direction around national guidance and legal aspects of the role (Szwed, 2007; Ekins, 2015; Winwood, 2016). The role is also perceived as solitary in nature, which may have an impact on retention and well-being (Curran, 2019) (see Chapter 10).

# SENCo role possibilities

This variation in expectations and interpretation of the role, together with the complexity and challenge of responsibility and accountability, has led to the suggestion that the role is unmanageable for one person (Morewood, 2012; Curran and Boddison, 2021). Indeed, it may be better fulfilled by the secondary school model where SENCos are placed within a larger SEND team, enabling them to delegate responsibilities (DfE, 2021). In such a model, elements of the role could be more widely distributed across staff to ensure inclusive provision and practice are the responsibility of all (Fitzgerald and Radford, 2020). This coheres with the Green Paper (DfE, 2022b) that contests the current situation, where financial resource and workforce capacity is pulled to the specialist end of the system, proposing instead that there is a need for much greater consistency in how needs are identified and supported across settings and lifespan.

There is also inconsistency and debate around the SENCo as strategic leader and/or manager. Tissot (2013) and Rosen-Webb (2011) suggest that SENCos must be skilled at both. The latter often dominates, however. With tasks including the management of budgets and specialist support, administration regarding policy and legislation, and deployment of human and physical resources (Robertson, 2012), the SENCo role is often largely 'operational' due to heavy bureaucratic demands and administrative burdens (Fitzgerald and Radford, 2017). Skilled practitioners are immersed in time-consuming paperwork, meaning that valuable resources are deflected from children's learning and from developing inclusive practices (Szwed, 2007; Tissot, 2013; Glazzard et al, 2019). In recognition of this, the Green Paper (DfE, 2022b) proposed a national SEND provision system and digitised education, health and care plan (EHCP).

Strategic leadership has been argued to be an essential part of the role (Ekins, 2015) and is widely stipulated as a key factor in effective inclusive practice which directly influences the extent to which a school embraces this ethos (Florian et al, 2011). However, the debate around what strategic leadership looks like within the quest for inclusion is an interesting one. Although it has been suggested that SENCos need to be part of the senior leadership team (SLT) to influence the development of policy for whole-school SEND and inclusion (DfES, 2001; Glazzard et al, 2019) this is not mandatory (DfE and DoH, 2015), with many being in middle management positions (Glazzard et al, 2019; Curran and Boddison, 2021). Research suggests that without the SENCo in a senior position and without the support of senior leaders, whole-school inclusive practice will be severely limited (Soan, 2017; Cowne et al, 2019; Glazzard et al, 2019). SLTs without a SENCo are without an advocate for SEND and inclusive policy. This may result in the loss of a strong voice and influence for strategic universal inclusive practice (Tissot, 2013) and representation of the experiences and views of parents and children with SEND (Oldham and Radford, 2011; Clarke and Done, 2021). Indeed, Clarke and Done (2021) identify this position as being vital within the leadership of a school for the realisation of the whole-school vision of inclusion (Clarke and Done, 2021), a reality that appears to be recognised in the Green Paper (DfE, 2022b). Certainly, where the role is valued and supported by the SLT, it can be a powerful one in relation to inclusion. In contrast, without the empowerment conferred through position, the role can be limited to and subsumed within bureaucratic and standardised SEND management duties and reactive approaches, limiting its ability to promote transformative change (Oldham and Radford, 2011; Liasidou and Svensson, 2012).

# The SENCo as leader

So far, this chapter has explored how leadership positions are integral to whole-school inclusion and has suggested that without embedded and shared understanding, values and ethos, barriers to inclusion cannot be addressed and reduced (Ainscow et al, 2006). This raises the following question: If all leaders collectively share a commitment to inclusion and SEND provision, then does the role of the SENCo need to exist, or should it be shared across leadership? An interesting perspective is proposed by Fitzgerald and Radford (2017), who suggest that a tension exists between the SENCo role and a universal response to SEND, a perspective recognised by the Green Paper (DfE, 2022b), which appears to be attempting to resolve this tension.

---

## *Critical questions* (?)

» Does the role of SENCo perpetuate a system that maintains the label of SEND within mainstream education, where effective SENCos act as a barrier to all educators enabling learning for all students with SEND?

» Without the role of SENCo, would opportunities for whole-school reflective, collaborative approaches help staff consider and remove barriers to learning and enable individual and collective responsibility and ownership of practice for all children?

---

To enable you to consider these questions further, the following case study explores the role of the SENCo by sharing an example of what can happen when a school does not have a SENCo. Some schools, for example those in multi-academy trusts (MATs), share a SENCo across many sites and so while the SENCo might not be physically present, they will at least complete statutory duties. However, we want to imagine what might happen without a SENCo and to consider the ways a setting would ensure inclusive practice and effective provision for pupils with SEND.

## CASE STUDY ⊖

### *Specific vs generic roles in SEND leadership*

The primary school has approximately 300 students and is situated in a socio-economically disadvantaged area. 24.2 per cent of its pupils are on the SEND register (national average = 12.8 per cent). The school has experienced instability in leadership over the last two years, having recently appointed a new headteacher and an inclusion leader, both of whom are currently leading inclusion and SEND provision in the absence of a SENCo. The historical context of the school's inclusive practice and SEND provision may be regarded as contentious due to the previous headteacher's ethos and practice, which focused on hierarchy and control, an approach which created many barriers and limited SEND provision.

In contrast, the new headteacher's views mean significant steps towards inclusive practice and provision for pupils are already happening, despite a SENCo not being in role. The headteacher demonstrates leadership that develops a team approach, motivates staff, focuses on teaching and learning, builds a school climate with a clear vision and embraces inclusive practice by improving outcomes for all children (Mortimore and Whitty, 2000). The absence of a SENCo has meant identification of children with SEND, interventions, provision mapping, specialist support and many of the other responsibilities a SENCo holds as specified by the SEND CoP (DfE and DoH, 2015) have had to be shared or distributed across the staff in order to assure the '*day to day operation of the school's SEND policy*' (DfE and DoH, 2015, p 108). It is not yet known how effective this is. However, the absence of a SENCo has prompted exploration and evaluation of the role, within an educational climate where inclusion and SEND are increasingly seen to be whole-school shared responsibilities, grounded in inclusive principles, values and commitment (Florian and Black-Hawkins, 2011; Ekins, 2015).

Furthermore, the absence of a SENCo has highlighted how this role is important in bringing together all the essential aspects that enable inclusion, but also how inclusion and SEND are collective and collaborative responsibilities that need to be led by transformational leaders, including the SENCo, and that these leaders empower staff and have a shared vision, commitment and ethos that creates a 'community of practice' around inclusion (Ainscow et al, 2006).

---

### Critical questions (?)

» How can SENCos build teams to share the balance between strategic leadership and managerial tasks?

» To what extent do we need to be more imaginative within school team building for SEND provision – and encourage all teachers to be part of the management of SEND processes, as well as drawing on their expertise?

---

## The SENCo as advocate: beyond compliance

Like the colleagues in this case study school, Fitzgerald and Radford (2020) assert that SENCos have a unique position that requires specific skills and are therefore essential to inclusion. They propose a conceptualisation of the role (Fitzgerald and Radford, 2020, p 12, Figure 1) that places it within the continuum of specialist and universal approaches.

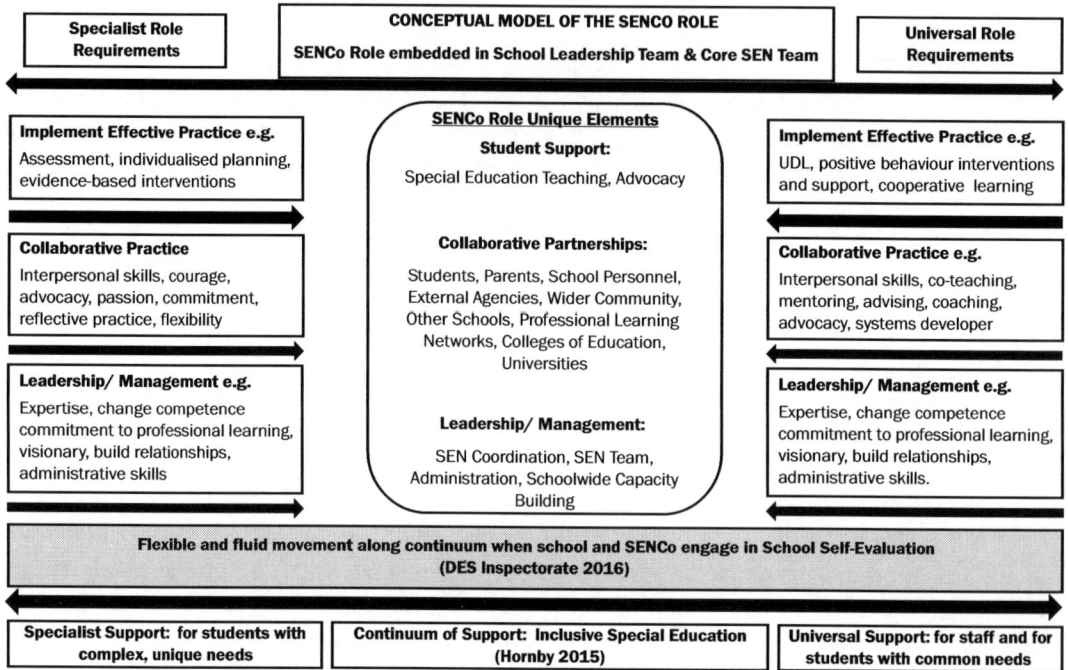

**Figure 1.1** *A conceptualisation of the SENCo role within an inclusive special education framework* (Fitzgerald and Radford, 2020, p 12, Figure 1).

The model outlines the complex and multifaceted role of the SENCo and encompasses the range of elements needed for effective collaborative practice, confirming the importance of the SENCo as a strategic leader, manager, advocate and administrator. However, Middleton and Kay (2021) recognise that there also needs to be a school-wide responsibility for, ownership of and approach to inclusion that engages all staff in the cycle of action, reflection, participation and collective practice. Such an inclusive, collective approach needs to be led in a transformative way, that is, by empowering all through a team approach, rather than in a transactional way that sustains hierarchy and control (Ainscow et al, 2006). We therefore argue, in line with Fitzgerald and Radford's (2020) identification of specialist and universal role requirements (see Figure 1.1), that if the SENCo is part of a transformational leadership team, they are in the best position to lead and develop inclusion.

Despite any merits of theoretical arguments for abolishing SENCos, a recent report about special educational needs (DfE, 2021) proposed that the role of the SENCo was integral to the identification and collation of need, as well as communication within educational settings. Significant in the decision-making process around SEND, SENCos were viewed as a *'conduit through which the school's SEND support activities were delivered'* (DfE, 2021, p 73). However, despite affirming that the role is essential within school contexts and other educational settings, the report failed to fully appreciate the role's multidimensional nature, as identified by research and perceived by SENCos themselves (Ekins, 2015; Fitzgerald and Radford, 2017). Indeed, perceptions and understanding of the SENCo role by others are key, since they can either act as a barrier or facilitator of inclusive practice (Ekins, 2015).

These differing expectations of the SENCo role often entail the belief of SENCo as 'expert' by parents and colleagues. Also, colleagues may see SEND as the sole remit of the SENCo, along with behaviour management, safeguarding, English as an additional language and other responsibilities that fall under the umbrella of inclusion (Rosen-Webb, 2011; Curran and Boddison, 2021). This varied interpretation not only depletes the time available for core SENCo responsibilities (see Table 1.1) (Ekins, 2015; Smith and Broomhead, 2019), but also increases workload, conflicts with a SENCo's self-perception and belief around the purpose of the role (Smith and Broomhead 2019; Fitzgerald and Radford, 2020; Hallet, 2022), and limits what could be achieved by a whole-school approach.

---

### Critical questions ❓

» How do you know how others perceive the SENCo role?

» How could you conduct small-scale research to discover this?

» How will you ensure that all staff have the same understanding of roles and responsibilities?

» How might you, as a whole setting, move beyond compliance with statutory and administrative requirements, to develop and progress your inclusive ethos and pedagogy? (see Chapter 3)

---

## Chapter summary 📝

This chapter concludes by suggesting that the SENCo role should be reframed as a leadership role supporting and developing colleagues' abilities to drive progress towards inclusion in their own classrooms. This appears to cohere with the White Paper by the Department for Education (DfE, 2022a) that identifies the need to pivot the system from 'looking through the lens of pupil's characteristics' (p 36), which means that sometimes 'the needs of children who do not acquire the label of having a special educational need or disability or being disadvantaged' (p 36) are missed, to a system that provides support at the point of need. Such a stance was identified by Norwich (1996), who argued that SEND provision is interconnected with education, since meeting the multiple needs of children is inherent to the purpose and practice of education. Certainly, the complex role of the SENCo encompasses many important elements that are essential for inclusive education and SEND.

However, the complexity of the role is challenging to manage for one person and there is the need for shared ownership and responsibility, as well as clarity about roles and responsibilities (Middleton and Kay, 2021). Therefore, linking to debate around whether, in practice, inclusion can be achieved solely through whole-school values, principles, policies and vision, the chapter suggests that the SENCo role needs to be recognised as being pivotal in developing both specialist and universal inclusive practice within educational settings (Glazzard et al, 2019; DfE, 2021), to enable and enhance learning for all.

## Further reading 📚

Hallett, F (2022) Can SENCos Do Their Job in a Bubble? The Impact of Covid-19 on the Ways in Which We Conceptualise Provision for Learners with Special Educational Needs. *Oxford Review of Education*, 48(1): 1–13.

- This article suggests that 'bubbles' of theoretical and professional knowledge and practice have existed for many years, critiquing such practice in England as being a product of broader systemic problems that create barriers for SEND support in practice.

## References 📚

Ainscow, M, Booth, T and Dyson, A (2006) *Improving Schools, Developing Inclusion*. Improving Learning Series. Abingdon: Routledge.

Clarke, A L and Done, E J (2021) Balancing Pressures for SENCos as Managers, Leaders and Advocates in the Emerging Context of the Covid-19 Pandemic. *British Journal of Special Education*, 48(2): 157–74.

Cowne, E A, Frankl, C and Gerschel, L (2019) *The SENCo Handbook: Leading and Managing a Whole School Approach*. 7th ed. London: Routledge.

Curran, H (2019) 'The SEND Code of Practice Has Given Me Clout': A Phenomenological Study Illustrating How SENCos Managed the Introduction of the SEND Reforms. *British Journal of Special Education*, 46(1): 76–93.

Curran, H and Boddison, A (2021) 'It's the Best Job in the World, but One of the Hardest, Loneliest, Most Misunderstood Roles in a School.' Understanding the Complexity of the SENCO Role Post-SEND Reform. *Journal of Research in Special Educational Needs*, 21(1): 9–48.

Department for Education (DfE) (1994) *Code of Practice for the Identification and Assessment of Special Educational Needs*. London: HMSO. [online] Available at: https://eric.ed.gov/?id=ED385033 (accessed 22 May 2023).

Department for Education (DfE) (2021) *Special Educational Needs (SEN) Support: Findings from a Qualitative Study*. [online] Available at: www.gov.uk/government/publications/special-educational-needs-sen-support-findings-from-a-qualitative-study (accessed 23 May 2023).

Department for Education (DfE) (2022a) *Opportunity for All: Strong Schools with Great Teachers for Your Child*. HM Government White Paper. [online] Available at: https://assets.publishing.service.gov.uk/government/uploads/system/uploads/attachment_data/file/1063602/Opportunity_for_all_strong_schools_with_great_teachers_for_your_child__print_version_.pdf (accessed 23 May 2023).

Department for Education (DfE) (2022b) *SEND Review: Right Support, Right Place, Right Time*. HM Government Green Paper. [online] Available at: https://assets.publishing.service.gov.uk/government/uploads/system/uploads/attachment_data/file/1063620/SEND_review_right_support_right_place_right_time_accessible.pdf (accessed 23 May 2023).

Department for Education (DfE) and Department of Health (DoH) (2015) *Special Educational Needs and Disability Code of Practice: 0 to 25 Years* [online] Available at: https://assets.publishing.service.gov.uk/government/uploads/system/uploads/attachment_data/file/398815/SEND_Code_of_Practice_January_2015.pdf (accessed 22 May 2023).

Department for Education and Skills (DfES) (2001) *Special Educational Needs Code of Practice.* Nottingham: DfES. [online] Available at: https://assets.publishing.service.gov.uk/government/uploads/system/uploads/attachment_data/file/273877/special_educational_needs_code_of_practice.pdf (accessed 23 May 2023).

Education Act 1993. [online] Available at: www.legislation.gov.uk/ukpga/1993/35/contents/enacted (accessed 23 May 2023).

Ekins, A (2015) *The Changing Face of Special Educational Needs: Impact and Implications for SENCos, Teachers and Their Schools.* 2nd ed. London: Routledge.

Equality Act 2010 [online] Available at: www.legislation.gov.uk/ukpga/2010/15/contents (accessed 13 June 2023).

Fitzgerald, J and Radford, J (2017) The SENCO Role in Post-Primary Schools in Ireland: Victims or Agents of Change? *European Journal of Special Needs Education*, 32(3): 452–66.

Fitzgerald, J and Radford, J (2020) Leadership for Inclusive Special Education: A Qualitative Exploration of SENCOs' and Principals' Experiences in Secondary Schools in Ireland. *International Journal of Inclusive Education.* https://doi.org/10.1080/13603116.2020.1760365

Florian, L and Black-Hawkins, K (2011) Exploring Inclusive Pedagogy. *British Educational Research Journal*, 37(5): 813–28.

Florian, L, Rouse, M and Black-Hawkins, K (2011) Researching Achievement and Inclusion to Improve the Educational Experiences and Outcomes of All Learners. *Spanish Education Review.* [online] Available at: https://redined.educacion.gob.es/xmlui/bitstream/handle/11162/208091/FLORIAN.pdf?sequence=1 (accessed 9 July 2023).

Glazzard, J, Stokoe, J, Hughes, A, Netherwood, A and Neve, L (2019) *Teaching and Supporting Children with Special Educational Needs and Disabilities in Primary Schools.* London: Sage Learning Matters.

Hallett, F (2022) Can SENCOs Do Their Job in a Bubble? The Impact of Covid-19 on the Ways in Which We Conceptualise Provision for Learners with Special Educational Needs. *Oxford Review of Education*, 48(1): 1–13.

Hallett, F and Hallett G (2017) *Transforming the Role of the SENCo.* 2nd ed. London: Open University Press.

Layton, L (2005) Special Educational Needs Coordinators and Leadership: A Role Too Far? *Support for Learning*, 20(2): 53–60.

Liasidou, A and Svensson, C (2012) Theorizing Educational Change within the Context of Inclusion. In Cornwall, J and Graham-Matheson, L (eds) *Leading on Inclusion* (pp 33–44). London: Routledge.

Middleton, T and Kay, L (2021) Uncharted Territory and Extraordinary Times: The SENCo's Experiences of Leading Special Education during a Pandemic in England. *British Journal of Special Education*, 48(2): 212–34.

Morewood, G D (2012) Is the 'Inclusive SENCo' Still a Possibility? A Personal Perspective. *Support for Learning*, 2(2): 73–6.

Mortimore, P and Whitty, G (2000) Can School Improvement Overcome the Effects of Disadvantage? In Cox, T (ed) *Combating Educational Disadvantage: Meeting the Needs of Vulnerable Children* (pp 156–76). London: Falmer.

Norwich, B (1996) Special Needs Education or Education for All: Connective Specialisation and Ideological Impurity. *British Journal of Special Education*, 23(3): 100–4.

Norwich, B (2013) *Addressing Tensions and Dilemmas in Inclusive Education: Living with Uncertainty.* London: Routledge.

Oldham, J and Radford, J (2011) Secondary SENCo Leadership: A Universal or Specialist Role? *British Journal of Special Education*, 38(3): 126–34.

Robertson, C (2012) Special Educational Needs and Disability Co-ordination in a Changing Policy Landscape: Making Sense of Policy from a SENCo's Perspective. *Support for Learning*, 27(2): 77–83.

Rosen-Webb, S M (2011) Nobody Tells You How to Be a SENCo. *British Journal of Special Education*, 38(4): 159–68.

Smith, M D and Broomhead, K E (2019) Time, Expertise and Status: Barriers Faced by Mainstream Primary School SENCos in the Pursuit of Providing Effective Provision for Children with SEND. *Support for Learning*, 34(1): 54–70.

Soan, S (2017) *The SENCo Essential Manual.* London: Open University Press.

Szwed, C (2007) Reconsidering the Role of the Primary Special Educational Needs Co-ordinator: Policy, Practice and Future Priorities. *British Journal of Special Education*, 34(2): 96–104.

Tissot, C (2013) The Role of SENCos as Leaders. *British Journal of Special Education*, 40(1): 33–40.

Teacher Training Agency (TTA) (1998) *National Standards for Special Educational Needs Coordinators.* London: TTA.

Warnock Report (1978). *Special Educational Needs.* Report of the Committee of Enquiry into the Education of Handicapped Children and Young People. London: HMSO. [online] Available at: www.educationengland.org.uk/documents/warnock/warnock1978.html (accessed 23 May 2023).

Winwood, J (2016) Leading and Managing for Inclusion. In Brown, Z (ed) *Inclusive Education: Perspectives on Pedagogy, Policy and Practice* (pp 23–33). London: Routledge.

# 2 SENCo professional identity and development

**HAZEL RICHARDS**

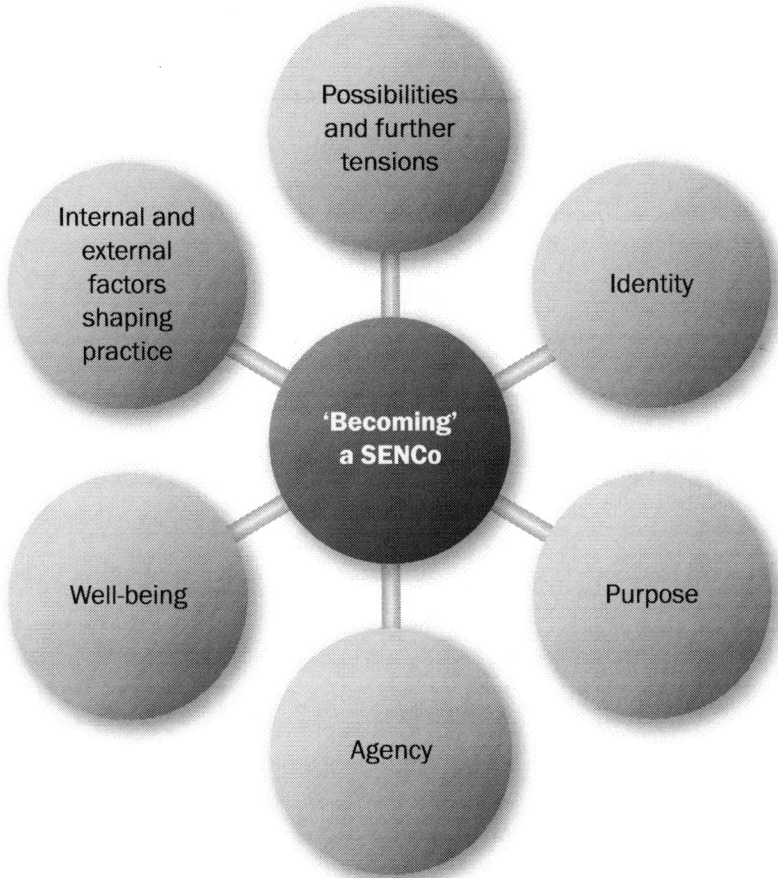

# Chapter objectives 🎯

This chapter explores personal and professional motivations for becoming a SENCo and considers the challenges of the role. The chapter:

- explores SENCo identity and purpose;

- poses critical questions to enable you to reflect on your own identity, well-being and development;

- investigates challenges, including to well-being and professional development;

- ponders the effects these challenges might have on your role, identity and practice, whether you are a SENCo or not.

## STARTING POINTS 🏁

» What is your current role in supporting children and young people with SEND?

» How do you see this developing over the short and long term?

» What personal values do you hold that contribute to your current role and future aspirations?

# Introduction

This chapter links notions of professionalism, postgraduate professional learning and expertise to the day-to-day work of SENCos. It considers differences between competency, compliance and advocacy, including the need for each of these, and how these might be operationalised in different combinations to galvanise change that supports positive outcomes for children and young people with SEND and their families.

# SENCo identity

The presence and status of SENCos varies between countries, including within the UK. Some countries, such as the United States, use external mechanisms where personnel outside the setting guide, lead and monitor the SEND support. In England, the external model is operative in the early years, in that area SENCos support early years SENCos in their settings (DfES, 2003). The internal model, where personnel from within the setting are designated to co-ordinate support, is more common (Poon-McBrayer, 2012) and is present in England in schools funded by a local education authority. SENCo role enactment also varies between settings, linked to the leadership, knowledge, training and ethos of settings and their staff (Maher and Vickerman, 2018). Such differences mean that SENCos and other setting staff can experience and perceive the role differently.

While there is a considerable body of knowledge about teacher identity (van Lankveld et al, 2017), including the recognition that clear ideas about the role contribute to effective joint working, the knowledge base about SENCo identity is much smaller. Like teachers, the identity of SENCos is also formed of several layers: collective, professional and personal. Collective identity is concerned with relating to a profession or team, with SENCos being involved with and functioning across several teams (Wenger, 1999). Commitment to the team is affected by one's sense of belonging, with collaboration being influenced by membership ties (see Chapter 9). SEND is seen by many as fundamentally an issue of human rights, equity and social justice, which can put SENCos in a difficult place because of how they conceptualise the aims and priorities of an education system situated in a neoliberal, standards-driven context. This has implications for the collective identities of SENCos due to their work across interconnected teams – who make sense of and prioritise things differently. This means it is necessary to consider other viewpoints while operating within their own settings, where alliances and loyalties contribute to well-being, commitment and effective practice.

Generally, professional identity is concerned with role identity, informed by subject knowledge, job responsibilities and perceptions of professional ideals, goals, interests and values (Callero, 1985). Strong professional identity constructions, which are formed when mismatches between who practitioners are as people and what they do in practice are worked through (Adioniou, 2016; Hellawell, 2017), have been found to both enable and empower successful transdisciplinary working (see Chapter 9). Professionalisation denotes the process '*of identity formation via socialisation and absorbing values that may be but are not necessarily in keeping with the professional*' (Phillips and Dalgarno, 2017, p 2), whereas professionalism is concerned with being an ethical, compassionate and virtuous person who practises in a moral and competent manner (Moore and Clarke, 2016). Qualifications, knowledge and autonomy contribute to this, and although there is debate about where SENCos position themselves in professional hierarchies (or are positioned by others), strong professional identity contributes to self-worth, with Richards (2019) finding that knowledge and confidence can be juxtaposed with feelings of vulnerability and self-doubt.

Alongside collective and professional identity, personal identity is also important since our experience, values and beliefs inform how practitioners construe and construct their work (Kelchtermans, 1993). For example, attitudes towards SEND are generally more positive when teachers have had personal experience with someone with SEND. Indeed, life events influence professional practice by informing knowledge and experience, as well as levels of energy, drive and morale (Bukor, 2015). Determination, perseverance and resilience are all personal qualities which can be called upon when working in the SEND workforce, and the challenges of SENCo work can result in changes to assertiveness and sense of achievement (Richards, 2019). However, Williams (2013) recognises the importance of considering the emotional labour involved, linked to stress, workload, value differences and being personally affected.

## SENCo purpose

SENCo purpose cannot be explored without considering the drivers and purpose of education. Neoliberalism and meritocracy currently underpin Western ideology (Liasidou and Svensson, 2014) so it can be argued that education is often driven more by economics and standards than values. Certainly, neoliberalism values competition rather than ethical approaches, prioritising efficiency over purposes and principles. Emphasising education for economic prosperity may therefore be at odds with the philosophy of inclusion, with its values of democracy, equality, care and justice. The inclusive education approach has been present in legislation and policy since 1994 (UNESCO, 1994), and whether this approach is limited to SEND or is about a wider egalitarian application or *'philosophy of acceptance where all pupils are valued and treated with respect'* (Carrington and Elkins, 2005, p 86) varies across settings. Certainly, how the SENCo role is viewed in terms of purpose and values can be linked to the priorities and ethos of individual settings, with these influencing the support, time and status bestowed on SENCos.

SENCo objectives may also be dual. That is, SENCos themselves often possess a strong sense of purpose and social justice, combined with a desire for career enhancement. The SENCo role can certainly facilitate career progression (Hellawell, 2017), with the literature also revealing a desire for equity, meaningful education and educational excellence for the pupils under their care (Hellawell, 2017; Maher and Vickerman, 2018; Richards, 2019). This involves passion and commitment and regarding the role as more than 'just a job', with the additional 'hearts and minds' layer enabling practitioners to go beyond just systemic delivery of assessment and provision. This is similar to the vocationalism identified by Plowden (1967), and to professionalism (Moore and Clarke, 2016), which is concerned with being ethical and compassionate as well as competent. Regardless of whether SENCos themselves are led by either values/ideas or data/abstract processes (Done et al, 2016), it can be argued that the experience and outcomes for individual children should be central to SENCo purpose. Furthermore, SENCos do not work in vacuums or blank spaces, meaning that their identity and purpose interact with facets present in the external environment.

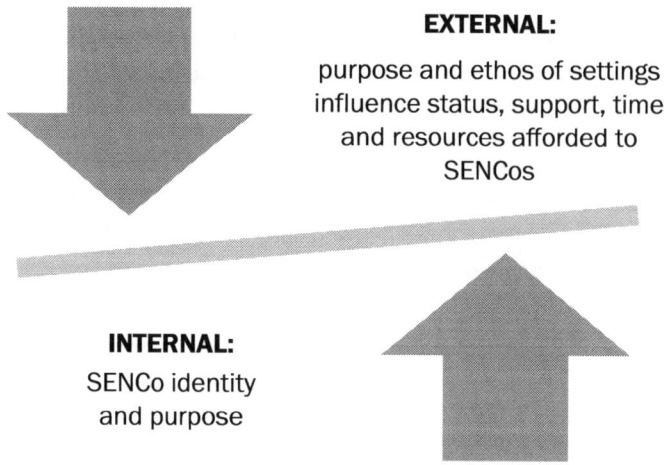

**EXTERNAL:**
purpose and ethos of settings
influence status, support, time
and resources afforded to
SENCos

**INTERNAL:**
SENCo identity
and purpose

**Figure 2.1** *External and internal influences on SENCo practice*

Figure 2.1 demonstrates how identity and purpose (internal factors) dynamically interact with SENCo agency in the ecological systems in which SENCos practise. That is, each setting in which SENCos practise has statutory and recommended duties as well as unique characteristics, with factors external to the SENCo, including the purpose and ethos of settings shaping how legislation and policy are enacted in terms of leadership, power and resources.

# New debates and developments

Traditionally, SEND has been viewed as less important than other areas of education (Social Mobility and Child Poverty Commission, 2014; Richards, 2022), which has implications for the status and function of the SENCo role. Some SENCos, especially those working in maintained settings and who are part of the senior leadership team (SLT), will be enacting the role at a strategic and managerial level. Others, especially those working in private, voluntary and independent (PVI) early years settings, where Qualified Teacher Status is not required and where achieving the National Award in Special Educational Needs Coordination (NASENCo) has not been mandatory, will be enacting the role at an operational level. These disparities in minimum training requirements have been identified as significant in the SEND and Alternative Provision (AP) Improvement Plan (DfE, 2023), which points out that early years practitioners can struggle to accurately identify SEND. While training in the early years is beginning to be addressed by level 3 early years SENCo training (Best Practice Network, 2022) (see Chapter 6), the Improvement Plan (DfE, 2023) will replace the current Master's-level NASENCo training, with a mandatory leadership-level SENCo National Professional Qualification (NPQ).

NPQs are designed to support the professional development of teachers and leaders (DfE, 2022b), and '*are part of a wider set of teacher development reforms which will together create a "golden thread" of high-quality evidence underpinning the support, training and development available*' to teachers throughout their whole career (DfE, 2022b, home page). These qualifications are consequently situated clearly in the domain of continuing professional development (CPD). It can be argued that this is a good thing, and that NPQs, which are underpinned by a specific content framework and where project work can be signed off by a school principal, will lighten the considerable additional workload placed on SENCos by the NASENCo qualification (Boddison et al, 2021). However, while it is argued that a carefully framed and designed NPQ will provide the knowledge, practical skills and leadership expertise needed for the role, will align with wider teacher training reforms (DfE, 2023) and enable SENCos to more routinely join SLTs (DfE, 2022b), concerns and challenges exist. For example, it will divest teachers wishing to pursue further Master's-level study of transferrable credits (Done et al, 2022), and impact the deep research-informed critical reflection inherent in Master's-level study (see Chapter 10). Also, it may not fully equip SENCos to challenge and change school culture (Done et al, 2022), meaning that inclusive education for SEND learners continues to be driven by individual settings' '*mode of governance and positioning within a quasi-marketised education system*' (Done et al, 2022, p 9) rather than interrogation of how learners experience inclusion and achieve their potential.

This is important to consider against the themes prevalent in the literature, including SENCo status, possession of the skills and power to systematically prioritise, evaluate, develop and monitor provision, and being able to practise effectively (Hellawell, 2017). This is because professionalisation (as opposed to de-professionalisation) requires re-conceptualisation of the aims and priorities of the education system (Liaisidou and Svensson, 2014), a process which requires deep levels of critical and ethical thinking. Against this backdrop, the Improvement Plan (DfE, 2023, p 93) aims to develop National Standards, '*setting clear and high expectations for good practice*' to progress provision that currently is not joined up, where tensions and challenges are rife, and when changes in legislation are not yet in sight.

## Implications for policy and practice: possibilities and further tensions

The SENCo role involves both practical and critical challenges. For example, in practice SENCos wear multiple hats, which may include being a member of the SLT, the designated safeguarding officer, and class, subject or phase lead. While compliance with legislative, policy and curriculum requirements is certainly necessary, competence (effectively meeting the demands of a role by adroitly using knowledge, skills and resources) is something SENCos new to the role, who may be highly experienced and proficient in other areas, often need to develop. This can impact confidence and identity. It can also impact agency.

Identity change is recognised as a core factor in educational change (Eteläpelto et al, 2017). Certainly, agents are more likely to effectively fulfil roles when they identify with the values and beliefs involved with them. This is because juxtaposing the demands and constraints inherent to this role with a clear sense of purpose facilitates strong agency. Professional agency represents the idea that professionals have the power to take stances, to make decisions and choices, and to influence things. Identity and agency therefore have important effects on SENCo work, including their involvement with and commitment to reform and change. While training, especially the mandatory NASENCo, has been identified as making a clear contribution to increased SENCo confidence and skill, Gu and Day (2013, p 22) recognise that individual teachers have different levels of confidence in, control over and resilience against demands within situations that are '*neither innate or stable*'.

---

### Critical questions (?)

» Who makes up your SLT and how do they influence the support provided for learners with SEND by your setting?

» How does your approach to supporting learners with SEND cohere with and differ from your setting's approach?

» What challenges has this created for your well-being, identity and professional development and what solutions can you implement to address these?

» What place does academic study have in SENCo training and what practical challenges has studying created for you?

## CASE STUDY ⊖

**Phil Rose, assistant headteacher and SENCo in a large comprehensive secondary school with above average numbers of SEND support and education, health and care plan (EHCP) students**

*I have been a teacher for over 26 years in five different schools and a senior leader for the last ten years. My last role was Head of School for Years 9 and 10 and Careers Leader, but in March 2021 my headteacher suggested I become SENCo to cover the maternity leave of the school's extremely experienced and long-standing SENCo. With no experience of SEND other than as a class teacher, I felt completely out of my depth, and have had to use all my leadership skills in the new role. As SENCo I am part of the 'Inclusion Team', which works hard to find creative solutions, and to remove barriers so that all students, regardless of SEND, gender, ability, ethnicity or background, feel part of the school community and can be successful. The fact that the school endeavours to be as inclusive as possible and that this comes from the top has made the transition more manageable.*

*My own values reflect a person-centred approach, which coheres with the ethos of the school. I've made a point of investing time to get to know students with SEND, and to understanding their needs. I have also built strong collaboration with external services and families. This has meant I have been able to develop my practice and meet the needs of students despite my lack of expertise.*

*Parents are involved from the get-go, and combined with school-based evidence they help shape the best provision and inform the graduated response. In the case of a new Year 7 student with autism, a transition programme involving parents, primary SENCo, the Outreach Service and myself began early, and the collaboration continues regularly now. This process has been absolutely necessary; the student was perceived to be 'too autistic for mainstream' by many members of staff but targeted and whole-school CPD on 'autism awareness' training, delivered by the external Outreach Service, developed a better understanding of the student's needs and empowered all staff to be more aware and responsible for effective provision for this student and other autistic students in the school.*

*I love my job as SENCo: I've been lucky enough to carry on in the role and continue to develop my expertise every day. Being SENCo has complemented and developed further my own natural leadership style of a person-centred approach, and has positively influenced my daily interactions with students, parents and colleagues.*

> **Critical questions** (?)
>
> »    How has Phil's confidence developed and what enabled this?
>
> »    Phil describes his personal values as aligning with those of his setting. Has compliance with your own setting's approach and/or requirements ever been at odds with a child's best interests?
>
> »    How might Phil's approaches of getting to know each student and of collaboration enable you to advocate for learners with SEND, and what aspects of your own identity and purpose would enhance this?

## Possibilities

SENCos often possess a strong sense of purpose and social justice, though achievement may be viewed both in terms of altruism and career enhancement opportunities (Hargreaves and Shirley, 2012). Certainly, the role offers opportunities for networking and multidisciplinary team working, postgraduate professional learning and development of expertise in the day-to-day work, including administrative and financial tasks. However, time and experience are needed to achieve competency. *Bildung* is a German term referring to a process of self-cultivation and maturation in which harmonisation of the individual's mind, heart and identity is achieved (Mollenhauer, 2014). This can involve challenges and changes to one's beliefs. Korsgaard (2008) talks of 'self-constitution' as being the task of identifying and orienting one's life around projects and values of one's choosing; practitioners are more likely to fulfil roles when they identify with the values and beliefs involved with them. Such practitioners are likely to be highly motivated, and if they are also able to evaluate and influence practice, they have the potential to go beyond mere compliance to actively develop their knowledge, understanding and attitudes, and thereby the support and intervention cultivated in their settings.

Changes that would enable SENCos to carry out their roles more efficiently and strengthen the quality of SEND provision in settings have been identified (Robertson, 2021; SEN Policy Research Forum, 2022).

- Strengthening accountability and governance to ensure all SENCos are supported to carry out their duties, reducing current variations in external factors and their impact (see Figure 2.1).

- Improving the availability of external support to children whose needs do not quite meet the benchmark of 'complex'.

- Teaming SENCos to create communities of practice (Wenger, 1999) and provide excellent opportunities for CPD within localities.

- Inspecting SEND provision at multi-academy or federation levels, not just at the levels of individual settings or local areas, in order to consider SEND networks and collaborative activity (see Chapter 6).

- Aligning SENCo training more closely to the Teachers' Standards (DfE, 2011), the early career framework (DfE, 2022a) and the forthcoming National Standards (DfE, 2023).

These have implications for both SENCo well-being and professional development. The role can be a lonely one, and professional support, collegiality and guidance for SENCos is lacking (Fitzgerald and Radford, 2022). The role can also involve a transition from competence in classroom or management practice to being a novice in relation to SENCo knowledge, networking and effective performance. While this can lead to a lack of confidence on the one hand, networks of support and expert advice, including participation in a community of practice (Wenger, 1999), can be enablers in practice, which in turn can reduce burnout, alleviate isolation, build relationships and so enhance well-being (Fitzgerald and Radford, 2022; Richards, 2022) (see Chapter 10).

## Further tensions

In reality, there may exist mismatches between who practitioners are as people and what they do or can achieve in practice (Callero, 1985, Adioniou, 2016; Hellawell, 2017). Recently, these have been exacerbated by the pandemic and by widespread post-pandemic economic challenges (Lin et al, 2022). Creative responses require space to think, and the increasing demands on SENCo capacity (Fitzgerald and Radford, 2022) are in danger of squeezing this. These authors advocate for the development of SENCos' leadership capacity within an integrated system promoting a collective approach to inclusive special education. De-coupling the dominant binary discourse of special and mainstream education (see Chapter 5) would move our thinking from 'othering' and 'specialised' to a continuum of need that includes all learners and which is encompassed in all training. Indeed, the existence of the SENCo role in its current social construction is at risk of perpetuating duality in the system, when instead we should be debating the situation explicitly and progressing perceptions of support. SENCos have a vital role to play in this, building school-wide systematic collaboration. Promoting school-wide responsibility for students with SEND requires leadership and collaboration (Fitzgerald and Radford, 2022). This will require SENCos to self-advocate if the role is to be moved from an isolated, marginalised position to one where contribution to pedagogy and learner outcomes across all diversities is fully operationalised. This has implications for how knowledge tends to be siloed or viewed as 'special' when instead the role should be strongly linked to the professional development of SENCos and colleagues (DfE, 2022c). The challenge though is to change thinking towards development of a curricular model that supports access to learning from a school-wide perspective (see Figure 1.1 in Chapter 1).

### Implications for the SENCo role, identity and practice

» Recognising identity and purpose, and their interaction with external factors, is important since existing differences in settings' purpose and ethos influence status, support, time and resources afforded to SENCos and their role enactment.

» Operating within a marketised education system can bring opportunities such as collegiate and team working; interrogating how learners experience inclusion and achieve their potential within our existing systems requires SENCos to be collaborators, educators, advocates and leaders.

$\longrightarrow$

» Both of the above have implications for SENCo well-being and professional development.

» SENCo training, in whatever form it takes going forward, needs to recognise and address these issues.

» This includes reconceptualising the role of education and the scope of inclusive education.

## Critical questions (?)

» How have your setting's values, ethos and drivers shaped the enactment of inclusion and the SENCo role in your setting?

» Using 360° feedback (feedback collected anonymously from all co-workers, see Further reading below), investigate your knowledge and understanding of inclusive practice and SEND. What does this reveal about your skills, knowledge and working relationships?

» Again using 360° feedback, investigate the knowledge and understanding of inclusive practice and SEND held by staff in your setting. Identify existing strengths and challenges, and consider how these interact with your setting's values, ethos and drivers to inform and shape practice.

» What practical and ideological challenges have you identified? Prioritise them and create a plan to change and develop perceptions, competency and advocacy for inclusion and support for diverse learners.

## Chapter summary 📝

The close link between SENCos' purpose of care for students and the burden that such commitment and emotional labour places on their professional and personal identity and development has been identified. SENCos themselves must interrogate their identity and purpose, recognise the difference between competency, compliance and advocacy, and consider how and when these are operationalised, or challenged and developed. Doing so will help galvanise SENCo agency and change, which is necessary if the ideology of inclusion and inclusive education is to progress.

## Further reading 📩

Fleenor, J W, Taylor, S and Chappelow, C (2008) *Leveraging the Impact of 360-Degree Feedback*. San Francisco: Pfeiffer, a Wiley Imprint.

• This book explains how to implement a 360-degree information gathering and feedback process, which engages co-workers in identifying and developing understanding and practice.

Lin, H, Grudnoff, L and Hill, M (2022) Agency for Inclusion: A Case Study of Special Educational Needs Coordinators (SENCos). *International Journal of Disability, Development and Education.* https://doi.org/10.1080/1034912X.2022.2137110

- Set in an international context, this article investigates SENCo agency, recognising transactions with the culture, structure and resources in individual settings, as well as with past, present and future actions.

# References

Adoniou, M (2016) Don't Let Me Forget the Teacher I Wanted to Become. *Teacher Development*, 20(3): 343–63.

Best Practice Network (2022) Early Years SENCO Level 3. [online] Available at: www.bestpracticenet.co.uk/early-years-SENCO (accessed 23 May 2023).

Boddison, A, Curran, H and Moloney, H (2021) *National SENCo Workforce Survey 2020: Time to Review 2018–2020.* Bath Spa University and Nasen. [online] Available at: www.bathspa.ac.uk/media/bathspaacuk/projects/National-SENCO-Workforce-Survey–Full-Report–24.06.21.pdf (accessed 23 May 2023).

Bukor, E (2015) Exploring Teacher Identity from a Holistic Perspective: Reconstructing and Reconnecting Personal and Professional Selves. *Teachers and Teaching: Theory and Practice*, 21(3): 305–27.

Callero, P L (1985) Role-Identity Salience. *Social Psychology Quarterly*, 48(3): 203–15.

Carrington, S and Elkins, J (2005) Bridging the Gap between Inclusive Policy and Inclusive Culture in Secondary Schools. *Support for Learning*, 17(2): 52–7.

Department for Education (DfE) (2011) *Teachers' Standards.* [online] Available at: www.gov.uk/government/publications/teachers-standards (accessed 5 September 2023).

Department for Education (DfE) (2022a) *Early Career Framework.* [online] Available at: www.gov.uk/government/publications/early-career-framework (accessed 23 May 2023).

Department for Education (DfE) (2022b) *Guidance: National Professional Qualifications (NPQs).* [online] Available at: www.gov.uk/government/publications/national-professional-qualifications-npqs-reforms/national-professional-qualifications-npqs-reforms#national-professional-qualifications (accessed 23 May 2023).

Department for Education (DfE) (2022c) *Opportunity for All: Strong Schools with Great Teachers for Your Child.* [online] Available at: https://assets.publishing.service.gov.uk/government/uploads/system/uploads/attachment_data/file/1063602/Opportunity_for_all_strong_schools_with_great_teachers_for_your_child__print_version_.pdf (accessed 23 May 2023).

Department for Education (DfE) (2023) *Special Educational Needs and Disabilities (SEND) and Alternative Provision (AP) Improvement Plan: Right Support, Right Place, Right Time.* [online] Available at: https://assets.publishing.service.gov.uk/government/uploads/system/uploads/attachment_data/file/1139561/SEND_and_alternative_provision_improvement_plan.pdfSEND and alternative provision improvement plan (accessed 22 May 2023).

Department for Education and Skills (DfES) (2003) *Area Special Educational Needs Co-ordinators (SENCOs) – Supporting Early Identification and Intervention for Children with Special Educational Needs.* [online] Available at: https://dera.ioe.ac.uk/9701 (accessed 23 May 2023).

Done, E J, Knowler, H, Richards, H and Brewster, S (2022) Advocacy Leadership and the Deprofessionalising of the Special Educational Needs Co-ordinator Role. *British Journal of Special Education*. https://doi.org/10.1111/1467-8578.12449

Done, L, Murphy, M and Watt, M (2016) Change Management and the SENCo Role: Developing Key Performance Indicators in the Strategic Development of Inclusivity. *Support for Learning*, 31(4): 281–95.

Eteläpelto, A, Vähäsantanen, K and Hökkä, P (2017) How Do Novice Teachers in Finland Perceive Their Professional Agency? *Teachers and Teaching: Theory and Practice*, 21(6): 660–80.

Fitzgerald, J and Radford, J (2022) Leadership for Inclusive Special Education: A Qualitative Exploration of SENCOs' and Principals' Experiences in Secondary Schools in Ireland. *International Journal of Inclusive Education*, 26(10): 992–1007.

Gu, Q and Day, C (2013) Challenges to Teacher Resilience: Conditions Count. *British Educational Research Journal*, 39(1): 22–44.

Hargreaves, A and Shirley, D (2012) *The Global Fourth Way*. Thousand Oaks, CA: Corwin, a Sage Company.

Hellawell, B (2017) 'There Is Still a Long Way to Go to Be Solidly Marvellous': Professional Identities, Performativity and Responsibilisation Arising from the SEND Code of Practice 2015. *British Journal of Special Education*, 44(4): 411–30.

Kelchtermans, G (1993) Getting the Story, Understanding the Lives: From Career Stories to Teachers' Professional Development. *Teaching and Teacher Education*, 9(5–6): 443–56.

Korsgaard, C M (2008) *Self-Constitution*. Oxford: Oxford University Press.

Liasidou, A and Svensson, C (2014) Educating Leaders for Social Justice: The Case of Special Educational Needs Co-ordinators. *International Journal of Inclusive Education*, 18(8): 783–97.

Lin, H, Grudnoff, L and Hill, M (2022) Agency for Inclusion: A Case Study of Special Educational Needs Coordinators (SENCos). *International Journal of Disability, Development and Education*. https://doi.org/10.1080/1034912X.2022.2137110

Maher, A J and Vickerman, P (2018) Ideology Influencing Action: Special Educational Needs Co-ordinator and Learning Support Assistant Role Conceptualisations and Experiences of Special Needs Education in England. *Journal of Research in Special Educational Needs*, 18(1): 15–24.

Mollenhauer, K (2014) *Forgotten Connections: On Culture and Upbringing*. Edited and translated by Friesen, N. London: Routledge.

Moore, A and Clarke, M (2016) 'Cruel Optimism': Teacher Attachment to Professionalism in an Era of Performativity. *Journal of Education Policy*, 31(5): 666–77.

Phillips, S P and Dalgarno, N (2017) Professionalism, Professionalization, Expertise and Compassion: A Qualitative Study of Medical Residents. *BMC Medical Education*, 17: 21.

Plowden, B (1967) *The Plowden Report*. London: HMSO. [online] Available at: www.educationengland.org.uk/documents/plowden/plowden1967-1.html (accessed 23 May 2023).

Poon-McBrayer, K F (2012) Implementing the SENCo System in Hong Kong: An Initial Investigation. *British Journal of Special Education*, 39(2): 94–101.

Richards H (2019) *Special Educational Needs Co-ordinator Perceptions of Practice and Potential: Investigating Education and Health Care Plan Implementation in Early Years and Primary Education.* Doctoral thesis. [online] Available at: https://ethos.bl.uk/OrderDetails.do?did=1& uin=uk.bl.ethos.817722 (accessed 23 May 2023).

Richards, H (2022) 'It Was Tough Making Sure It Happened': SENCo Experience of the Reality and Risk of Education and Health Care Plan Implementation. *Educational Review*: 1–22. https://doi.org/ 10.1080/00131911.2022.2033703

Robertson, C (2021) Points from the SENCo-Forum: England's SEND Review and the Role of the SENCo. *British Journal of Special Education*, 48(4): 519–23.

SEN Policy Research Forum (2022) Response from the Lead Group to the SEND Green Paper/ Review: Right Support, Right Place, Right Time. [online] Available at: https://senpolicyresearchforum. co.uk/send-green-paper-review-right-support-right-place-right-time-response-from-the-lead-group-of-the-national-sen-policy-research-forum (accessed 22 May 2023).

Social Mobility and Child Poverty Commission (2014) *State of the Nation 2014: Social Mobility and Child Poverty in Great Britain.* [online] Available at: www.gov.uk/government/uploads/system/ uploads/attachment_data/file/365765/State_of_Nation_2014_Main_Report.pdf (accessed: 23 May 2023).

UNESCO (1994) *The Salamanca Statement and Framework for Action on Special Needs Education.* [online] Available at: www.european-agency.org/sites/default/files/salamanca-statement-and-framework.pdf (accessed 23 May 2023).

van Lankveld, T, Schoonenboom, J, Volman, M, Croiset, G and Beishuizen, J (2017) Developing a Teacher Identity in the University Context: A Systematic Review of the Literature, *Higher Education Research and Development*, 36(2): 325–42.

Wenger, E (1999) *Communities of Practice: Learning, Meaning and Identity.* Cambridge: Cambridge University Press.

Williams, A (2013) Hochschild (2003) – the Managed Heart: The Recognition of Emotional Labour in Public Service Work. *Nurse Education Today*, 33: 5–7.

# 3 Pedagogy, inclusion and the SENCo's role

**TUNDE ROZSAHEGYI AND MIKE LAMBERT**

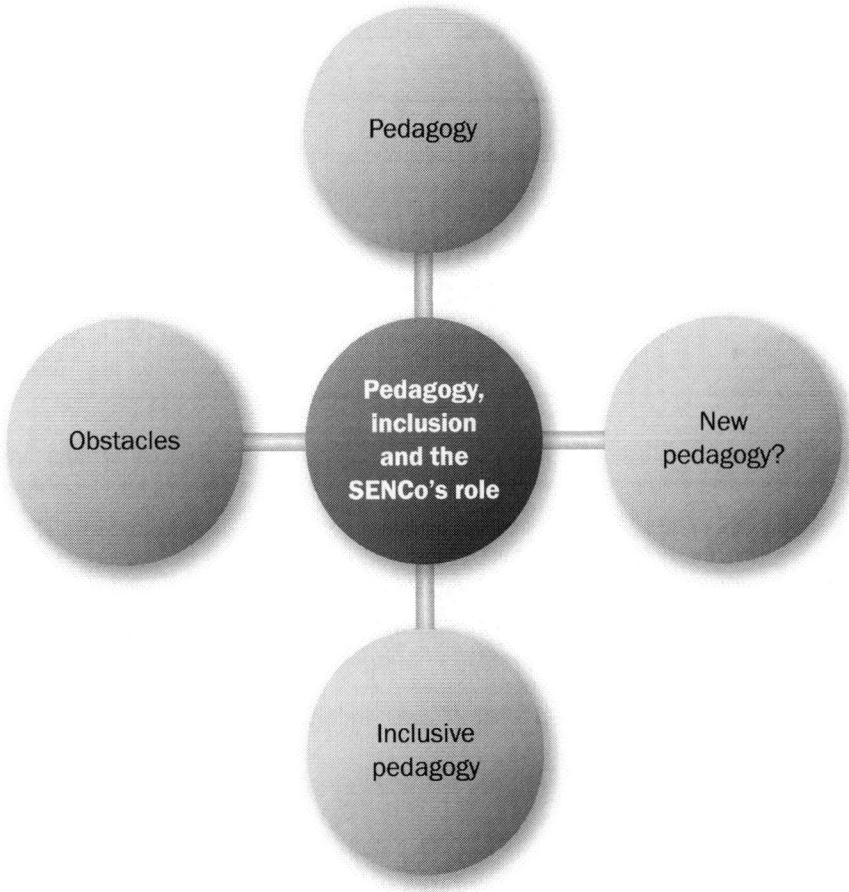

Pedagogy

Obstacles

Pedagogy, inclusion and the SENCo's role

New pedagogy?

Inclusive pedagogy

# Chapter objectives 🎯

This chapter invites readers to explore how the notion of pedagogy in general, and of inclusive pedagogy in particular, may strengthen the role of SENCos within efforts to develop and deliver inclusive education. The chapter:

- considers the nature of pedagogy and its significance in formulating, organising and carrying out successful education;

- considers the nature of inclusive pedagogy, and ways in which this contributes to understanding and realisation of inclusive teaching and learning;

- encourages readers to explore the strengthening of pedagogy and inclusive pedagogy as central concerns of SENCos;

- offers case studies to raise pedagogical issues for discussion by concerned educators and by prospective or actual SENCos.

## STARTING POINTS 🏁

» What do the terms 'pedagogy' and 'inclusive pedagogy' mean to you?

» To what extent do these notions play a part in your professional activity?

» In your opinion, to what extent are they relevant to the role of SENCos?

# Introduction

Brewin and Knowler's detailed and comprehensive treatise on the roles of SENCos (see Chapter 1) mentions an important word: 'pedagogy'. The term occurs twice : the first is early on in the chapter, when it is associated with historical evolution of the SENCo role, which has *'developed over time from support for learners and developing pedagogy towards a role that is multi-faceted'* (p 11); the second comes later, where pedagogy is advocated not in terms of history, but as an element of future professional and structural advancement: *'How might you, as a whole setting, move beyond compliance with statutory and administrative requirements, to develop and progress your inclusive ethos and pedagogy?'* (p 17).

This use of this word in the chapter, with its reference both to past and future, is interesting. The notion of pedagogy indeed has a long history, and in some educational cultures is a fundamental and frequently cited basis for developmental and educational thinking and practice. However, the concept also has a history of being disregarded or poorly judged in Western discourse, an issue examined – together with the kind of political and practical confusions which can result – by Alexander (2008). More specifically, it rarely plays a meaningful part in outlooks on the SENCo's role in England and Wales. Yet, if anyone was likely to have 'pedagogy' high up in their list of concerns, it would aptly be the SENCo, whose role incorporates particular responsibility for learners whose education in many ways can raise the most challenging pedagogical concerns.

# Pedagogy

'Pedagogy' unites in a single notion and a single word the values, principles and both the formal and creative processes of instruction and learning. It denotes the merging of the 'science' of teaching with its 'art', as seminally described by Gage (1978), cited by Galton et al (1999, p 189) and others. Alexander (2004, p 11) usefully encompassed both values and principles in a solitary, more graspable concept of 'attendant discourse', evoking not just philosophy, literature, research and grand political speeches but also thoughtful conversations in meetings, staff rooms and even, at times, at school or nursery gates.

Basically, pedagogy is a macro view of what constitutes teaching and child development (an equivalent word for adults is 'andragogy'). For Daniels (2016, p 1), it broadly incorporates *'forms of social practice which shape and form the cognitive, affective and moral developments of individuals'*. For Leach and Moon (1999, pp 268–9) it more specifically is a *'view of mind, of learning and learners, of the kind of knowledge that is valued and above all by educational outcomes that are desired'*. The term can also imply a broad perspective on learning, whereby *'commitment to children's overall development, attributes and personality are a vital addition to concern for formal learning outcomes normally associated with education'* (Rozsahegyi and Lambert, 2016, p 15).

'Nurturing' and 'overall development' are important words here as involvement in pedagogy extends more widely than among college, school or nursery educators, also taking in home, wider agencies and other stakeholders, as evident in Vygotsky's (1991, p 37) seminal dictum: *'Pedagogika – nauka o vospitanii detyei' – 'Pedagogy is the science of the upbringing of children'*. And despite the talk of 'values' and 'principles', pedagogy is by no means static. Instead, it is responsive to changes in moral, social and even political conditions. Its nature can therefore vary in relation to different social and international contexts, different belief systems and even different epochs.

That is not to say that pedagogy is forever the slave of location and time. It is malleable and can, and perhaps should, be purposefully and deliberately proposed, formulated, espoused – and challenged – as a common basis for teaching, learning and social development: *'Pedagogy is never neutral ... [educators] make choices in the pedagogies they adopt'* (Armstrong, 1998, p 58). In short, pedagogy needs to be worked out, debated and – ultimately and ideally – collectively owned.

---

### *Critical questions* (?)

» How does what you have read here (and in your own further reading or discussion) strengthen or change your understanding of 'pedagogy'?

» How might you now consider this concept when pursuing your professional work and your SENCo aspirations?

# New pedagogy?

From the above, one can deduce that with new times, new philosophies and new beliefs comes new pedagogy. The desire for inclusive education and, indeed, more broadly an inclusive society, is one such relatively recent evolution: *'Regular schools with [an] inclusive orientation are the most effective means of combating discriminatory attitudes, creating welcoming communities, building an inclusive society and achieving education for all'* (UNESCO, 1994, p ix). Such change in the UK and elsewhere in the last three decades has indeed required close examination of how an 'inclusive pedagogy' is formulated and how it should be put into practice. Four main components of these developments have become evident.

## Rights

Pedagogy should recognise common, non-negotiable rights and societal obligations, as encapsulated in international agreements, law, philosophy and the best of human thinking. An example is the right of all children to child-centred and empowering education (OHCHR, 2001), and that of those with disabilities to enjoy *'fundamental freedoms on an equal basis with other children'* (CRPD, 2006). In England and Wales there is legal presumption of mainstream education for children with special educational needs (Children and Families Act 2014) and educators are urged to maintain a *'focus on inclusive practice'* (DfE and DoH, 2015, p 25).

## Values

Pedagogical values are the reasons for thinking and acting in desirable ways. The values chosen are likely to apply to all learners, not just those whose educational needs are regarded as extra or special. For example, oft-advocated values are the respecting, indeed the cherishing, of diversity among learners, together with positive regard for what each child can bring to the collective learning process (for example, Baglieri and Shapiro, 2017).

## Principles

Principles are rules to live by, models to be acted upon. One important principle for inclusive education is that children, wherever possible, should receive their education together, under an all-encompassing ethos of equity and the intrinsic worth of all individuals.

## Practice

Practice is when rights, values and principles meet reality in an educational or developmental context. The question will constantly be: How should instruction and learning be organised and delivered to help all children to learn and develop – socially, emotionally, physically, academically – in the very best way they can? Importantly, for a well-developed and mature pedagogy, all the elements must link with each other, without mismatch or contradiction. For instance, rights must align with values, which must align with principles, and all must be evident in the *'rough ground of the practical'* (Schwandt, 2003, p 362), most importantly in the everyday actions of educators and others.

> ### Critical questions (?)
>
> Four levels in the make-up of pedagogy are assumed here: rights, values, principles and practice.
>
> » To what extent do the descriptions match your own understanding as an aspiring or practising SENCo?
>
> » How can their relevance to learners who have a range of special needs or disabilities be further explained?

# Inclusive pedagogy

As we have seen, the nature of pedagogy is not fixed – its elements are subject to further critical discovery and understanding. In terms of learners with disabilities, many societies have moved from social separation to integration and to inclusion, although elements from all of these, described by Wilde and Avramidis (2011), may still be evident, even in current perspectives. There has also been a move from concern with deficiencies in individuals ('handicaps') to concern for deficiencies in social attitudes, policies, organisation and provision, accompanied by a desire to change and improve these in order to strengthen inclusive outlooks and practices.

Inclusive pedagogy can thereby be defined as a shared deliberated stance, aimed at collective, successful nurturing and learning in mixed and mingled community settings. The actual process of change towards this is, of course, far from straightforward, and in reality there are considerable differences in how inclusive pedagogy is advocated and especially in the ways it is (or is not) borne out in practice. With this in mind, here are three not wholly distinct pedagogical scenarios for learners whose needs are seen as additional to those of their 'non-special' or 'non-disabled' peers.

## Dispersed

Standard educational approaches cover a majority of children (those seen or presumed to have customary needs for teaching and learning), alongside different approaches for those defined or identified as having educational needs further to or outside of this majority. Such needs may include the need for expert assistance and input or oversight by a SENCo. This distributed approach may involve specialist educational methodologies, available only in specialist settings, or separated location and provision in one mainstream site ('special units'). Despite this partition, and its potentially divided focus on *most and some learners* rather than on *everyone* (Florian and Linklater, 2010, p 370), a single value system may still claim to cover all learners, for instance the right of every child to an education which meets their 'individual needs'. A claim may also be made that separated, 'specialised' learning improves the disabled child's prospects for an inclusive adult life.

## All-embracing (all-inclusive)

A stance which embraces all learners in expression of common values and principles and in collective delivery in practice. Rights are paramount, locations are inclusive (and are designed to be so), as are actions of teaching and learning (albeit with facilitative differences).

## Mottled

A mixture or amalgamation of dispersed and all-embracing approaches, combining separated and collective arrangements under an umbrella of common values and beliefs. Location is shared (or mainly so); the actions of teaching and learning are differentiated and diverse.

---

### *Critical questions* (?)

» What are your views on the three scenarios outlined above? Which of these most closely reflects your own professional context?

» The first scenario suggests potential arguments about means and ends: can education be separate but still have inclusive purposes, or can only inclusive child education properly help social inclusivity in later life? What is your view?

» Florian and Beaton (2018, p 870) note the following: '*Inclusive pedagogy... is a pedagogical response to individual differences between pupils that avoids the marginalisation that can occur with differentiation strategies that are designed only with individual needs in mind*'. To what extent and in what ways does this statement relate to each of the scenarios described above?

---

### *Implications for the SENCo's role, identity and practice*

Adherence to the notion of pedagogy in general, and to inclusive pedagogy in particular, has major implications for the role of SENCos and, it has to be said, can present some major challenges as well. Here, to start with, is an imagined, four-faceted ideal.

1. The SENCo is a visionary, philosopher, theorist and creative thinker; far-sighted and able to see what the future holds, wide-sighted in the here and now.

2. The SENCo is an activist; protector of rights and values; voice of the unvoiced and overlooked; campaigner for learners, parents and others; speaking, urging, acting and deciding on behalf of others, using knowledge, empathy, beliefs and understandings.

3. The SENCo is an enthusiast for pedagogy itself and for inclusive pedagogy in particular; a principal designer, player and protector of togetherness in the curriculum; a believer in what is to be learnt and how that can best be done.

4.      The SENCo is a day-to-day pragmatist, doer, logician and realist; guided by practical considerations of the real world; evaluator of pedagogical theories in terms of success in their practical application.

Four ideals, but actual SENCos themselves may at this point be scratching their collective heads. In real life, a SENCo's role is likely to be more organisational and administrative than philosophical; more follower of official edict than formulator of values; more solver of problems than guardian of rights; and more used to managerial compromise than to pedagogical ideals. Most crucially, a SENCo's relatively humble position within the school's leadership structure, and even a sense of isolation within the school as a whole (Curran et al, 2018), may mean that pursuing grand aims such as those listed above appears largely unrealistic.

This reality is indeed evident in much of the official literature. The most recent Code of Practice (CoP) (DfE and DoH, 2015, pp 108–9) lists oversight, co-ordination, liaison, advising and other managerial roles among a SENCo's obligations but does not mention pedagogical responsibilities in any meaningful way. The closest the requirements for the SENCo National Award come to inclusive pedagogy are that SENCos should know and understand the implications of '*relevant theory, research and inspection evidence about effective practice in including pupils with SEN and/or disabilities*' and that they should '*advise on and influence the strategic development of a person-centred and inclusive ethos, policies, priorities and practices*' (National College for Teaching and Leadership, 2014, pp 6, 7).

## *Critical questions* ?

»      If you are aspiring to become a SENCo, what elements of the above descriptions do you consider should be most prevalent in your future role? Which should be least prevalent?

»      What kind of other, more specific, roles would you expect to fulfil when you become a SENCo? To what extent do these echo the ideal roles described above?

# Obstacles

The remark from Papatheodorou (2007, p 40) that '*diversity in... education is not without its challenges*' was perhaps an understatement. Indeed, formulating inclusive pedagogies in ideas, as you are encouraged to do in this chapter, may be the easier part – acting them out in practice and making them work for children, families and communities is probably much more difficult. Here are three of the obstacles which can stand in the way, each accompanied by a short personal case study which illustrates the point in question.

# Constraint

Cynics might point out that official commitment to inclusive education is relatively skin-deep. More important than human rights and pedagogical values are the political agenda, financial budgets and (let's face it) the result of the next election. The more sympathetic would point out that change, especially paradigmatic change, which is what inclusion requires, is difficult, that money is not limitless (although Ainscow et al, 2019, and others have pointed out that education together is less costly than education divided), and that concern with winning elections is a price we pay for living democratically. Whatever one's stance, it is clear that official direction does not always facilitate the strengthening of inclusive pedagogy and inclusive systems of education.

## CASE STUDY ⊙

### Constraint

*It is very difficult to see beyond attainment and achievement when it is such a huge focus and when, as a teacher in England, my performance and worth are measured against results within my class. Teaching in Year 2 (children aged six to seven) includes SATS (standardised assessment tests, required in the English educational system), which heighten the heavy pressure of gaining good academic outcomes. It is evident that we cannot talk about this kind of standardised assessment and inclusion together, where individual differences are not celebrated and instead children are compared and set against averages and figures. Some SEND children do not sit assessments due to school scores and this will be the case for two learners in my class.*

## Critical questions ❓

» To what extent is this teacher and aspiring SENCo justified in perceiving the impossibility of combining performance-oriented, standardised assessment with an inclusive approach?

» What other elements of school systems can act as barriers to the development and implementation of inclusive pedagogies?

» What position can SENCos take in the face of apparently rival agendas and incompatible demands?

# Scope

Another issue is when we start to ask ourselves if the focus of inclusion in relation to learners who have special needs related to disability is really the best and most useful one to have. From this perspective, disability is far from being the only 'difference' an educator needs to take into account: cultural, linguistic, gender, social class and other elements of diversity can all be associated with disadvantage or difficulty if an educational system lacks discernment and flexibility. Why should 'inclusive pedagogy' (and indeed a SENCo's role) not consciously embrace them all?

## CASE STUDY ⊖

### Scope

*I am a teacher in Nigeria, and SEND documentation there, as in England and Wales, focuses solely on learning difficulties associated with specified disabilities. Yet the first form of 'special needs' I see in Nigeria derives from material deprivation. For example, some of the students in my class are hungry and need food; others do not have proper clothing or writing materials and need these – why do they not qualify as students with 'special educational needs'? I posit that the definition of 'special needs' needs to be broadened; it should be all-encompassing.*

### Critical questions ⑦

» How might the widening of scope, which this teacher suggests, help or hinder the development of inclusive pedagogy and successful education for all?

» What practical implications would it have for the role of SENCos within the managerial structure of schools and other contexts?

» In relation to this and to other case studies in this chapter, what literature or research can you find which discusses or expresses opinion on this issue?

# Stresses and strains

As indicated earlier, concern about the management burdens of SENCos are long-standing. The SEND CoP (DfE and DoH, 2015, p 109) may have good intentions in this regard: SENCos should have '*sufficient time and resources... administrative support and time away from teaching*', but complaints about excessive workload are well rehearsed (for example, by Tirraoro, 2018).

To stresses and strains one might add frustration, as the relatively low standing of many SENCos within leadership structures means that influence in strengthening inclusive pedagogy is very difficult to achieve. Westwood (2007), among others, long ago pointed out that successful inclusion was most likely to come about with strong leadership and supportive whole-school policy and commitment. Research by Tissot (2013, p 34) concluded that failure to make membership of the senior leadership team a requirement for SENCos '*supports a tension between the theoretical agreement that [they] are senior leaders and the day-to-day work done when making school-wide decisions on priorities and practice*'. This leadership requirement, together with a protected, full-time role, continues to be urged, for example by Lamb (2021).

## CASE STUDY ☺

### *Stresses and strains*

*I am a SENCo in a large primary school. I am also a classroom teacher and have responsibility for science as well. I often find that issues about children with special educational needs, which I want to discuss, are ignored or side-stepped by more senior colleagues. So as well as getting all the extra SENCo work, I get discouraged as well. On one occasion I became particularly upset because a child got into trouble for violence against another child, but no action was taken at senior level to prevent it happening again and the second child's parents blamed me. My understanding of inclusion is that it should involve the whole school, especially management, and including parents, children and other agencies. I feel that SENCos should not be left on their own to deal with things like this.*

### Critical questions ❓

» What practical and pedagogical issues are raised in this short account?

» What improvements or solutions would you suggest a) for the SENCo and b) for leadership in the school?

## Chapter summary 📝

Formulating inclusive pedagogy forces us to determine relevant social values and purposes in the design of education, as well as in the actions of educators. This chapter has raised some of the issues and options involved in strengthening thoughtful and meaningful developments of this kind in individual professionals, including prospective SENCos, and in systems as a whole. These include:

• the function of pedagogy in creating a macro view of what constitutes teaching and child development;

• the particular significance for SENCos of new and inclusive pedagogy, encompassing rights, values, principles and educational practices;

• challenging implications for hard-pressed SENCos, involving issues of outlook, status and influence, as well as how to address the constraints, stresses and strains which accompany their work.

# Further reading 📖

Hart, S, Dixon, A, Drummond, A J and McIntyre, D (2004) *Learning without Limits*. Maidenhead: Open University Press.

- Radical concepts of inclusive pedagogy seek a conceptualisation of learners which is not based on ability. The case for this is persuasively presented in this book. Whether or not you are convinced by its arguments, they might just help you tone down a professional obsession with the vocabulary and acronyms of 'SEN' and now 'SEND', both of which serve largely to disconnect some learners from their peers.

Winwood, J (2016) Leading and Managing for Inclusion. In Brown, Z (ed) *Inclusive Education: Perspectives on Pedagogy, Policy and Practice* (pp 22–33). Abingdon: Routledge.

- This book chapter provides a carefully argued overview of how the SENCo can become a 'knowledgeable guide', close to pedagogy as part of distributed leadership and sharing of responsibilities within a whole-school approach. This involves a more encompassing and affirmative emphasis on inclusion, above and beyond the restricted and often deficit-focused field of special educational needs and disability.

# References 📚

Ainscow, M, Slee, R and Best, M (2019) Editorial: The Salamanca Statement: 25 Years On. *International Journal of Inclusive Education*, 23(7–8): 671–6.

Alexander, R (2004) Still No Pedagogy? Principle, Pragmatism and Compliance in Primary Education. *Cambridge Journal of Education*, 34(1): 7–33.

Alexander, R (2008) *Essays on Pedagogy*. Abingdon: Routledge.

Armstrong, F (1998) Curricula, 'Management' and Special and Inclusive Education. In Clough, P (ed) *Managing Inclusive Education: From Policy to Experience* (pp 48–63). London: Paul Chapman.

Baglieri, S with Shapiro, A (2017) *Disability Studies and the Inclusive Classroom: Critical Practices for Embracing Diversity in Education*. 2nd ed. Abingdon: Routledge.

Children and Families Act 2014. [online] Available at: www.legislation.gov.uk/ukpga/2014/6/contents/enacted (accessed 16 April 2023).

Committee on the Rights of Persons with Disabilities (CRPD) (2006) *United Nations Convention on the Rights of Persons with Disabilities*. 6 December 2006. [online] Available at: www.un.org/esa/socdev/enable/rights/convtexte.htm (accessed 18 April 2023).

Curran, H, Moloney, H, Heavey, A and Boddison, A (2018) *It's about Time: The Impact of SENCO Workload on the Professional and the School*. Bath Spa University/Nasen/National Education Union. [online] Available at: www.bathspa.ac.uk/media/bathspaacuk/education-/research/senco-workload/SENCOWorkloadReport-FINAL2018.pdf (accessed 14 April 2023).

Daniels, H (2016) *Vygotsky and Pedagogy*. 2nd ed. Abingdon: Routledge.

Department for Education (DfE) and Department of Health (DoH) (2015) *Special Educational Needs and Disability Code of Practice: 0 to 25 Years*. [online] Available at: https://assets.publishing.service.gov.uk/government/uploads/system/uploads/attachment_data/file/398815/SEND_Code_of_Practice_January_2015.pdf (accessed 22 May 2023).

Florian, L and Beaton, M (2018) Inclusive Pedagogy in Action: Getting It Right for Every Child. *International Journal of Inclusive Education*, 22(8): 870–84.

Florian, L and Linklater, H (2010) Preparing Teachers for Inclusive Education: Using Inclusive Pedagogy to Enhance Teaching and Learning for All. *Cambridge Journal of Education*, 40(4): 369–86.

Galton, M, Hargreaves, L, Comber, C, Wall, D, with Pell, A (1999) *Inside the Primary Classroom: 20 Years On*. London: Routledge.

Lamb, B (2021) The Future of SEND Legislation in England: What Next? In Beaton, M C, Codina, G N and Wharton J C (eds) (2021) *Leading on Inclusion: The Role of the SENCo* (pp 35–44). Abingdon: Routledge.

Leach, J and Moon, B (1999) Recreating Pedagogy. In Leach, J and Moon, B (eds) *Learners and Pedagogy* (pp 265–75). London: Paul Chapman.

National College for Teaching and Leadership (2014) *National Award for SEN Co-ordination: Learning Outcomes*. [online] Available at: www.gov.uk/government/publications/national-award-for-sen-co-ordination-learning-outcomes (accessed 14 April 2023).

Office of the United Nations High Commissioner for Human Rights (OHCHR) (2001) *General Comment No. 1: The Aims of Education (Article 29)*. [online] Available at: www.ohchr.org/en/resources/educators/human-rights-education-training/general-comment-no-1-aims-education-article-29-2001 (accessed 15 April 2023).

Papatheodorou, T (2007) Difference, Culture and Diversity: Challenges, Responsibilities and Opportunities. In Moyles J (ed) *Early Years Foundations: Meeting the Challenge* (pp 40–59). Maidenhead: Open University Press.

Rozsahegyi, T and Lambert, M (2016) Pedagogy for Inclusion? In Brown, Z (ed) *Inclusive Education: Perspectives on Pedagogy, Policy and Practice* (pp 14–22). Abingdon: Routledge.

Schwandt, T A (2003) 'Back to the Rough Ground!' Beyond Theory to Practice in Evaluation. *Evaluation*, 9(3): 353–64.

Tirraoro, T (2018) The Devastating Impact of the SENCo Workload. *Special Needs Jungle*, 30 November. [online] Available at: www.specialneedsjungle.com/the-devastating-impact-of-the-senco-workload/ (accessed 16 April 2023).

Tissot, C (2013) The Role of SENCos as Leaders. *British Journal of Special Education*, 40(1): 33–40.

UNESCO (1994) *Salamanca Statement and Framework for Action on Special Needs Education*. United Nations Educational, Scientific and Cultural Organization. Salamanca, Spain, 7–10 June 1994.

Vygotsky, L S (1991) Pedagogika i psikhologiya. In Davydova, V V (ed) *Pedagogicheskaya Psikhologiya*. Moscow: Pedagogika.

Westwood, P (2007) *Commonsense Methods for Children with Special Educational Needs*. 5th ed. Abingdon: Routledge.

Wilde, A and Avramidis, E (2011) Mixed Feelings: Towards a Continuum of Inclusive Pedagogies. *Education 3–13*, 39(1): 83–101.

# 4 The SENCo as advocate: speaking up and speaking out

**KITTY HUTHWAITE AND LAURA HOWIESON**

SENCos as managers

Skills for advocacy leadership

**SENCo as advocate**

SENCo as advocacy leader

Working with others and making change

# Chapter objectives 🎯

This chapter explores the capacity of SENCos to work as advocates for pupils and their families by embracing advocacy leadership in the SENCo role. The chapter:

*   critically reflects on the advocacy leadership dimension of the SENCo role in relation to SEND practice;

*   explores the challenges for SENCos transitioning from management into advocacy leadership over time;

*   critically investigates examples of SENCos challenging inequalities in their roles.

---

### STARTING POINTS 🏁

»   What do you think are the key differences between managing and leading as a SENCo?

»   Reflecting on your current role, are you working more as a manager or as leader?

»   If you feel your role is 'one-sided', what skills do you need to develop to balance your profile as an influencer of policy in your school and strategic leader?

---

# Introduction

Liasidou and Svensson (2014) note that there are many challenges in leading SEND provision in schools and while the specifics of *doing* the SENCo role from an administrative perspective might be clear for someone new to the role, the challenges of transitioning from management to leadership are more complex and require further reflection (Clarke and Done, 2021). SENCos work across subject boundaries, across age phases and collaborate with many differing professionals, both internally and externally (see Chapter 9). This chapter is premised on the idea that while SENCos need to be organised and engaged, considering the balance between administration and advocacy leadership offers useful avenues for reflection and possibilities for doing things differently. In our experience, SENCos can have limited agency to enact change and challenge practices that are not supporting inclusive provision. Therefore, this chapter invites readers to see beyond the role of the SENCo as a manager or administrator and to think about the skills, values and experiences that support advocacy leadership (Clarke and Done, 2021).

# The SENCo as advocacy leader

The idea that a SENCo is a leader in their school has developed in SEND policy over time (Sobel, 2016). Leadership was not foregrounded in the 1996 and 2001 iterations of the SEND Code of Practice (CoP), where the focus was on the managerial accountability a SENCo could bring to administrative processes of SEND provision (Tissot, 2013). This retrospective nature of the inclusion of strategic capacities for the SENCo role in the most recent iteration of the SEND CoP (DfE and DoH, 2015) has led to many professionals reporting that they struggle to fulfil the expectations of the wider school community and their involvement in their work (Curran and Boddison, 2021). Kearns (2005) found that SENCos adopt multiple, sometimes concurrent, approaches or roles, including that of arbiter, rescuer, auditor, collaborator and expert, making the notion of a coherent identity for SENCos very difficult (if not undesirable) to achieve.

Transitioning into an advocacy leadership orientation in the role of SENCo is relevant, because as Winwood (2016) asserts they have many opportunities to demonstrate advocacy approaches to their work in ways that classroom teachers do not. For example, a SENCo can take an active role in building partnerships with staff, parents and external organisations, and in ensuring learners' full participation and engagement by setting a clear direction for school policies and practice. Supporting the development of staff and other stakeholders using all available evidence, experience and expertise to collaboratively create and sustain the learning community and support everyone to achieve the best possible outcomes sits within an advocacy leadership orientation in recognising that leadership is a collective and co-ordinated effort. Oldham and Radford (2011) point out that there is a danger of the SENCo being seen as 'heroic' and while efforts to be an advocate are laudable, SENCos do need to be strategic about the use of advocacy skills so that this work is properly recognised and supported. Advocacy leadership is not about solving issues and challenges on behalf of everyone within a school community, but as Anderson (2009) points out it is an orientation towards leadership centring social justice outcomes for pupils, rather than outcomes designed for accountability measures (such as league tables). Done et al (2022) argue that adopting an advocacy leadership position means that SENCos will be working against neo-liberal discourses that can position the role as only administrative, with excessive workloads and lack of time for reflection or professional learning, instead demonstrating the ways that SENCos' specialist knowledge and skills can support the development of inclusive cultures.

We would argue, in the vein of Pearson et al (2014, p 54), that SENCos need to have *'a vision of inclusive schools, in which there is a collective responsibility for the achievement of all learners'*. As explored in Chapters 7 and 11 in this book, the development of the SENCo as an advocacy leader is important for very specific reasons, such as moving away from deficit notions of SEND towards ideals of inclusion by recognising that effective teaching works for all pupils. Additionally, this positionality encourages joint ownership of SEND-related tasks, potentially creating communities of practice around needs, topics or provision, all of which can positively contribute to staff development. Crucially, many of the managerial tasks which SENCos can feel overwhelmed by could be distributed to class or subject teachers, again encouraging positive experiences of developing inclusive communities.

---

### *Critical questions* (?)

» How would you describe your vision for SEND and inclusion within your school and how close are you to achieving it?

» Consider how you will develop your leadership with respect to your SENCo role.

» How might you develop communities of practice to take joint responsibility for SEND and inclusion school policy and practice?

# Facing challenges as a SENCo

We landed on the concept of 'speaking up and speaking out' as we were reflecting on the ways that SENCo work is so often conceptualised as an administrative or managerial role (Smith, 2022). Many of the SENCos we have supported in our professional development roles have their 'ear to the ground', particularly in terms of schools' abilities to support learners – they know the strengths and areas for development of the organisation and keep up to date with the latest statutory developments in SEND policy. SENCos are often acutely aware of the ethical imperatives of being effective in observing and learning about good practice because of the direct relationship between teaching and learning effectiveness and learner outcomes (Akram, 2019). This ethical positioning means that SENCos can usefully reflect on ways to 'speak up and speak out' about the ethical processes of developing inclusive provision, and that this reflection will not only support their development as an advocacy leader but also their school's ability to enact inclusive cultures (Cole, 2005). Drawing on the work of Loretta Ross (Ross, 2021), speaking up and speaking out is not an unintentional and random strategy for 'calling out' colleagues who are perceived as 'uninclusive.' Rather, Ross sees effective advocacy work as the process of 'calling in' our colleagues and fellow professionals and inviting them to a conversation about inclusion and pupil experiences and outcomes.

One strategy for SENCos to develop the ability to speak up and speak out is to utilise research-informed ways of advocating for learners and their families. This promotes an ability to speak up using evidence-based suggestions and signposting (as explored in Chapter 12), rather than cherry picking actions that seem easy and might solve barriers to inclusion in short-term ways. Speaking up and speaking out means developing the ability to ask questions with respect and professional curiosity, especially the questions that parents and families might not have the courage to ask. It means having data and information to hand so that complex problems and experiences are appropriately acknowledged by schools and teachers. Linked to this, a more curious approach to information seeking would also help in finding different ways to avoid confrontations that can arise when working with sensitive and emotive aspects of provision such as one-to-one supporting, EHCP processes and transition points such as the moves between Year 6 and Year 7.

---

### *Critical questions* (?)

&raquo; Think about a time when a decision you made in your role went well– what factors helped you to feel this way?

&raquo; CPD for teachers and SENCos is ongoing and dynamic. Does this make you feel excited and challenged positively? Or does this make you feel anxious?

&raquo; Take some time to consider and reflect on this aspect of your work and discuss further with a trusted colleague.

If the SENCo is to lead on strategy and process, we would encourage SENCos to explore notions of trust in the wider school team. It goes without saying that we would favour a collaborative approach to teaching and learning development, with the SENCo and other senior leaders ensuring that those children and young people with SEND have effective and timely support to achieve the learning. There is an interesting intersection here between teaching and learning development and accountability (Beauchamp et al, 2015), and sitting in this space can be uncomfortable for SEND teams as they support and challenge their colleagues. Development opportunities can include information sharing, team planning, team teaching, coaching and formal feedback and adaptive teaching. Where these have not been successful, and children and young people with SEND are still not making expected progress, it may be necessary to move towards individual accountability for ineffective practice. This can involve difficult conversations and the SENCo may need the support of other senior leaders. Knowledge and tolerance of bad educational practices is not only unfair to the pupils in the school because it might lead to exclusion (Done and Knowler, 2020), but is also unfair to the staff as others will need to fill gaps in learning or provide emotional support to a pupil who thinks they may be failing. Bomber (2022) argues that the teacher needs to know the pupils that they teach to set appropriate challenges in the learning. If the challenge is not at the right level, disengagement or disruption is likely to occur (Bomber, 2022). The SENCo can support teachers to focus on scaffolding for the pupil to achieve success.

In the following section, we share three short case study examples of SENCos working around complex issues. We have selected examples of advocacy leadership and considered the kind of dilemmas (Rose, 2011) SENCos experience in their daily work. Each case study is followed by a short 'so what?' discussion. The purpose of the examples is to support reflection and discussion that will lead to further questions for colleagues or the senior leadership team at school.

## CASE STUDY

### The SENCo as advocate

*Autism doesn't always present itself clearly in schools; some pupils are adept at masking and have just enough social functionality to make it difficult for education professionals to spot in the day-to-day bustle of a school. Mahdi is the SENCo in a school situated in an affluent urban area but, as with most schools, there are pockets of deprivation that the catchment area encompasses. During his first week, Mahdi receives a request to meet a parent; he seeks information from staff so that he can prepare for the meeting. Staff report nothing of note: the pupil is progressing well and, other than an increasing absence rate, there are no concerns. Mahdi looks further at the attendance data and spots that there may be a pattern: absence is usually on a Monday and anxiety is the usual reason given.*

*During the meeting, the mother describes her daughter differently to the pupil seen in school. She describes frequent aggressive outbursts, both physical and verbal; refusals to leave the home; destruction of possessions; obsessions over patterns of speech; a lack of reciprocal*

→

*friendships; a fussiness over certain foods and some risky behaviours such as contacting unknown persons online and self-harming. The mother breaks down and confides that her marriage is suffering and that she is beginning to resent her daughter. Mahdi reassures the mother that she has done the right thing in bringing this to the school as there are things that can be done that may relieve some of the tensions at home. He also decided to gently broach the topic of autism and how this may present in females on the basis of what the mother has described and his past experiences – he is careful to state that he is not offering a diagnosis. Mahdi is familiar with the research evidence that most females with autism possess an innate social drive, and this motivates them to use social techniques such as masking (Tierney et al, 2016); Mahdi feels this may explain why the school isn't reporting any issues at the moment.*

*Mahdi briefs staff about the meeting but some staff are unwilling to adapt for a pupil that presents no problems in the classroom. Mahdi's role here is to advocate for the family: he needs staff to understand how school may be causing the problems at home. He decides to equip staff with the knowledge of how autism presents in females and the palpable difference that simple provisions could make. He shares The Girl with the Curly Hair (2018) website as a basis to create change in a staff meeting.*

Smith (2022) suggests that speaking up and speaking out – to advocate for learners – does not need to be made up of large-scale change or radical reform to make a difference. This case study demonstrates that a decision to share knowledge about SEND with parents and staff had the potential to make a positive impact. Mahdi recognised that assumptions, lack of knowledge and maybe even a lack of professional curiosity can lead to inequitable provision for some learners, and simple information sharing and exploring possibilities has opened new possibilities. Crucially, Mahdi took responsibility for locating a potential issue with school systems, rather than within the pupil or their family – something that is central to the development of inclusive cultures and practices (Azorin and Ainscow, 2020).

## CASE STUDY 🎧

### The SENCo as advocate for inclusive cultures

*James has worked as a SENCo for five years in a busy secondary school in an urban area of England. He decided to train as a SENCo as he enjoys working with staff on 'wicked problems' (Armstrong, 2017) in education. He has invested a lot of time in arranging training and development for teaching assistants (TAs). On reflection, James has realised that the focus on the knowledge and understanding of TAs in relation to creating positive behaviour cultures has resulted in a split between the practices of teachers and TAs. For example, James started to observe instances where teaching staff had strong expectations that TAs will deal with behaviour. He wondered whether this means they do not take on board the concept of every teacher is a teacher of SEND (DfE and DoH, 2015). He has also noticed that the TAs have developed strong consistency of approach when they work with pupils and that since they attended training together, they have developed a shared language in relation to school rules and expectations.*

*James thinks that there are several barriers to inclusive practice in this scenario. First, the differences between expectations around pastoral support is not conducive to team working and shared responsibility for care and safeguarding. James reflects that in the future, for some aspects of SEND training he needs to do whole-school training where all staff are involved. He thinks he could develop a training needs analysis so that he can offer a more differentiated and bespoke training programme to better gauge when staff training is more beneficial done together or in job-role groups.*

In this example, we see evidence that James has reflected on how to better understand the attitudinal barriers to inclusion within his school (Lindner et al, 2023). However, in developing approaches to one challenge in his setting, another has emerged. This is a reality of change management and though James could try to move on to other issues, he has remained committed to working through the difficult conversations; these challenge colleagues' negative attitudes towards children's needs and are a necessary step towards inclusive culture and practice. This is likely to support better targeting of training topics, because James has work to do around supporting a staff culture where all staff understand their roles and responsibilities under the Teacher Standards (specifically Part One: Teaching – Standard 5). James needs to think about further professional learning around having difficult conversations with staff that do not share the school's ethos outlined in behavioural and pastoral policies. However, James is clearly demonstrating an important dimension of strategic thinking within his role that is vital to be able to observe a different culture in the school.

## CASE STUDY ↻

### The SENCo empowering others

*Louise is a SENCo in a large primary school in the south of England. Initially, Louise found the role extremely demanding and so carefully analysed how she was spending her time. A clear and dominant factor was that although the SEND CoP (DfE and DoH, 2015) clearly states that all teachers are responsible for children with special needs, staff were not always equipped with the knowledge and understanding of how best to support children with special needs as part of a graduated response. Many were using Louise as a 'font of all knowledge' and would ask copious questions about best approaches for different groups of children.*

→

*Some teachers felt disempowered by their limited ability to identify learning differences and the strategies to use with children with different needs.*

*Although the answers to many concerns could be addressed in the longer term through CPD activities, Louise noticed that many staff used ad hoc approaches (such as quick internet searches) if they could not get hold of her quickly. She reflected on the risk, when staff explore approaches for themselves, that this could lead to an inconsistent set of strategies being used across different settings. Louise wanted to focus on strategies that could offer flexibility for staff in their specific contexts, but also that were based on robust research. Like many SENCos, Louise needed to make decisions about how best to direct her time and resources. She decided that a centralised online resource for all staff which explained different types of special needs and a graduated response to them would be ideal for her school and others in the Academy Trust. In consultation with her senior leadership colleagues, Louise built a website as a centralised resource for colleagues. In considering who would have access to the website, she decided that parents as well as staff should be encouraged to use it. Her website was launched, and feedback suggested it was a useful tool for staff and parents. It also forms a crucial part of the induction of teachers who are new to the Trust.*

In this case study, Louise demonstrates the importance of careful non-judgemental scrutiny of the situation across her school – she did not seek to blame or shame her colleagues, despite understandable frustration that staff seemed to rely on her for solutions to their day-to-day challenges. Louise also demonstrates a degree of courage in suggesting a strategy that at first glance appeared to be very time-consuming, but that had the potential to impact the ways that colleagues learned about SEND. The website offered a viable way of understanding the training and support needs of both staff and parents by tracking engagement with the website content. Louise did this by looking at clicks and downloads and asking for user comments on website content. The website offers the clear potential to drive consistency across the school in terms of process of identification, planning and evaluation, as well as definitions, inclusive pedagogies and even sharing successful approaches between colleagues. Although these aspects are not guaranteed and would require ongoing website oversight by Louise, there is no doubt that fostering more sustained knowledge and understanding of inclusive pedagogies (see Chapter 3) is important in the development of inclusive cultures.

## Implications for the SENCo role, identity and practice

The case studies demonstrate how far the skills of SENCos go beyond management and administration, and how it is impossible for a SENCo to deal individually with all the issues that arise in their school. For this reason, we would argue that behaving tactically is a crucial skill. These strategic approaches involve thinking in the long term and empowering others within the school community to feel a sense of agency. This is important as many SENCos report the challenges of having to keep reacting to day-to-day issues, rather than strategic issues in their school (Clarke and Done, 2021). Savill-Smith and Scanlan (2022) demonstrate that this continual responsiveness can lead to burnout, which eventually impacts the ability to cope with the challenges of the SENCo role. Advocacy SENCos will:

» invoke the support of colleagues from both within and outside their school;

» allow the needs of the child, rather than compliance with legislation, to drive their work;

» identify common goals and encourage dialogue rather than conflict;

» seek to recognise the voice of the child and their family, and of the school, even when these are in tension;

» be able to justify decisions, especially when these are problematic;

» promote discourse around advocacy rather than accountability.

# Chapter summary

We have argued that while SENCos are in an ideal position to lead on SEND practices in their school, this also extends to thinking about the ways that their role supports advocacy-based practices, such as having a commitment to socially just approaches to intervention design and implementation. While some SENCos arguably do work from a values-based perspective, Clarke and Done (2021) demonstrate that SENCos need to go beyond the expectations of the SEND CoP (DfE and DoH, 2015) to claim that school support and resources are truly inclusive. Fundamentally, this requires SENCos to recognise practices that are counterproductive or that damage families' trust in the school. SENCos need to have a multi-pronged approach to speaking up and speaking out. This is something that needs to be intentionally developed; it takes time and will be context specific for each SENCo. Also, basic principles of good communication, the ability to form productive relationships and building trust and warmth are crucial. When these skills are underpinned by up-to-date knowledge, understanding and evidence, SENCos will be working as advocates for the learners in their school.

# Further reading

Devi, A and Bowers, J (2023) *Journeying to the Heart of SENCo Wellbeing: A Guide to Enable and Empower SEND Leaders*. Abingdon: Routledge.

• This engaging and accessible text forefronts well-being for SENCos and centres the relational dimensions of the role. This is important as advocating for pupils and their families is sometimes difficult work and SENCos need to be able to prioritise care and health to do their role to the best of their ability.

# References

Akram, M (2019) Relationship between Students' Perceptions of Teacher Effectiveness and Student Achievement at Secondary School Level. *Bulletin of Education and Research*, 41(2): 93–108.

Anderson, G (2009) *Advocacy Leadership: Towards a Post-Reform Agenda in Education.* New York: Routledge.

Armstrong, D (2017) Wicked Problems in Special and Inclusive Education. *Journal of Research in Special Educational Needs*, 17(4): 229–36.

Azorin, C and Ainscow, M (2020) Guiding Schools on Their Journey towards Inclusion. *International Journal of Inclusive Education*, 24(1): 58–76.

Beauchamp, G, Clarke, L, Hulme, M, Jephcote, M, Kennedy, A, Magennis, G, Menter, I, Murray, J, Mutton, T, O'Doherty, T and Peiser, G (2015). *Teacher Education in Times of Change*. Bristol: Policy Press.

Bomber, L M (2022) *Know Me to Teach Me: Differentiated Discipline for Those Recovering from Adverse Childhood Experiences*. London: Worth Publishing.

Clarke, A L and Done, E J (2021) Balancing Pressures for SENCos as Managers, Leaders and Advocates in the Emerging Context of the Covid-19 Pandemic. *British Journal of Special Education*, 48: 157–74.

Cole, B (2005) Mission Impossible? Special Educational Needs, Inclusion and the Re-conceptualization of the Role of the SENCO in England and Wales. *European Journal of Special Needs Education*, 20(3): 287–307.

Curran, H and Boddison, A (2021) 'It's the Best Job in the World, but One of the Hardest, Loneliest, Most Misunderstood Roles in a School.' Understanding the Complexity of the SENCO Role Post-SEND Reform. *Journal of Research in Special Educational Needs*, 21(1): 39–48.

Department for Education (DfE) (2011) *Teachers' Standards*. [online] Available at: www.gov.uk/government/publications/teachers-standards (accessed 12 June 2023).

Department for Education (DfE) and Department of Health (DoH) (2015) *Special Educational Needs and Disability Code of Practice: 0 to 25 Years*. [online] Available at: https://assets.publishing.service.gov.uk/government/uploads/system/uploads/attachment_data/file/398815/SEND_Code_of_Practice_January_2015.pdf (accessed 8 June 2023).

Done, E J and Knowler, H (2020) Painful Invisibilities: Roll Management or 'Off-Rolling' and Professional Identity. *British Educational Research Journal*, 46(3): 516–31.

Done, E J, Knowler, H, Richards, H and Brewster, S (2022) Advocacy Leadership and the Deprofessionalising of the Special Educational Needs Co-ordinator Role. *British Journal of Special Education*. https://doi.org/10.1111/1467-8578.12449

Kearns, H (2005) Exploring the Experiential Learning of Special Educational Needs Coordinators. *Journal of In-service Education*, 31(1): 131–50.

Liasidou, A and Svensson, C (2014) Educating Leaders for Social Justice: The Case of Special Educational Needs Co-ordinators. *International Journal of Inclusive Education*, 18(8): 783–97.

Lindner, K, Schwab, S, Emara, M and Avramidis, E (2023) Do Teachers Favor the Inclusion of All Students? A Systematic Review of Primary Schoolteachers' Attitudes towards Inclusive Education. *European Journal of Special Needs Education*. https://doi.org/10.1080/08856257.2023.2172894

Oldham, J and Radford, J (2011) Secondary SENCo Leadership: A Universal or Specialist Role? *British Journal of Special Education*, 38(3): 126–34.

Pearson, S, Mitchell, R and Rapti, M (2014) 'I Will Be "Fighting" Even More for Pupils with SEN': SENCOs' Role Predictions in the Changing English Policy Context. *Journal of Research in Special Educational Needs*, 15(1): 48–56.

Rose, J R (2011) Dilemmas of Inter-Professional Collaboration: Can They Be Resolved? *Children and Society*, 25(2): 151–63.

Ross, L (2021) Don't Call People Out – Call Them In. TED talk. [online] Available at www.youtube.com/watch?v=xw_720iQDss (accessed 12 June 2023).

Savill-Smith, C and Scanlan, D (2022) *The Teacher Wellbeing Index.* Education Support. [online] Available at: www.educationsupport.org.uk/media/zoga2r13/teacher-wellbeing-index-2022.pdf (accessed 19 July 2023).

Smith, A (2022) The Experiences of New Primary School Special Educational Needs Coordinators: Presenting the SENCO Voice through Concept-Drawing and Personal Narratives. *Support for Learning*, 37(1): 91–107.

Sobel, D (2016) The Changing Role of SENCO. *SecEd*, 2016(27): 14.

The Curly Hair Project (2018) The Girl with the Curly Hair. [online] Available at: https://thegirlwith thecurlyhair.co.uk (accessed 8 June 2023).

Tierney, S, Burns, J and Kilbey, E (2016) Looking behind the Mask: Social Coping Strategies of Girls on the Autistic Spectrum. *Research in Autism Spectrum Disorders*, 23: 73–83.

Tissot, C (2013) The Role of SENCos as Leaders. *British Journal of Special Education*, 40(1): 33–40.

Winwood, J (2016) *The Changing Role of the SENCo: Policy into Practice.* Chico, CA: Scholars' Press.

# 5  SENCos engaging with theory

**LIZ DONE**

Identifies the influences shaping current thinking and policy

Foucault (power, discourses and identity)

**Theory**

Informs professional stances and learning related to inclusion, exclusion and disability

The concept of praxis

Provides 'tools' for exploring and developing our thinking

# Chapter objectives 🎯

This chapter invites SENCos to think about the relationship between theory and practice in relation to issues of inclusion, exclusion, disability and professional learning. The chapter:

*   draws on the ideas of Foucault and others to consider issues of power;

*   challenges the notion of theory-neutral knowledge or policy guidance;

*   explores how foundational assumptions about 'knowledge' can limit our thinking about practice;

*   explores the theory–practice binary and introduces the concept of praxis;

*   considers the implications of applying theory for the professional learning of SENCos.

---

### STARTING POINTS 🏁

»   How confident do you feel in using theory on a scale of 0 (not at all) to 5 (very)?

»   Identify some key theories you know about and use in your practice, for example, you may use developmental or pedagogic theories.

»   Identify a time you have used theory to interrogate your work – how did it inform, challenge and develop your thinking?

---

# Introduction

The role of theory in discussions about inclusion is not always recognised or valued. Yet appreciation of theory can empower practitioners to fulfil their role in advocating for the rights of children and young people with disabilities and additional needs to equitable educational opportunities. This chapter explores the relationship between theory and practice for SENCos and suggests that holding theoretically informed perspectives on the understandings that inform educational provision and learners' experiences will assist SENCos to advocate for marginalised learners (Clarke and Done, 2021).

Theoretical assumptions are not always recognised or explicit, particularly in policy, statutory guidance or practice guidelines. This chapter therefore examines some key presuppositions that inform current thinking and policy in the field of inclusive education and SENCo practice. The traditionally accepted bio-medical model of disability presupposes that it is the individual in which deviations from some normative standard are located. For Foucault (2008), this model describes one way in which individuals may be categorised and pathologised and how populations and sub-populations are managed.

For Foucault, however, it is precisely the individual or sense of ourselves as embodied, rational and autonomous individualised entities which must be accounted for rather than taken and responded to as pre-given. This means we must question assumptions to discover the systems of power, discourse and identity that produce the 'objects' or responses we are concerned with. Foucault (1982, p 778) was interested in the 'subject' and its social production: individual and professional identities are produced or constituted through numerous discourses (political, social and cultural), conceived as habitual practices and normative narratives about who we are and who we should be. SENCos, for instance, are caught up in recently revised discourses of teacher professionalism (Moore and Clarke, 2016; Wilkins, 2020) which, according to Ball (2003), have transformed the nature of caring and SENCo practice. This has resulted in expectations that SENCos are individualised professionals who will attend to, for example, matters of performance data, cost-efficiency, resource management and strategic planning. This discourse may be in tension with their personal values and beliefs, and some of the policies they are required to implement (Moore and Clarke, 2016), leading them to strive to influence policy at school level and through national organisations.

## Responsibilisation

A familiar mode of the social production of subjects as individuals capable of rational choice is 'responsibilisation' (Foucault, 1982). An example of this in policy discourse is the choice parents are offered between 'mainstream' or 'special' school: the choice is individualised and it is the individual who must take responsibility for getting a decision right or wrong. Likewise, SENCos have been responsibilised for inclusion in that they are charged with ensuring an inclusive school ethos regardless of school-specific contexts such as the support, or otherwise, of school leaders. Indeed, it could be argued that invitations to SENCos to engage in critical self-reflection also serve to individualise their performance in their role, thus deflecting attention away from systemic, structural, cultural or socio-political issues which constrain or condition that performance. Foucault (1982, p 777) describes such processes linked to subject formation as *'dividing practices'* and such division not only captures the *'dilemmas of difference'* outlined by Norwich (2009) but also something about the difference between *structuralist* and *poststructuralist* theorising, which will be explained below.

---

*Critical questions* (?)

Norwich (2009, p 448) identified several *'dilemmas of difference relevant to students with disabilities'*, namely:

* *identification (whether to identify and how or not);*

* *curriculum (how much of a common curriculum was relevant to them);*

* *placement (to what extent they learn in regular or ordinary classes or not).*

» What dilemmas have you encountered in practice, and have you found ways of reconciling them?

# Power and identity

Although Foucault (1982) is concerned with the control or management of populations and sub-populations, power should be understood as relational, meaning there are always opportunities to resist control even when we feel powerless to change the course of events. Advocacy leadership (Clarke and Done, 2021) and the concept of agency (see Chapter 2) assume that SENCos can resist, and work to alter, an existing state of affairs to the benefit of specific groups or individuals. This is possible but not always easy because power is exercised at different levels (Foucault, 1982): there are micro-practices of power (which can be experienced when interacting with school principals or parents), and at the level of government there are technologies of power through which populations and sub-populations are organised or controlled, such as the early identification imperative found in policy discourse and statutory guidance directed towards SENCos. In its Code of Practice guidance aimed at SENCos in early childhood education, the Department of Education includes '*early identifier*' of additional needs as integral to the SENCo's role and ascribed professional identity despite teacher resistance to labelling children at such a young age (DfE, 2014; Done et al, 2018).

# Discourse

The medium through which control is exercised is discourse which, for Foucault (1977), includes not only speech and written texts but also routinised practices. Discourses can be thought of as narratives or stories that govern what we do by setting limits on what we consider to be possible. The fact there are discourses relating to 'inclusion' which are contested is testimony to the agency we retain. SENCos are, for example, familiar with debates around labelling and the potentially negative effects of segregating children from their peers for ameliorative interventions (Power and Taylor, 2020). The social model of disability is a discourse that recommends environmental adaptations to reduce the disability experienced and to meet the needs of those with SEND. Yet, legislation simultaneously dictates that these must be limited to what are considered to be '*reasonable adjustments*' (Disability Discrimination Act 1995) or bound by financial thresholds and administration (education, health and care plans needed for complex needs and most specialist provisions).

# Foundational assumptions

Foucault (2008) insists there are multiple realities or truths that are socially produced through discourse and that reality comprises our interpretations of events. In broad terms, the knowledge SENCos can draw on when seeking to influence events or school policies and decision making is of two types; both are rule governed since their claim to legitimacy depends on certain rules of knowledge production being followed.

First, SENCos will be aware of the scientific paradigm since the diagnostic categories used to identify certain conditions derive from medical, neuroscientific, psychiatric or psychological discourses. Calls for evidence-based practice in education (see Chapter 12 for further discussion) can be overly reliant on the assumption that education can emulate such discourses in producing knowledge understood as 'truth' or with demonstrable statistical validity which can be generalised to all settings. This scientific or positivistic paradigm also encourages linear thinking or a linear understanding of causal relations (as in A causes B). It assumes there is an objective world, or single truth, that is independent of our consciousness but which we can access by following prescribed rules of knowledge production. It could be argued that it is naive to assume the use of numerical values must mean something real is being measured. SENCos should be aware of concepts such as reification whereby something like incremental 'progress' is assumed to be real and measurable when, in fact, it may be better understood as a social construct (Hacking, 2006; Bradbury and Roberts-Holmes, 2017).

The second paradigm is known as interpretivism. It does not assume a single objective reality that exists outside of discourse and experience. Reality here is complex and causality is rarely linear. Knowledge production involves acknowledging the complexity of situations and contribution of context. For SENCos, this might mean identifying and analysing the varied and sometimes competing discourses through which their practice is organised. It could involve consideration of historical discourses which continue to influence attitudes towards inclusion today. It might involve exploring 'how' and 'why' questions such as how and why the nature of caring in the SENCo role seems to have changed as the wider policy context has become more focused on 'interventions' and evidencing 'progress'.

---

### Critical questions (?)

»  Which paradigm do you prefer and why?

»  When is one paradigm more useful than another and why?

»  Can you think of situations when both paradigms might be useful?

»  What types of knowledge are presented as value free, and what types can be described as political?

---

SENCos are likely to encounter situations where it is beneficial to draw on knowledge derived from either or both of the paradigms described above and can choose to do so strategically. Advocating for children and young people categorised as having SEND might be more effective where prevalence statistics such as standardised test results or published quantitative research can be cited to underline the need for change at school level, whereas describing behavioural or sensory responses might contribute to our understanding of what changes are needed or would be most helpful.

# Theory, practice, praxis

## Past, present and future

Foucault (1977, p 30) referred to critical analyses of discourse as a *'history of the present'*, suggesting we look at the past in order to understand the present and change the future. The identifying of ironies or paradox is a feature of such analyses, particularly in relation to the language found in policy discourse. It has been observed that the term 'inclusion' logically, and paradoxically, presupposes that some individuals and groups are excluded in some way, and so we risk reinforcing that exclusion or marginalisation by repeatedly referring to them as in need of inclusionary policies and actions (Done and Andrews, 2019; Done and Knowler, 2023). Norwich (2009, p 447) summarises such paradoxical scenarios as demonstrating '*dilemmas of difference*' (see above). Others refer to exclusionary inclusion (Done and Knowler, 2023), an example of which is differentiated group teaching provided to learners with SEND which involves their separation from peers while facilitating learning and placement in a mainstream setting. Certainly, SENCos might identify and challenge school or classroom practices which are difficult to reconcile with their school's official policy around inclusion – practices that are ironic given that policy.

SENCos may be well positioned to contest certain practices which are not included in statutory guidance for SENCos such as the home education of children. Some parents report being coerced by the school into doing so, rather than home education being truly elective (OSA, 2018; Done, Knowler, Warnes and Pickett-Jones, 2021). SENCos could also familiarise themselves with the concept of intersectionality – how it has evolved and why it is relevant to SENCos' efforts to lead change at school level. This involves considering multiple factors which overlap to create interdependent systems of discrimination, disadvantage or challenge, such that identifying one factor in isolation risks a misguided response. The emphasis on behaviour in decisions to formally exclude deflects attention from how children can be subject to multiple disadvantages, meaning behaviour is isolated from context in a way that works against them receiving the support they need (Done, Knowler and Armstrong, 2021).

## Assumptions of neutrality and structuralism

Foucault's theorising challenges reliance on the scientific paradigm and the search for a single de-contextualised truth. It is described as poststructuralist because it rejects the assumptions of structuralist theories that social arrangements are organised and reproduce themselves according to timeless and universal rules. Such rules neglect context and are presented as ahistorical and non-ideological. Gough (2010) argues that the influence of structuralist thought is rarely recognised in education; however, it is pervasive and evidenced in curricula design which assumes learning occurs in a staged and linear way, and that it is non-ideological. SENCos in England will be aware of statistically generated age-related expectations that children with additional needs are measured against, and of policies encouraging intervention where they are found to be 'behind' this normative standard. It is assumed that their 'progress' in narrowly defined curriculum areas will be measurable over a specified time frame. Gough (2010) analyses what are widely promoted as basic principles of curriculum and instruction design and identifies several features of structuralist theorising. Specifically:

- learning objectives that are only meaningful as elements of a systematic structure of staged learning experiences and evaluation;
- language that works to valorise purpose, organisation and accountability;

- curriculum design process that is presented as non-ideological and relevant to an immediate present with no indication of its historical antecedents;

- it is the structural relations between objectives that determine their meaning or being the diametric opposite of the other (black/white, right/wrong – applying this to areas of SEND: 'working within age-related expectations'/'falling below age-related expectations').

## Binaries and poststructuralism

In poststructuralist theorising, 'binaries' are oppositions that are hierarchically arranged, working to valorise the first term and denigrate the second or, at best, indicate a lesser value, for example, 'very good' as opposed to 'good'. The overall structure of language and prevailing social relations function to underline which term is socially valued or de-valued. Applying this to practice, terms used informally in some settings to describe children and young people with additional needs is a case in point, for example, the word 'challenging'. SENCos should be aware that such terms not only reinforce an embodied sense of difference (Done and Andrews, 2019); they also implicitly convey social hierarchies or social (de)valuations linked to stigmatisation and discrimination.

---

### *Critical questions* (?)

» Which interventions and processes present in your setting reproduce binary rules that are taken to be timeless and universal?

» Which interventions and processes in your setting:

   a) are linked to the perspective and experience of those implementing them?

   b) Consider the multiple factors at play, the interplay between these and how these should be prioritised or addressed?

» How can we use our knowledge and systems of knowledge to shape and develop our work and identity as SENCos (if we think of these as objects themselves, uproduced by the systems of knowledge)?

---

Foucault and other poststructuralist theorists developed concepts intended to overcome binaries that they viewed as unhelpful if social change was to be achieved, particularly around issues of social justice and equity. SENCos may be aware of international policy discourse in which the concept and aspiration towards 'full inclusion' was intended to address the 'mainstream' and 'special' binary in schooling (UNESCO, 1994). They will also be familiar with the binary of theory and practice which presupposes a rigid boundary and the undervaluing of practice. The concept of praxis in poststructuralist theorising is designed to overcome any presupposition that these are entirely different realms of activity.

## Praxis

In poststructuralist theorising, *praxis* denotes resistance to a situation which is understood to be unjust, oppressive or discriminatory, highlighting how actions of resistance can be informed by theory (Buchanan, 2012). Actions that SENCos take to challenge the inequitable allocation of resources, either socially or in their own schools, or to end discriminatory practices, can be read as *praxis* where they are driven by, for example, an understanding of the distinction between equality of opportunity and equity (see 'Critical questions' below), and of the relative and/or intersectional disadvantage of specific demographic groups. For instance, during the period of school closures due to the Covid-19 pandemic in England, SENCos in schools within areas of high social deprivation were likely to be involved in wider school efforts to provide material support for families that lacked ICT and other resources, in addition to supporting the families of children with additional needs (Done and Knowler, 2021).

These SENCos were acutely aware that inclusion on a school register, once parents had exercised their legal right to select a 'mainstream' school for their child, supports a political rhetoric around inclusive education despite resources being inequitably spread across the education system and local communities (Montacute and Cullinane, 2021). SENCos who recognise the disproportionately high representation of school students classified as having SEND in school exclusion data, and who seek to transform their school's policies, practices and ethos, are engaging in *praxis* since their actions are conceptually informed and can be conceived as resisting or problematising (Garland, 2014, p 365). This contrasts with presuppositions that an authentically inclusive education has already been achieved.

---

### *Critical questions* (?)

» If equality of opportunity differs from equity, which means offering resources appropriate to individual needs such that all can reach equal outcomes, how can drawing attention to this distinction help you advocate for those categorised as having SEND?

» The concept of intersectionality acknowledges that any individual has multiple identities, which can interact in complex ways to produce discrimination and disadvantage. Such identities may be associated with categories such as gender, ethnicity and socio-economic status, as well as disability. What identities and overlapping factors should you be aware of and consider when identifying and prioritising a course of action for an individual child?

## CASE STUDY ⊖

**Sue is a primary classroom teacher and soon to be assistant SENCo, part way through the National Award**

*I'm finding the course challenges my perception of things; it's made me reflect on the experience of my learners and theories that I hadn't encountered before are giving me new strategies and angles to consider and use in the classroom. I'm also slowly beginning to think more strategically and consider how my provision is meeting the needs of our learners and how I could be part of shaping our approach. In short, I'm beginning to think more critically about the concept of inclusion.*

*Discovering various theoretical perspectives on the course has helped me take a step back from day-to-day events and consider them in different ways. For example, through lengthy discussion with one colleague, she now theorises inclusive practice for dyslexic learners very differently; she sees how creating the right environment and learning opportunities for him are enabling him to flourish, where before all she could focus on were his 'deficits' in a very 'medical model' kind of way.*

*Being introduced to Lesson Study (see Chapter 12) was also a game changer for me. I now feel empowered to make a case for my learners with SEND, knowing I have evidence to support my proposals to the school leadership team. Understanding how different kinds of evidence can be used in different ways and have different strengths (evidence-based practice, in other words) gives me an edge my practice didn't have before. I now engage with pupil voice in a much more conscious and planned way (whether as part of the Lesson Study process or not); this has helped me persuade colleagues of the importance of hearing – and more importantly, valuing – what even very young learners say. Their views should 'count' every bit as much as our attainment statistics. I can't say I've won this battle yet, but there is definitely a gradual shift in school perceptions and discourses over the last year. As a team we now recognise where we need to robustly challenge policies when we see them disadvantaging our learners with additional needs.*

The case study above shows how SENCos have some scope - however constrained it may be - to resist the pressures on inclusion that are so prevalent in the current educational climate.

## Implications for the SENCo role, identity and practice

If SENCos and others are to effectively transform policy and practice, they need to develop a strong critical literacy to recognise and challenge the managerialist discourse so prevalent in schools today. Teachers may experience little autonomy within this performative culture which emphasises accountability and carefully monitored performance indicators. Yet, the fight against inequality and discrimination, and the questioning of privilege – in other words, critical literacy, is central to the professional identity of SENCos.

A commitment to professional learning can be regarded as a form of resistance within a managerialist environment, especially scholarly or academic study that promotes critical literacy. Paradoxically, it should also be recognised that critical literacy has been co-opted by this same managerialist discourse, through explicitly identifying performance criteria such as those required for a Master's-level qualification, in which the student: '*Selects and applies advanced principles, concepts, theoretical frameworks and approaches to critically develop systematic responses to existing discourses and methodologies, suggesting new ideas in unpredictably complex contexts*' (Seec, 2021, p 16). The context in which SENCos practice is, undoubtedly, both complex and full of conflicting agendas (see Chapter 10).

# Chapter summary

The emphasis in this chapter has been on critical literacy conceived as a readiness to question the assumptions which inform knowledge production, policy and professional discourses, political rhetoric and practice at local level. For Foucault, the value and purpose of critique is to recognise and embrace opportunities for thinking and doing otherwise. It must be acknowledged that such questioning or problematising by SENCos may not be easy given the managerialist discourse (Kay et al, 2022) and ever-shifting policy landscape that has resulted in what Curran (2019, p 90) describes as a '*confused and contested*' SENCo role. Yet, there are numerous instances where SENCos do successfully challenge discourses and practices that conflict with their understanding of a socially just education system; that is, where SENCos have rejected a common-sense and taken-for-granted binarised assumption that theorising and practice are separate realms of activity or that theoretical concepts lack relevance in their practice. It is the poststructuralist concept of *praxis* which challenges such assumptions.

# Further reading

Aubrey, K and Riley, A (2019) *Understanding and Using Educational Theories.* 2nd ed. Los Angeles: Sage.

- This book gives a clear overview of additional key thinkers on education, whose theories and writings have helped shape our views on teaching and learning.

Ball, S J (2013) *Foucault, Power, and Education.* London: Routledge.

- Ball is an eminent scholar in the sociology of education and this book offers an interpretation of how Foucault's ideas can be applied to contemporary educational issues.

Besic, E (2020) Intersectionality: A Pathway towards Inclusive Education? *Prospects*, 49(3–4): 111–22.

- This article argues for an expanded definition of inclusive education which encompasses all children, not just 'children with disabilities', using the theoretical lens of intersectionality.

# References

Ball, S J (2003) The Teacher's Soul and the Terrors of Performativity. *Journal of Education Policy*, 18(2): 215–28.

Bradbury, A and Roberts-Holmes, G (2017) Creating an Ofsted Story: The Role of Early Years Assessment Data in Schools' Narratives of Progress. *British Journal of Sociology of Education*, 38(7): 943–55.

Buchanan, I (2012) Power, Theory and Praxis. In Buchanan, I and Thoburn, M (eds) *Deleuze and Politics* (pp 13–34). Edinburgh: Edinburgh University Press.

Clarke, A L and Done, E J (2021) Balancing Pressures for SENCos as Managers, Leaders and Advocates in the Emerging Context of the Covid-19 Pandemic. *British Journal of Special Education*, 48(2): 157–74.

Curran, H (2019) Are Good Intentions Enough? The Role of the Policy Implementer during Educational Reform. *Practice*, 1(1): 88–9.

Department for Education (DfE) (2014) *Early Years: Guide to the 0 to 25 SEND Code of Practice.* London: DfE.

Disability Discrimination Act 1995. [online] Available at: www.legislation.gov.uk/ukpga/1995/50/contents (accessed 23 May 2023).

Done, E J and Andrews, M J (2019) How Inclusion Became Exclusion: Policy, Teachers and Inclusive Education. *Journal of Education Policy*. https://doi.org/10.1080/02680939.2018.1552763

Done, E J and Knowler, H (2021) *Exclusion and the Strategic Leadership Role of Special Educational Needs Coordinators (SENCos) in England: Planning for COVID-19 and Future Crises.* Education and Covid-19 series. British Educational Research Association. [online] Available at: www.bera.ac.uk/publication/the-experiences-ofautistic-young-people-their-parents-of-lockdown-the-reopening-of-schools (accessed 18 July 2023).

Done, E J and Knowler, H (eds) (2023) *International Perspectives on Exclusionary Pressures in Education: How Inclusion Became Exclusion.* Cham: Palgrave Macmillan/Springer.

Done, E J, Andrews, M J and Evenden, C (2018) (C)old Beginnings and Technologies of Rectification in Early Years Education: The Implications for Teachers and Children with Special Educational Needs. *International Journal of Early Years Education*, 30(2): 434–47.

Done, E J, Knowler, H and Armstrong, D (2021) 'Grey' Exclusions Matter: Mapping Illegal Exclusionary Practices and the Implications for Children with Disabilities in England and Australia. *Journal of Research in Special Educational Needs*, 21(1): 36–44.

Done, E J, Knowler, H, Warnes, E and Pickett-Jones, B (2021) Think Piece on Parents, 'Off Rolling' and Wavelength Methodology: Issues for SENCos. *Support for Learning*, 36(1): 69–8.

Foucault, M (1977) *Discipline and Punish*. New York: Vintage.

Foucault, M (1982) The Subject and Power. *Critical Inquiry*, 8, 777–95.

Foucault, M (2008) *The Birth of Biopolitics: Lectures at the College de France 1978–1979*. New York: Palgrave.

Garland, D (2014) What Is a 'History of the Present'? On Foucault's Genealogies and Their Critical Preconditions. *Punishment and Society*, 16(4): 365–84.

Gough, N (2010) Structuralism. In Kridel, C (ed) *The SAGE Encyclopedia of Curriculum Studies* (pp 817–21). New York: Sage.

Hacking, I (2006) Making Up People. *London Review of Books*, 28(16): 23–6.

Kay, V, Chrostowska, M, Henshall, A, Mcloughlin, A and Hallett, F (2022) Intrinsic and Extrinsic Tensions in the SENCo Role: Navigating the Maze of 'Becoming'. *Journal of Research in Special Educational Needs*, 22(4): 343–51.

Montacute, R and Cullinane, C (2021) *Learning in Lockdown: Research Brief*. [online] Available at: www.suttontrust.com/wp-content/uploads/2021/01/Learning-in-Lockdown.pdf (accessed 23 May 2023).

Moore, A and Clarke, M (2016) Cruel Optimism: Teacher Attachment to Professionalism in an Era of Performativity. *Journal of Education Policy*, 31: 666–77.

Norwich, B (2009) Dilemmas of Difference and the Identification of Special Educational Needs/ Disability: International Perspectives. *British Educational Research Journal*, 35(3): 447–67.

Office of the Schools' Adjudicator (OSA) (2018) *Annual Report: September 2017 to August 2018*. [online] Available at: www.gov.uk/government/publications/osa-annual-report (accessed 23 May 2023).

Power, S and Taylor, C (2020) Not in the Classroom but Still on the Register: Hidden Forms of School Exclusion. *International Journal of Inclusive Education*, 24: 867–81.

Seec (2021) *Credit Level Descriptors for Higher Education*. [online] Available at https://seec.org.uk/wp-content/uploads/2021/05/MDX_SEEC-Descriptors_Update-May-2021_Version-2_For-screen_AW13885.pdf (accessed 23 May 2023).

UNESCO (1994) *The Salamanca Statement and Framework for Action on Special Needs Education*. Paris: UNESCO. [online] Available at: https://unesdoc.unesco.org/ark:/48223/pf0000098427 (accessed 18 July 2023).

Wilkins, A (2020) Technologies in Rational Self-Government. In Allan, J, Harwood, V and Jøorgensen, C (eds) *World Yearbook of Education 2020* (pp 100–12). London: Routledge.

# Part 2 The SENCo at work

# 6 The SENCo role across ages and settings

**HAZEL RICHARDS, SELENA HALL, JENNIFER WELLS AND ZOE STUART**

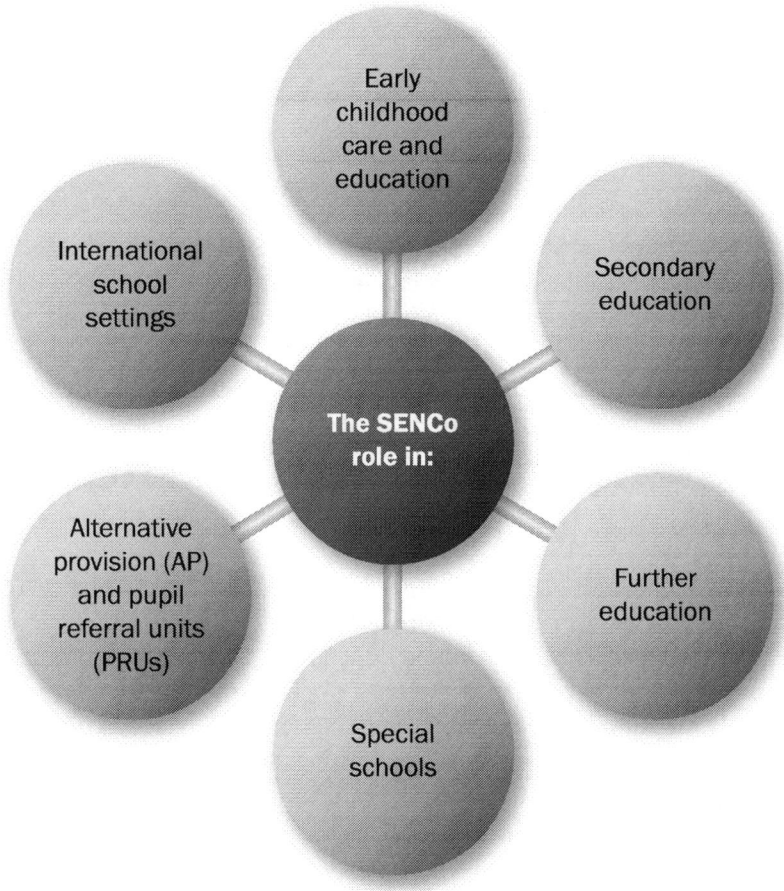

Diagram showing "The SENCo role in:" at the centre, with connected circles: Early childhood care and education, Secondary education, Further education, Special schools, Alternative provision (AP) and pupil referral units (PRUs), International school settings.

## Chapter objectives 🎯

This chapter explores the context and enactment of the SENCo role across age phases and setting types less commonly covered. The chapter:

• identifies commonalities as well as challenges particular to these contexts;

• explores the core implications for the SENCo role in these contexts;

• highlights the most significant factors to consider for SENCo identity and practice in these contexts.

### STARTING POINTS 🏁

» Which age phase and setting types do you have most experience of? And which the least?

» Which age phase and setting types do you receive from/transfer children and young people to and what might you need to know about each?

## Introduction

In England, the SENCo role is well established within maintained early years settings (DfE and DoH, 2015) and the compulsory education years (ages 5–16) (Gov.uk, 2012) but enactment in other age phases and setting types is less well established (Lamb and Blandford, 2017; Robertson 2022) and explored in the literature. This chapter addresses these gaps by exploring the role in early childhood care and education, secondary, further education, special school, alternative provision and international school settings. Each is addressed in turn, identifying the contextual differences and challenges peculiar to each, including implications for the SENCo role, identity and practice.

## Early childhood

The SENCo practising in early childhood (birth to five years) has a particularly important role. However, in England, early childhood care and education (ECCE) settings that are private, voluntary or independent (PVI) have different funding systems and qualification requirements to government-maintained nurseries. This has implications for early childhood practitioners (ECPs), who are uniquely placed to shape how childhood is supported and enhanced. This includes the identification of additional needs and investing early in the life of a problem, which leads to greater long-term benefits (Easton and Gee, 2012). The extensive and additional duties of the SENCo are undertaken alongside or within the capacity of an ECP's daily routine, with responsibilities which must be maintained in the capacity of each role. This creates challenges for practitioners to fully dedicate themselves to identifying and supporting children with additional needs, despite it being central to practice that the unique needs of the child are not compromised. Indeed, continued commitment to valuing and respecting the diversity of individuals, families and communities sits at the heart of early years practice (*Birth to 5 Matters*, 2021).

Inclusion acknowledges that all children learn differently, and settings must be structured and resourced to facilitate full and meaningful access and participation for all (Ofsted, 2021). Meeting the unique needs of the child, including how we value, advocate for and appropriate the early years to shape, support and enable the next generation, requires a depth of knowledge of children's development. Well trained, qualified and engaged practitioners are instrumental contributors to rich, meaningful educational environments (Sollars, 2022). The benefits of ECCE can be long-lasting, and educational investments and remedial interventions later in life are less cost-effective (Buckley et al, 2020). This aligns with the 1001 Critical Days manifesto, which acknowledges that providing support during this rapid period of development makes a significant contribution to achieving the best life outcomes for the child (DHSC, 2021). A shared contention for settings and practitioners, however, is that changes to legislative guidance, delayed referrals, funding concerns and time constraints, as well as complicated and time-consuming systems and processes to gain funding and support for the child, continue to be prevalent in the sector.

The ECP is ideally placed to identify early indicators of atypical development, providing support at the point of need before formal recognition or diagnosis is in place. However, if early help and support is to be truly successful, pedagogy and values regarding improving outcomes need to be shared and reflect the expertise of all agencies. Partnership working, while undoubtedly beneficial, presents notable challenges, which must be overcome, often through shared values and reciprocal collaboration (Allen, 2011) (see Chapter 9). Partnership working should foreground collaborating and co-operating with parents and families and recognise the child's voice. This is an imperative ecological influence that contributes to the holistic consideration and support of the child (Musgrave, 2017). ECPs routinely lead and contribute to discussions with parents through both formal processes to share the observations and informal discussions integral to this age phase. However, frustrations due to policy and legislative requirements can impact upon quality partnerships, with challenges around the agency and involvement of parents and children in the decision processes surrounding SEND support, and inconsistency of practice between settings being recognised (Hutchinson, 2021). ECPs and SENCos must recognise the benefit of, and actively develop rapport with, parents, as they are most often best placed to provide information regarding their child, and so contribute to early identification and intervention (Richards, 2021). Given the depth of knowledge and skill required in these roles, continuing professional development (CPD) is imperative to ensuring the ECP is current and contemporary in the capacity of their role. To this end, SENCo specific training at level 3 for early years practitioners is now available (Best Practice Network, 2022).

## CASE STUDY ⟲

### Sally Ramsbottom: nursery manager, West Midlands

*With over 25 years' experience working in early childhood, I have undertaken the SENCo role alongside the role of nursery manager. I have the responsibility to work with my staff team to gather documentation and evidence about each child in order to best support the*

→

child's current and future development. More recently, challenges in the sector, such as staff shortages, rising child:staff ratios and a lack of resources are concerning. A huge concern has been accessing support services – children need to wait longer for support, which has implications for the staff, setting, families and most importantly the child. In a team approach, we are guided by our initial concerns and then the process of Assess, Plan, Do, Review begins. It takes time to work as a team to set targets for each child and the support from the local authority special needs early years services worker (SNEYS) in addition to Team-Around-the-Child (TAC) meetings is invaluable, especially where extra funding or an education, health and care plan (EHCP) is needed. From professional reflections and observations, our children's needs are also altering. In our 2022/23 nursery intake we have 50 per cent more children requiring early help. Due in part to the Covid-19 pandemic, this has widened the gap further and exacerbated delays in children's holistic development. Specifically, we are noting from our observations that behaviour, communication and social skills are an increasing area of concern.

---

### Implications for SENCos working in private, voluntary or independent early childhood care and education settings

» Time allocations to perform the SENCo role can be informal.

» Partnership working with parents and professionals is key.

» Numbers and complexity of children with SEND are rising.

» The process and procedures for funding, provision and diagnosis are complex and often time-consuming.

» A depth of knowledge surrounding child development, inclusion and SEND is needed and should be provided routinely in level 3 training and CPD.

---

## Secondary education

As a child enters secondary education, the partnership between the SENCo, parents and children often changes. The SENCo may not feel as accessible to parents and as the range of teachers supporting the child increases, parents may feel communication around SEND support is slower. The larger school building and range of specialist subject staff can make the SENCo role challenging since provision must be co-ordinated with an increased number of teaching and support staff in addition to external agencies (Fitzgerald and Radford, 2022).

The SENCo will be accountable for a large cohort of pupils and the role needs to be flexible to meet the needs of both the school cohort and context of the school. As a result, a SENCo in the secondary phase is more likely to have support from a deputy SENCo or a dedicated administrator than their counterparts in the primary phase (Curran et al, 2021). The management of a large team of support staff, budgets and provision planning for a wide range of pupil needs makes the secondary SENCo role a complex one. Deployment of support staff is a challenging element as the number of pupils with an education, health and care plan (EHCP) has risen by 50 per cent since 2016. The number of pupils with SEND support has also increased by 14 per cent since 2016 (Gov.uk, 2022). However, the number of teaching assistants in UK state secondary schools is significantly less than state primary settings – only 18 per cent of the teaching assistant workforce are employed in secondary settings (EPI, 2020). Organising of timetables and opportunity for support staff to co-plan with teaching staff is essential in creating a co-operative and supportive staff team.

Ensuring staff are adequately trained to support learner needs in a range of subjects is a multifarious task and requires the consideration of activities a learner may find challenging. Experiments in science, machinery in design and technology and changing facilities in PE are examples of specialist subject components that subject staff may need support with when planning for SEND pupils. While core and enrichment subjects are often taught in similar styles (Galton et al, 1980; Galton et al, 2002), specialist rooms and facilities, and the movement to access them, require careful consideration. Additionally, specialist subject staff are often asked to teach outside of their specialism, meaning that the SENCo, as well as subject staff, may need to support non-specialists navigating unfamiliar lesson content to ensure staff have the confidence to support children with SEND. There are also concerns for teaching staff around workload generally, as well as how planning additional support and participating in training will impact well-being. The SENCo may also need to provide strategies and support for several early career teachers (ECTs) who are still completing training and developing their subject knowledge and pedagogical practices (Gov.uk, 2019).

In primary education, parents will most often communicate with the class teacher as the person who sees the child for most of the school day. In secondary, parents will more often communicate with the form tutor or SENCo. Children with SEND transitioning to secondary need to adapt to new learning environments and routines and transition arrangements are often co-ordinated by the SENCo to ensure this is a positive experience. However, experiencing a range of new classrooms, subjects, teaching staff, lesson times, uniform and personal responsibilities can be overwhelming and the SENCo role is crucial to ensure children who struggle with these new expectations are supported rather than sanctioned.

Terminal examinations also raise issues for the SENCo. The removal of coursework assessment, pressure on schools to achieve progress measures across eight subjects (DfE, 2020) and the increase in terminal examination entries has coincided with an increase in applications for access arrangements (Hipkiss et al, 2021). Organisation of support staff for examinations is a crucial time as often a balance needs to be struck between the support for those in examinations and support for SEND children in lower year groups. This is a period of high stress for all secondary pupils, and many SEND children require a change to their support as the examination period approaches.

As pupils journey through puberty, the support required may change and the secondary SENCo co-ordinates a range of provision and external services which may not have been required at an earlier stage of development. Adolescence brings changes in emotions, friendships and communication needs. Pupils with SEND will experience the same changes as pupils without SEND, including experiencing sexual desires. The SENCo and external agencies may need to work in partnership with parents to ensure changes in puberty, hygiene and sex are discussed in a way that is appropriate to the individual pupil. Furthermore, children and young people with SEND are at greater risk of abuse (Jones et al, 2012; Brown, 2014) due to barriers in communication, misinterpretation of the signs of abuse or a lack of education in how to stay safe (Garbutt et al, 2010). An important role of secondary schools is therefore providing specialist support and education as part of preparation for adulthood and keeping pupils safe.

---

### Implications for SENCos working in secondary education

» Implementing positive transition arrangements to support both the change in setting and routine transitions around the school.

» Managing a high number of specialist teaching and support staff as part of supporting diverse pupil needs, including supporting subject staff with workload issues and staff cover.

» Providing ongoing training to teaching staff, contextualised by subject.

» Organising exam arrangements.

» Managing personal, social, health and relationship training and support in preparation for adulthood and to keep pupils safe.

---

## Further education

A significant challenge in further education (FE) is the variety of options for young people moving to post-16 education. Possibilities include sixth forms attached to schools, specialist provision and large, university-style campuses which often provide real-life working environments for vocational training and employability. The FE sector is undergoing significant change, with mergers being a pervasive feature in a challenging financial climate where funding per student has fallen by 8 per cent in real terms since 2010 (DfE, 2019). Consequently, there has been a rise in the number of large colleges spread across different geographical locations and the rationalisation of administrative support in a drive for greater cost-efficiency. Departments that support students with SEND may therefore work with more than one local authority. Exacerbating this economic climate is the additional challenge of funding students without an EHCP, achieved via the college disadvantage fund which also needs to provide for a range of support needs including re-sits and mental health services. To contextualise this, in England FE currently caters for 64,000 students with EHCPs and 240,000 without EHCPs (Maudslay, 2021).

Unlike schools, there is no specific designation of SENCo in FE but rather the requirement for a 'named person' (DfE and DoH, 2015); the interpretation and expectations of the role may differ between settings and there is no requirement for Qualified Teacher Status. Therefore, in the current financial climate of FE, the role of co-ordinating SEND provision is often viewed as one of financial management and compliance without any requirement for a background in education. Perhaps an advantage in this context is that the role is usually within the senior leadership team, which allows for strategic development without the demands of an additional teaching workload (Curran and Boddison, 2021). This also may mean different areas of responsibility can be delegated within a team of specialists. However, *how* the areas of responsibility are delegated is key to outcomes for young people (Hallett and Hallett, 2017) and the challenge is to have robust systems in place with clear lines of communication and responsibility. Challenges for the strategic lead of SEND in FE therefore include the need to consider financial efficiency, liaison with outside agencies across local authorities, assessment of student needs with a possible age range of 14–25 and quality of provision from both teaching and support staff.

All teachers within an FE setting should be working in line with the Education and Training Foundation Professional Standards (ETF, 2022), which include the need to '*develop and apply... knowledge of [SEND] to create an inclusive learning experience*'. However, the requirement for newly appointed teachers to hold a formal teaching qualification was lifted in 2013, allowing FE organisations to employ industry specialists for their professional rather than teaching experience. Furthermore, with the introduction of apprenticeships and workplace training (House of Commons, 2015), observations are likely to be carried out by vocational and work-based practitioners. Managing quality assurance so all staff are engaging in inclusive provision and practice is therefore a key challenge for the SEND lead. Additionally, '*the successful implementation of any inclusive policy is largely dependent on educators being positive about it*' (Avramidis and Norwich, 2016, p 129), which for the SEND lead in FE means developing a shared ethos among a number of qualified and unqualified teaching staff, across different campuses, teaching on a range of programmes from specialist entry-level provision to level 6 academic and vocational programmes of study.

Implementing effective support and a meaningful learning experience for young people is a complex endeavour. However, at the heart of any consideration of how provision is managed should be the young people themselves. For any designated SEND lead, the most important focus is to develop robust systems for listening to students and placing them at the heart of shaping their experience. This is a time for many of 'becoming' as they transition to adulthood and enter a new social world where making friends and feeling valued is pivotal to a positive experience. Lawson and Parker (2019) highlight the importance placed by young people on empowerment and the importance of relationships which mediate change. Therefore, any designated SEND lead in FE may find the place to start designing provision is by taking a person-centred approach so that professional practice is rooted in the concerns and aspirations of its young people.

## CASE STUDY ↺

**Kelly Kensett, learning difficulties and disabilities (LDD) lead, apprenticeship training provider**

*My job role of LDD lead focuses on practitioner knowledge, standardised processes, reporting and impact for learners. Work-based learning apprenticeships are quite different to traditional educational settings as employers hold a high level of responsibility for an apprentice's qualification. This means training providers only contribute a percentage of the overall learning journey. Also, apprenticeships don't feature in the SEND Code of Practice (CoP) (2015) in the way other educational providers do. Providers catering for apprentice learners with SEND are therefore making an ethical choice rather than meeting a legal requirement and our processes and ways of working are vital to support this.*

*I was trusted with an 'open canvas' approach to identify and appropriately develop awareness of supporting learners with SEND to increase their inclusion and success. Discussions were held with each contract on an individual basis to ensure any enhanced processes around the awareness of the learners' needs fitted into the individual contract processes rather than having a one-size-fits-all approach. It was also agreed that there would be a review at the six-month stage of any process. This ensured all contracts within the business were on board with this development.*

*We found practitioners' knowledge needed to be developed to increase their competency and confidence in supporting learners with SEND. As I knew a culture change was required, I asked them how they would prefer to do this. This included completing the apprentice provider training sessions myself to allow myself to be seen by all and allow practitioners to provide feedback to me at these opportunities. I also implemented surveys to gain information from practitioners about how to create a proactive plan relative to the needs of the staff. Asking for their involvement in this way resulted in higher participation and engagement from trainers and so changes in culture. It was also important to create a quality assurance process. This reinforces the revised ways of working to ensure we are delivering continued support from the point we become aware of learner need, as well as providing regular opportunities for the learner to disclose any information they need to through the tripartite system of reviews.*

### ⚇ Implications for SENCos working in further education

» How a culture of inclusion can be embedded into the setting among all staff.

» Challenges related to lack of specificity in the role and approaches to managing provision, though these also present an opportunity to shape provision around student needs.

> » How relationships with feeder schools and employers can be managed so there is a seamless transition for students.
>
> » How the voice of students with SEND can be captured so it authentically shapes provision.

# Special schools

Special schools provide education and support to children and young people with complex needs that are best met by specialist provision and support, and who have EHCPs. Although tensions around how special school provision relates to definitions of 'inclusive' education, citizenship (Hakala, 2010) and the 'industry' (Tomlinson, 2014) exist, it is also argued that such schools can specialise according to SEND category (communication and interaction; cognition and learning; social, emotional and mental health; sensory and physical needs (SEND CoP: DfE and DoH, 2015)) or specific need, for example, autism, visual impairment or speech, language and communication needs. SENCos in special schools are more often part of the senior leadership team, with co-ordination of cross-professional working being a key part of the role. This requires high levels of partnership and collaborative working (see Chapter 9) between the setting and external staff, all of whom should possess good levels of knowledge and expertise (Hellawell, 2018). These may include speech and language therapists, physiotherapists, occupational therapists, family support workers, school nurses and social workers, each of whom contribute to practice within the school and to individual pupil programmes.

SENCos will be involved with differentiating the curriculum to ensure it is broad, progressive, relevant and promotes personalised learning opportunities. Partnership working with schools that pupils are transferring from and to, as well as with schools in the area to share and develop expertise is also an important part of the role. Additionally, special schools support children with increasingly complex needs (due to advances in medical science and higher survival rates in extremely premature babies) and are due to receive an average 3.4 per cent per place funding increase in 2023–4, or 10.6 per cent for pupils with complex SEND (DfE, 2022b) to meet, in part, their higher staffing and equipment needs.

## *Implications for SENCos working in special schools*

> » A need for EHCPs to be in place (or agreement with local authority) to ensure funding.
>
> » High partnership and collaborative working levels with professionals from a range of disciplines.
>
> » Differentiating the curriculum to ensure relevance.
>
> » Co-ordinating and developing the expertise of staff.
>
> » Complexity of students' needs, with implications for staffing, training, resources and advice.

# Alternative provision and pupil referral units

The phrase alternative provision (AP) encompasses pupil referral units (PRUs). The main reason for attendance at a PRU is the risk of exclusion or actual exclusion, though sometimes pupils may be placed there while waiting for a school place because of a medical condition or school refusal. AP schools can support children and young people whose behaviour or other needs can present a barrier to learning because:

- smaller class sizes allow teachers and support staff to get to know each student individually and to tailor teaching to suit their needs;
- there is curriculum flexibility;
- staff bring a wealth of professional experience and skills (PRUsAP, n d).

However, the role of AP can be unclear; it may be used too late, or the particular AP may not be focused specifically on a child or young person's needs. Significantly, there has been a sharp rise in the number of pupils taken out of their primary school and referred to AP settings. Parts of the sector are poorly regulated, giving concern about standards of educational provision and outcomes (House of Commons, 2018; Spielman, 2021; Weale, 2021). In recognition of this, the Green Paper on SEND (DfE, 2022a) proposes a single national SEND and AP system (DfE, 2023) to set nationally consistent standards for how needs are identified and met, to include:

- early intervention;
- a bespoke performance framework which sets robust standards focused on progress and tracking of children and young people's movement in and out of AP;
- an AP-specific budget;
- reintegration into mainstream education or sustainable post-16 destinations.

However, changes in legislation are not identified in the Green Paper, meaning issues around accountability and governance are likely to persist. SENCos in AP and PRUs work to ensure each pupil has their needs met, though literature specific to these setting types is limited. Belli (2021) identifies the benefit of a modified and enhanced curriculum for more vulnerable learners and of flexible and early access to AP with the vision for SEND driven by the senior leadership team. Certainly, working together with mainstream settings could and should be part of the AP SENCo's role, including: best practice support with behaviour management; working to reduce exclusions and absences by identifying contributing factors and providing early and targeted support; improving the quality and standards in AP and unregistered provision, including co-ordination and links with local SEND systems; optimising student outcomes; easing transitions in and out of mainstream education and on into post-16 training and employment (PRUsAP, n d).

---

### Implications for SENCos working in PRUs and APs

» The significant rise in both the number of AP settings and the number of pupils being referred to them.

» The previous educational experience of pupils and the need for restorative (repairing harm by building supportive and respectful behaviour) and/or more tailored teaching (Briscoe et al, 2017).

» Collaborating with settings, including those sending and receiving pupils, to aid pupil transitions and develop practice.

» Improving provision in PRUs and APs with a view to improving pupil educational outcomes and futures.

---

## International schools

International schools are accredited by, for example, the Council of British International Schools (COBIS) or the Council of International Schools (CIS) and follow internationally recognised curricula to make it easy for children to transfer between schools or back to a school in the UK. There is a mobile population of multinational and multilingual students taught by teachers who have trained in different countries with varied cultural understandings of SEND. International inclusive policy states that '*all children should learn together, wherever possible, regardless of any difficulties or differences they may have*' (UNESCO, 1994, p 11). However, local SEND practices may vary, with the SENCo in an international school setting tasked both with fostering effective learning support and facilitating inclusion for students with SEND. In many countries, SENCos also take a leading role in identifying SEND, applying for resources related to SEND, advising classroom teachers, and liaising with families and outside agencies. This requires effective SENCo agency (see Chapter 2), which involves advocacy for students, commitment to the role, professional competence, self-efficacy, participation in decision making and collaboration with a wide range of people (Lin et al, 2022), all of which involves engagement with culture, structure and resources in specific contexts and interactions with past, present and future actions.

## CASE STUDY ⊖

***Hannah Grange, SENCo in training academy for a consortium of international schools, Abu Dhabi***

*SENCos in international settings face some of the same challenges as in England and elsewhere, as well as additional ones. Abu Dhabi, where I work, is making steps to advance inclusion. The creation of my role shows commitment to professional development and*

→

recognition that in-school SENCos need support in terms of their capacity to deliver staff INSET. Working across 29 schools, my remit is to deliver centralised and bespoke training for each school in high-quality teaching (DfE and DoH, 2015). Heads of Inclusion can contact the Training Academy and request personalised workshops for specific groups or whole-school training, created for classroom teachers, assistants, students and parents, and delivered bilingually in English and Arabic.

One of the main barriers to getting the correct support for students is gaining parental consent for assessment by educational psychology. Resistance to accept a child may have SEND may be related to:

- cost (most often borne by the family) and availability of reliable testing;

- cultural and religious interpretation of SEND and what that means for a child's future (Otieno, 2009), including the potential hindrances a diagnosis can bring to their career prospects.

Meeting the needs of all students requires a great deal of trust building by schools. Abu Dhabi's progress towards increased inclusion began with a 2019 decree announcing that all schools must have a qualified SENCo with four years' experience of working in special education (Gov.ae, 2022). The government body for education (Abu Dhabi Education and Knowledge Department) delivers after-school online sessions for professional development purposes, with each teacher working in a public school required to complete 25 hours per academic year. These hours are certificated and audited when schools are inspected. All shadow teachers supporting students in a one-to-one capacity are expected to be degree-holders, have two years' experience of working in a school environment, and an English language test (IELTS) score of 6.5. In return, they can command a generous minimum salary. These stipulations mean schools can demand quality support for 'Students of Determination' – a terminology change made to recognise staff achievements, strengths and skills. As awareness, acceptance and admissions grow, so does my role. We have partnered with a local teacher training school, the Best Practice Network and The International Education Group, meaning our schools can offer early career teacher placements, help deliver training to student teachers, deliver the training for the proposed National Professional Qualification for SEND (DfE, 2022a), and ensure every classroom assistant attains a NCFE CACHE qualification to help them support all students.

## Implications for SENCos working in international schools

» Mobile pupil population necessitating information exchange between educational settings.

» Differing training and cultural understandings within staff body.

> » SENCo must engage with the culture, structure and resources of specific contexts.
>
> » SENCo agency required to foster effective learning support and resources, and facilitate inclusion for students with SEND, which must consider past, present and future needs and actions.

## Chapter summary 📝

Consideration of the six different setting types (early childhood care and education, secondary, further education, special school, alternative provision and international school settings) reveals issues specific to each. The following conclusions can be made.

- The SENCo role cannot be uniformly defined as the context contributes significantly to enactment.

- SENCos need to know what happens at each stage of education/type of education so they can see where they fit in. Each phase/setting must therefore know about what has gone before, and what will come after and be building on this reality.

- SENCos can therefore identify and play their part in a meaningful joined-up transition pathway that enhances the educational journey and outcomes for each individual child and young person with SEND.

## Further reading 📩

Alzahrani, N (2020) The Development of Inclusive Education Practice: A Review of Literature. *International Journal of Early Childhood Special Education*, 12(1): 68–83.

- This article identifies what has informed current inclusive early years education practice.

Lawson, K and Parker, R (2019) How Do Young People with Special Educational Needs Experience the Transition from School to Further Education? A Review of Literature. *Pastoral Care in Education*, 37(2): 143–61.

- This article highlights themes such as learner voice, adjusting to change and feeling valued, offering important thinking points for anyone in a designated lead role or SENCo team in FE.

Lin, H, Grudnoff, L and Hill, M (2022) Agency for Inclusion: A Case Study of Special Educational Needs Coordinators (SENCos). *International Journal of Disability, Development and Education*. https://doi.org/10.1080/1034912X.2022.2137110

- Set in an international context, this article investigates SENCo agency, recognising transactions with the culture, structure and resources in individual settings, as well as with past, present and future actions.

## References 📚

Allen, G (2011) *Early Intervention: The Next Steps*. [online] Available at: https://assets.publishing.service.gov.uk/government/uploads/system/uploads/attachment_data/file/284086/early-intervention-next-steps2.pdf (accessed 22 May 2023).

Avramidis E and Norwich B (2016) Special Educational Needs: The State of Research; from Methodological Purism to Pluralistic Research Progress. In Peer, L and Reid, G (eds) *Special Educational Needs: A Guide for Inclusive Practice* (pp 28–44). London: Sage.

Belli, C (2021) Commitment to Inclusion: A Review of SEND Provision across Mainstream Secondary Schools in Southampton. *Support for Learning,* 36(1): 43–68.

Best Practice Network (2022) Early Years SENCO Level 3. [online] Available at: www.bestpracticenet. co.uk/early-years-SENCO (accessed 24 April 2023).

*Birth to 5 Matters* (2021) *Non-statutory Guidance for the Early Years Foundation Stage.* [online] Available at: www.birthto5matters.org.uk/wp-content/uploads/2021/03/Birthto5Matters-download. pdf (accessed 24 April 2023).

Briscoe, F, Okilwa, N and Khalifa, M (2017) *The School to Prison Pipeline: The Role of Culture and Discipline in School.* Bingley: Emerald Publishing Limited.

Brown, R L (2014) Psychological Distress and the Intersection of Gender and Physical Disability: Considering Gender and Disability-Related Risk Factors. *Sex Roles,* 71(3–4): 171–81.

Buckley, L, Martin, S and Curtin, M (2020) A Multidisciplinary Community Level Approach to Improving Quality in Early Years' Settings. *Journal of Early Childhood Research,* 18(4): 433–47.

Council of British International Schools (COBIS) (n d) [online] Available at: www.cobis.org.uk (accessed 22 May 2023).

Council of International Schools (CIS) (n d) [online] Available at: www.cois.org (accessed 22 May 2023).

Curran, H and Boddison, A (2021), 'It's the Best Job in the World, but One of the Hardest, Loneliest, Most Misunderstood Roles in a School.' Understanding the Complexity of the SENCO Role Post-SEND Reform. *Journal of Research in Special Educational Needs,* 21: 39–48.

Curran, H, Moloney, H, Heavey, A and Boddison, A (2021) *National SENCO Workforce Survey 2020: Supporting Children and Young People with SEN and Their Families during the Coronavirus (COVID-19) Pandemic. A National Survey of SENCOs.* Bath Spa University. [online] Available at: www. bathspa.ac.uk/schools/education/research/senco-workload/ (accessed 22 May 2023).

Department for Education (DfE) (2019) *The Impact of College Mergers Research Report.* [online] Available at: https://assets.publishing.service.gov.uk/government/uploads/system/uploads/ attachment_data/file/904406/The_impact_of_college_mergers_in_FE.pdf (accessed 24 April 2023).

Department for Education (DfE) (2020) *Secondary Accountability Measures: Guide for Maintained Secondary Schools, Academies and Free Schools.* [online] Available at: https://assets.publishing. service.gov.uk/government/uploads/system/uploads/attachment_data/file/872997/ Secondary_accountability_measures_guidance_February_2020_3.pdf (accessed 16 April 2023).

Department for Education (DfE) (2021) *The Early Years Healthy Development Review Report. The Best Start for Life: A Vision for the 1,001 Critical Days.* [online] Available at: https://assets.publishing. service.gov.uk/government/uploads/system/uploads/attachment_data/file/973112/The_best_ start_for_life_a_vision_for_the_1_001_critical_days.pdf (accessed 24 April 2023).

Department for Education (DfE) (2022a) *SEND Review: Right Support, Right Place, Right Time – Government Consultation on the SEND and Alternative Provision System in England.* SEND Green Paper. [online] Available at: www.gov.uk/government/consultations/send-review-right-support-right-place-right-time (accessed 22 May 2023).

Department for Education (DfE) (2022b) Thousands of Children to Benefit from Schools Fit for the Future. [online] Available at: www.gov.uk/government/news/thousands-of-children-to-benefit-from-schools-fit-for-the-future (accessed 22 May 2023).

Department for Education (DfE) (2023) *Special Educational Needs and Disabilities (SEND) and Alternative Provision (AP) Improvement Plan: Right Support, Right Place, Right Time.* [online] Available at: https://assets.publishing.service.gov.uk/government/uploads/system/uploads/attachment_data/file/1139561/SEND_and_alternative_provision_improvement_plan.pdf (accessed 19 July 2023).

Department for Education (DfE) and Department of Health (DoH) (2015) *Special Educational Needs and Disability Code of Practice: 0 to 25 Years.* [online] Available at: https://assets.publishing.service.gov.uk/government/uploads/system/uploads/attachment_data/file/398815/SEND_Code_of_Practice_January_2015.pdf (accessed 22 May 2023).

Department of Health and Social Care (DHSC) (2021) *The Best Start for Life: A Vision for the 1,001 Critical Days.* [online] Available at: www.gov.uk/government/publications/the-best-start-for-life-a-vision-for-the-1001-critical-days (accessed 15 August 2023).

Easton, C and Gee, G (2012) *Early Intervention: Informing Local Practice.* [online] Available at: www.local.gov.uk/sites/default/files/documents/early-intervention-inform-d12.pdf (accessed 22 May 2023).

Education and Training Foundation (ETF) (2022) *Professional Standards for Teachers and Trainers in the Further Education and Training Sector.* [online] Available at: www.et-foundation.co.uk/professional-standards (accessed 22 May 2023).

Education Policy Institute (EPI) (2020) Understanding School Revenue Expenditure. Part 5: Expenditure on Teaching Assistants. [online] Available at: https://epi.org.uk/publications-and-research/understanding-school-revenue-expenditure-part-5-expenditure-on-teaching-assistants (accessed 22 May 2023).

Fitzgerald, J and Radford, J (2022) Leadership for Inclusive Special Education: A Qualitative Exploration of SENCOs' and Principals' Experience in Secondary Schools in Ireland. *International Journal of Inclusive Education,* 26(10): 992–1007.

Galton, M, Comber, C and Pell, T (2002) The Consequences of Transfer for Pupils: Attitudes and Attainment. In Hargreaves, L and Galton, M (eds) *Transfer from the Primary Classroom, 20 Years On* (pp 131–58). London and New York: Routledge Falmer.

Galton, M J, Croll, P and Simon, B (1980) *Inside the Primary Classroom.* Abingdon: Routledge.

Garbutt, R, Boycott-Garnett, R, Tattersall, J and Dunn, J (2010) *Talking about Sex and Relationships: The Views of Young People with Learning Disabilities.* [online] Available at: http://eprints.hud.ac.uk/id/eprint/23513/1/change-final-report-read-copy.pdf (accessed 22 May 2023).

Gov.ae (2022) Policy 26: Licensing and Qualifications. [online] Available at: https://pass.adek.gov.ae/Auth/en/DocumentUpload/GetFileURL?sectionType=ResourceDocs&parentId=1036&masterDocID=0 (accessed 22 May 2023).

Gov.uk (2012) *Education System in the UK.* [online] Available at: https://assets.publishing.service.gov.uk/government/uploads/system/uploads/attachment_data/file/219167/v01-2012ukes.pdf (accessed 22 May 2023).

Gov.uk (2019) Early Career Framework. [online] Available at: www.gov.uk/government/publications/early-career-framework (accessed 1 June 2023).

Gov.uk (2022) Special Educational Needs in England. [online] Available at: https://explore-education-statistics.service.gov.uk/find-statistics/special-educational-needs-in-england (accessed 22 May 2023).

Hakala, K (2010) Discourses on Inclusion, Citizenship and Categorizations of 'Special' in Education Policy: The Case of Negotiating Change in the Governing of Vocational Special Needs Education in Finland. *European Educational Research Journal*, 9(2): 269–82.

Hallett, F and Hallett, G (eds) (2017) *Transforming the Role of the SENCO: Achieving the National Award for SEN Coordination*. 2nd ed. Maidenhead: Oxford University Press.

Hellawell, B (2018) An Ethical Audit of the SEND CoP 2015: Professional Partnership Working and the Division of Ethical Labour. *Journal of Research in Special Educational Needs*, 19(1): 15–26.

Hipkiss, A, Woods K A and McCaldin, T (2021) Students' Use of GCSE Access Arrangements. *British Journal of Special Education*, 48(1): 50–69.

House of Commons Education Committee (2018) *Forgotten Children: Alternative Provision and the Scandal of Ever-increasing Exclusions*. [online] Available at: https://publications.parliament.uk/pa/cm201719/cmselect/cmeduc/342/342.pdf (accessed 22 May 2023).

House of Commons Library (2015) *Apprenticeships Policy, England 2010–2015*. [online] Available at: https://researchbriefings.files.parliament.uk/documents/CBP-7278/CBP-7278.pdf (accessed 19 July 2023).

Hutchinson, J (2021) *Identifying Pupils with Special Educational Needs and Disabilities*. [online] Available at: https://epi.org.uk/wp-content/uploads/2021/03/SEND-Indentification_2021-EPI.pdf (accessed 24 April 2023).

IELTS (n d) [online] Available at: www.ielts.org (accessed 22 May 2023).

Jones, L, Bellis, M A, Wood, S, Hughes, K, McCoy, E, Eckley, L, Bates, G, Mikton, C, Shakespeare, T and Officer, A (2012) Prevalence and Risk of Violence Against Children with Disabilities: A Systematic Review and Meta-Analysis of Observational Studies. *The Lancet*, 380(9845): 899–907.

Lamb, B and Blandford, S (2017) *Review of the Special Educational Needs Co-ordination Function in Early Years and Further Education Settings with Recommendation for the National Award for Special Educational Needs Co-ordination*. Achievement for All. [online] Available at: https://educationendowmentfoundation.org.uk/projects-and-evaluation/projects/achievement-for-all (accessed 22 May 2023).

Lawson, K and Parker, R (2019) How Do Young People with Special Educational Needs Experience the Transition from School to Further Education? A Review of Literature. *Pastoral Care in Education*, 37(2): 143–61.

Lin, H, Grudnoff, L and Hill, M (2022) Agency for Inclusion: A Case Study of Special Educational Needs Coordinators (SENCos). *International Journal of Disability, Development and Education*. https://doi.org/10.1080/1034912X.2022.2137110

Maudslay, L (2021) AoC – Students with SEND in Further Education. [online] Available at: www.wholeschoolsend.org.uk/blog/aoc-students-send-further-education (accessed 22 May 2023).

Musgrave, J (2017) *Supporting Children's Health and Wellbeing*. London: Sage.

Ofsted (2021) *The Special Educational Needs and Disability Review: A Statement Is Not Enough*. [online] Available at: https://assets.publishing.service.gov.uk/government/uploads/system/uploads/attachment_data/file/413814/Special_education_needs_and_disability_review.pdf (accessed 22 May 2023).

Otieno, P A (ed) (2009) *Biblical and Theological Perspectives on Disability: Implications on the Rights of Persons with Disability in Kenya*. Disabled Shakespeares / Disability in Kenya: The Nairobi Workshop on Disability, Culture, and Human Rights. [online] Available at: https://dsq-sds.org/article/view/988 (accessed 22 May 2023).

PRUsAP (n d) [online] Available at: www.prusap.co.uk/home (accessed 22 May 2023).

Richards, H (2021) Influences on SENCo Practice in Early Care and Education Settings in England. *New Zealand International Research in Early Childhood Education Journal*, 23(1): 24–38.

Robertson, C (2022) Points from the SENCo-Forum: Strengthened Role for SENCos across Different Phases of Education. *British Journal of Special Educational Needs*, 49(2): 299–304.

Sollars, V (2022) Reflecting on 'Quality' in Early Childhood Education: Practitioners' Perspectives and Voices. *Early Years: An International Research Journal*, 42(4–5): 613–30.

Spielman, A (2021) A Loophole Is Leaving the Most Vulnerable Pupils in England at Risk. *The Guardian*, 5 November. [online] Available at: www.theguardian.com/commentisfree/2021/nov/05/loophole-vulnerable-pupils-england-risk-alternative-provision-registered (accessed 22 May 2023).

Tomlinson, S (2014) *The Politics of Race, Class and Special Education*. Abingdon: Routledge.

UNESCO (1994) *The Salamanca Statement and Framework for Action on Special Needs Education*. Paris: UNESCO. [online] Available at: https://unesdoc.unesco.org/ark:/48223/pf0000098427 (accessed 22 May 2023).

Weale, S (2021) Ofsted Investigates Rise in Primary-age Children in Alternative Provision. *The Guardian*, 5 November. [online] Available at: www.theguardian.com/education/2021/nov/05/ofsted-investigates-rise-in-primary-age-children-in-alternative-provision (accessed 22 May 2023).

# 7 Working with children and young people experiencing additional challenges

## CATHERINE LAMOND

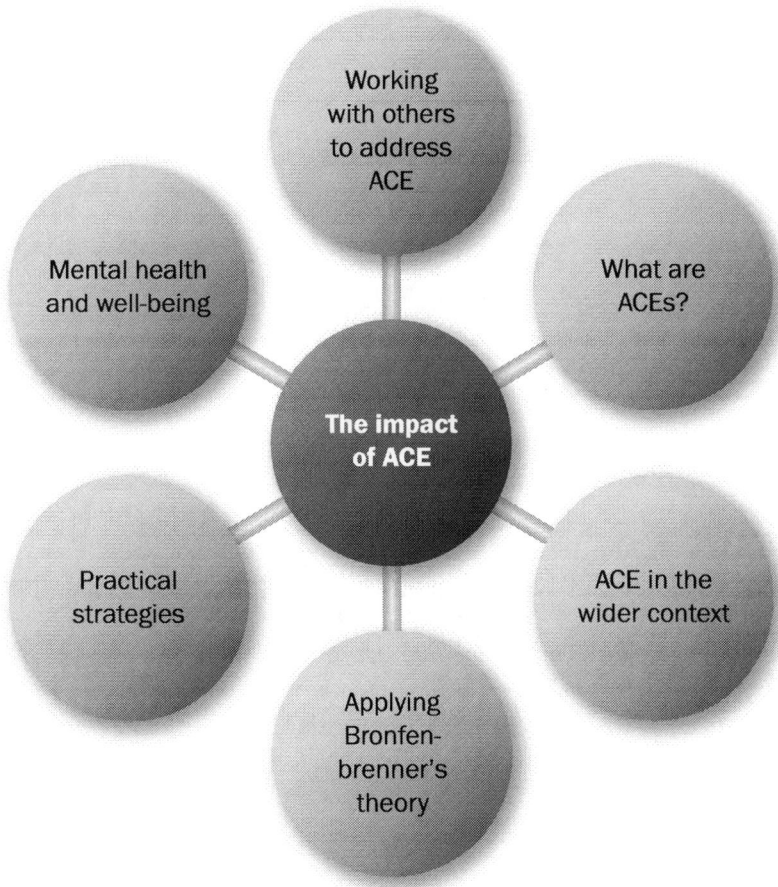

- Working with others to address ACE
- What are ACEs?
- Mental health and well-being
- The impact of ACE
- ACE in the wider context
- Practical strategies
- Applying Bronfenbrenner's theory

# Chapter objectives 🎯

Children identified as having SEND frequently also experience other challenges which can adversely affect their development, learning and well-being. The chapter:

- explores the definition of adverse childhood experiences (ACE) and their links to SEND;

- introduces you to a critical analysis of ACE and their impact;

- applies Bronfenbrenner's (1979) ecological systems theory to schools;

- encourages you to think holistically about the context of children's lives, their families and communities;

- discusses practical strategies to become a trauma-aware setting;

- suggests ways in which you, as SENCo, can lead others in developing effective responses to difficult situations.

---

## STARTING POINTS 🏁

» What mechanisms are in place in your setting to support children, young people and families with adverse life experiences?

» What is your current role in supporting these children, young people and families?

» What is in place to support staff, including you?

---

# Introduction

Concerns have been raised about the long-term consequences of ACE (Bellis et al, 2019). While much of the focus has been on health outcomes, the impact of ACE on education has also been recognised (DfE, 2022b) with apprehension that trauma leads to social, emotional and mental health needs. Offerman et al (2022) list social, emotional and academic difficulties resulting from ACE, which '*include aggression and anxiety, psychiatric problems according to the DSM* [Diagnostic and Statistical Manual], *such as ADHD* [attention deficit hyperactivity disorder], *ASD* [autism spectrum disorder] *and post-traumatic stress disorder (PTSD), as well as significant delays in cognitive development and academic achievement*'. Bomber (2020, p 31) explicitly links ACE to growing numbers of pupils being taught in behaviour units and pupil referral units. As SENCo, you should be involved in leading a co-ordinated approach to promoting the well-being of every child and young person in your setting, with an understanding of the impact of ACE (Estyn, 2020, p 5). A vital component is ensuring your setting is a safe space where children and young people know they can talk to trusted adults about events in their lives and where they can share their feelings when they are ready (Bomber, 2020).

Bronfenbrenner's ecological systems model (1979) helps conceptualise the factors which impact a child. Applying this theory to specific children can help us shift from an individualised focus on deficits to a recognition of systemic disadvantage and unlock a new approach to supporting children.

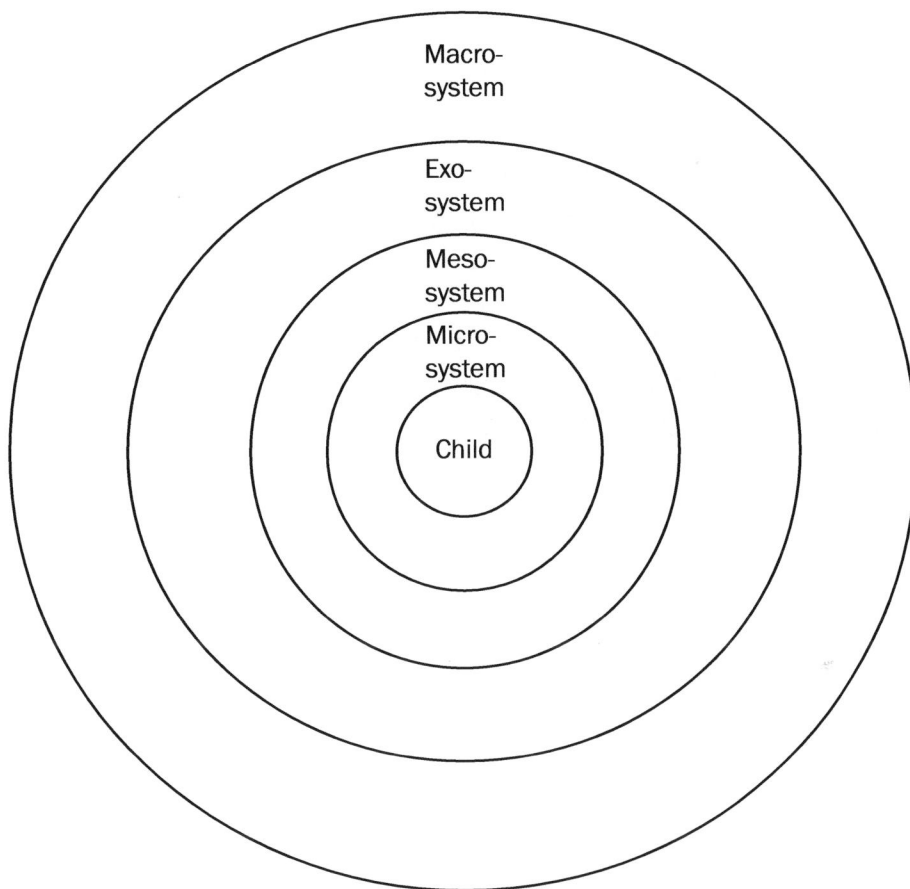

*Figure 7.1* *Bronfenbrenner's ecological systems theory*

In Bronfenbrenner's model, the child is an individual at the centre of a multi-layered, interactive and dynamic system. The first layer is the micro-system – the child's family, home, school and neighbourhood. The child is not passive but engages with this layer and influences it. The next layer is the meso-system, which relates to the interactions between, for example, parents' work and school, and between family and neighbourhood. Note that the different levels interact with and influence each other. Then there is the exo-system, which includes community services and mass media. Finally, the macro-system includes cultural values and beliefs. In some versions Bronfenbrenner also includes the chrono-system, which shows how changes over time affect all the other layers. A key point is that an individual child may seem to have a small number of interactions within their daily lives, but as they develop they are influenced by many layers of external factors. The model is useful in conceptualising education in a way which allows analysis through different layers, placing a child in context, and recognising that the child also influences those around them.

---

### Critical questions (?)

» What does the phrase 'adverse childhood experience' mean to you? List examples you have encountered in your career so far. What impact did they have, particularly in relation to SEND?

» To what extent does your setting take account of the context of children and young people's lives?

» Select a pupil you have recently begun working with. Apply Bronfenbrenner's model to their situation to identify different perspectives. How might these different perspectives change your intervention?

» What steps have you taken to ensure your setting is a safe space where children and young people have the time and opportunity to talk to trusted adults?

---

## Defining adverse childhood experiences and links to Bronfenbrenner

ACEs have been defined as '*highly stressful, and potentially traumatic, events or situations that occur during childhood and/or adolescence. They can be a single event, or prolonged threats to, and breaches of, the young person's safety, security, trust or bodily integrity*' (Young Minds, 2018). More specifically, Estyn (2020, p 1) defines ACEs as:

- *verbal and or mental abuse;*
- *physical abuse;*
- *sexual abuse;*
- *hostile parental separation;*
- *domestic violence;*
- *parental mental illness;*
- *alcohol abuse;*
- *drug use;*
- *neglect;*
- *parental incarceration.*

Reading through this list, you may think of children and young people being taken into care because of these experiences: an important group to consider in relation to overcoming disadvantage. Other groups may also have been impacted by disadvantage: young carers; children from the Gypsy, Roma and Traveller community; and asylum seekers, for example. Considering the final group, it has been suggested that children learning English as an additional language (EAL) are disadvantaged, and clearly there is a need to provide appropriate support to encourage language development – but being bilingual is beneficial for further language learning and children and young people should not be viewed as having SEND because English is not their first language (NALDIC, 2023). Mowat (2019) highlights intersectionality, stating that mental health needs often arise from a complex range of factors.

Given the high rate of marital relationship breakdown in the UK, it is unsurprising that the NHS (2022a) states that 47 per cent of children will have experienced an ACE, with many having multiple overlapping experiences. Trauma causes physical changes to the brain, which can have long-lasting effects on relationships. ACE can therefore be linked to SEND: trauma can lead to sensory impairments, with children and young people being hyper- or hypo-sensitive, with potential impacts on cognition, communication, social and emotional development, and mental health.

The list of ACEs above is not exhaustive. For example, disabled children and those with health conditions can experience segregation and loneliness as they grow up and these adverse experiences can be both long term and damaging. Challenges associated with parenting children with SEND can also lead to stresses on a relationship, so the link between ACE and SEND is bi-directional. Children and young people not having access to a nutritious diet is an issue of current concern (Lalli, 2022) which impacts physical and mental health and well-being.

Linking the definition above of ACE with Bronfenbrenner suggests these experiences all occur at the level of the micro-system, with a focus on the child and their immediate environment. Examining each category in more depth, however, we see that other levels are also important: physical, sexual and emotional abuse can all be linked to societal problems such as sexism and homophobia – individuals or groups may be targeted. Children of a same-sex couple may experience discrimination, not because of any neglect or abuse in their home lives but because of wider prejudice. The Joseph Rowntree Foundation (2022) explains the harmful effects of child poverty, giving the shocking statistic that 550,000 children are living in destitution.

Bronfenbrenner's model (see Figure 7.1) also highlights that schools do not operate in isolation. Links to families, the wider community and to support services mean different levels of the system can be drawn upon to address disadvantage; for example, many schools work closely with food banks (Lalli, 2022).

# Critique of adverse childhood experiences

Some have argued that the widespread use of the concept of ACE is not necessarily helpful.

*The current popularity of the ACE narrative should not lead us to ignore the limitations in the current evidence base or be allowed to create the illusion that there are quick fixes to prevent adversity or to help people overcome it.*

(EIF, 2020)

As well as the danger of focusing too much on the individual and psychological approaches, '*the concept of ACEs has been critiqued for taking inadequate account of the socio-political and economic inequalities that influence family functioning*' (Goding et al, 2022, p 2). Smith (2018) argues that there are positive perceptions of interventions designed to support children and young people who have experienced ACE, but a lack of robust evidence of what works. The impact of the Covid-19 pandemic must also be considered, and it could be argued that most children had adverse experiences due to lockdowns and restrictions, with some children with SEND being particularly negatively impacted. It is necessary, therefore, to address the consequences of the pandemic with a holistic approach rather than focusing on individuals.

The concept of ACE can also be criticised for positioning the child or young person as a passive recipient of experiences rather than as having any agency. This concern has also been raised in relation to children and young people with SEND. Since the United Nations Convention on the Rights of the Child (UNICEF, 1989), there has been a widespread focus on listening to the views of children and young people and involving them in decisions about their lives. There are challenges, however, with concerns about tokenism and the extent to which children can really be given autonomy in decision making within existing structures of imbalanced power. It is especially important to engage authentically with children who face additional challenges in their lives (Bomber, 2020, p 88), such as SEND and living through ACE, but the barriers which may be erected through issues including lack of trust may make building relationships more difficult. It is also important to note that a focus on listening to children could potentially place them in a position where they are re-living trauma without access to appropriate support such as trained counsellors. Strudley-Brown and Prowle (2022) provide comprehensive guidance on how to approach talking to children about difficult experiences.

As well as the impact of ACE on mental health, Strudley-Brown and Prowle (2022) also suggest that they can lead to sensory processing difficulties, linking to sensory and physical impairment, and communication difficulties, which can lead to challenges in engaging with learning. Examining the figures, however, can raise questions about how helpful these different methods of categorising children and young people are.

The NHS (2022a) quotes the Bellis et al study of 2014, which found that 47 per cent of children will have experienced at least one ACE, while the DfE (2022b) suggest that 15.8 per cent of children and young people have SEND. '*In 2022, 18 per cent of children aged seven to 16 years and 22 per cent of young people aged 17 to 24 years had a probable mental disorder*' (NHS, 2022b); and the Joseph Rowntree Foundation (2022) found that almost a third of children are growing up in poverty. Many of these figures are increasing, and all children, young people and families have been affected by the Covid-19 pandemic. In addition, children and young people, or their families, may possess other '*protected characteristics*' (Equality Act 2010) such as being from an ethnic minority. Intersectionality of these factors means ACE can only be one perspective to use in trying to understand their lived experience. It can be questioned how useful these figures are, and how complex the Venn diagram would be if trying to portray the relationship between the overlapping categories.

This can be illustrated by focusing on looked after children – 0.7 per cent of the population of children (DfE, 2022a), which is much lower than the suggested figure for ACE. For most children who are taken into care, the primary reason is abuse or neglect, so the stark difference between the figures for looked after children and those experiencing ACE suggests that only those having the most severe experiences are picked up by the care system. There is concern, however, about the attainment gap between pupils in care and those in the general population, which is initially wide and further increases as pupils progress through school (Goding et al, 2022). It is suggested that, while it may be helpful to address trauma, it is also necessary to examine what the education system is offering these children and young people. They are being failed too often. As a SENCo, it is important to work with the designated teacher for looked after children, the local Virtual School (which has responsibility for all looked after children within each local authority), and other agencies such as the child or young person's carers and social worker to identify any SEND or gaps in learning as early as possible. Targeted support can help looked after children to overcome disadvantage such as disrupted schooling (Goding et al, 2022).

# Theory into practice

So far, this chapter has defined ACE and the ecological systems theory of Bronfenbrenner (1979). It has also explored some other potential challenges for children and young people. While it is important to consider the long-term impact of ACE, it is also useful to view a child or young person in a wider context which can be analysed using the different levels. It is also vital to consider the views of children and young people and to be aware of the complexities of their lives (Bomber, 2020). The following case study interweaves some of these factors.

## CASE STUDY ☺

### Tom

Tom (aged ten) is in Year 5 in a small village primary school. He lives with his dad, his step-mum and his siblings in a rural location. Tom's dad is a lorry driver and is sometimes away overnight, while his step-mum is currently at home with their young baby. Tom and his sister do not have contact with their birth mother, as the relationship broke down when she was in prison. Although Tom's family are economically disadvantaged, their supportive relationships are vital in promoting Tom's well-being.

Tom is good at maths and enjoys practical subjects. He has found reading harder, however, and is sometimes frustrated that his strength with calculations can be held back when he struggles to read number problems. Tom has asthma, which is treated with an inhaler but has led to repeated absences from school. He has a lively sense of humour and likes playing

→

sports, including football, with the other children at break times. Tom can be quick to lose his temper and sometimes other children will provoke him, knowing he will react. In the past, this has led to Tom being punished at school with sanctions such as detention. He has a personal education plan (PEP) for dyslexia-type characteristics and for behaviour support. The language used in the PEP is in the style critiqued by Bomber (2020, p 73), who stresses the need to use the approach of '*regulate, relate, reason and repair*' when working with pupils who have experienced ACE.

Tom has reported being bullied by older children and by others in his class, and his parents are very concerned about this. In the last few years, they have contacted the school several times to complain about incidents of bullying, where Tom's parents felt his class teacher '*always blamed him*' and '*never took his side*'. This led to some heated meetings where the headteacher became involved and resulted in a rather confrontational relationship between Tom's parents and some of the school staff. Tom's parents expressed the view that '*everyone always has it in for our family*'. This is not in line with the requirement for practitioners to offer support to families (Strudley-Brown and Prowle, 2022).

On occasions, Tom and his sister are late for school or arrive without their packed lunch or required equipment. The children and their parents are very apologetic when this occurs, explaining the baby has been unwell or there have been difficulties with transport. Tom's parents are very proud of his abilities in maths, practical subjects and sports. The family are discussing options for Tom moving to secondary school. One concern they have raised is that Tom will have to take the bus to secondary school in a bigger town and they are worried about him being bullied on these journeys. Tom's parents would like him to have a fresh start when he changes school.

## Critical questions (?)

» How can an understanding of ACE help to explain Tom's situation?

» How can Bronfenbrenner's ecological systems model be used to gain different perspectives on Tom?

» As SENCo, how would you give Tom a voice to be able to share his lived experience?

» What concerns would you have and how would you address these?

» What plans can you put in place to prepare Tom for his next steps?

» How can you work effectively with Tom's family?

## ⚛ *Implications for the SENCo role, identity and practice*

A range of challenges can affect children and young people's readiness to learn. ACE, SEND, economic disadvantage, bullying and practical issues such as being hungry can all mean pupils arrive in school distracted and unsettled. Some of these can be addressed with appropriate intervention but this chapter does not suggest the focus should be solely on 'fixing' children. As SENCo you will lead on planning whole-school approaches. For example, if your school supports reading for pleasure and ensures diverse reading material for all pupils, this can help children to explore what is going on in their own lives (National Literacy Trust, 2022). This section will suggest ways of working with children and young people who have experienced ACE at different levels, in line with Bronfenbrenner's ecological systems model. The focus is on the system rather than the individual child.

In response to concerns about behaviour, many writers have advised building relationships with the child or young person displaying challenging behaviour (eg O'Regan, 2020). It has been suggested that a key person is vital to provide stability for the pupil, but this can lead to difficulties if the member of staff is unavailable, and does not prepare the pupil for transitions to other classes or schools. Minahan (2019) provides many useful suggestions on how to improve the relationship between any member of staff and a child or young person who has experienced trauma, thereby strengthening support at the level of the micro-system. It could be helpful to consider training all the adults in your school community on this trauma-aware approach, with some suggestions given below.

» Expect unexpected behaviours. This insight shows why a system based on rules, sanctions or rewards may not be sufficiently flexible to respond to an individual who feels threatened or abandoned.

» Employ thoughtful interactions. These include giving choice; avoiding being authoritarian; giving reasons for requests; and allowing time for reactions. An individual who has experienced ACE may feel they do not have control over their own lives, so allowing some agency can avoid confrontation.

» Teach strategies to 'change the channel'. A pupil who is becoming angry is often sent for time out to allow them to calm down. Minahan argues that frequently this only leads to the child or young person thinking about what has happened and becoming more frustrated, so she suggests having distraction activities instead such as a quiz or *Where's Wally?* to change the focus.

To return to Bronfenbrenner (1979), it is also important to consider the other layers of the ecosystem impacting on the lives of children and young people. At the level of the meso-system, professionals can work together to develop supportive classroom

→

and school environments. Bomber (2020, pp 259–73) suggests many activities to build links with the community while providing positive experiences for pupils, with, for example, animals, creative activities, gardening and sport.

At a wider level, education settings have an important role to play in teaching children and young people about the values and culture of society – the macro-system. Education can lead positive change. As a SENCo, you can be part of that leadership.

> *School improvement and social mobility policies that focus overwhelmingly on examination results largely disregard the potential impact of schools on other policy areas acknowledged nationally as in need of amelioration, such as managing mental health, supporting parents, and building community cohesion.*
>
> (McIntyre and Hall, 2020, p 596)

## Critical questions (?)

» Review your school's behaviour policy. To what extent is there a balance between providing structure, routine and clear expectations, while allowing for individuality?

» How can you build capacity in all members of staff to respond to pupils in a trauma-aware way?

» What are the possibilities for promoting values of empathy and inclusion among the pupils at your school?

» How can your setting promote positive links with its community?

# Chapter summary 📝

This chapter has critically analysed the concept of ACE and has suggested that Bronfenbrenner's ecological systems theory model can provide a valuable approach to addressing challenges faced in schools. As a SENCo, your role can be to lead in the development of a portfolio of responses to changing situations in school. The portfolio could include:

• strategies to develop positive relationships with all pupils;

• plans to promote a positive atmosphere within the classroom;

• training for all staff on the impact of ACE;

• ideas on how to engage collaboratively with families and the wider community;

• resources (books, information leaflets, posters) which reflect the diversity of your pupils, families and staff;

- guidelines on how to work effectively with other agencies involved in the school;

- a commitment to taking seriously the ethos, culture and values of the school and how they are experienced by the whole school community.

It may seem daunting that there are many issues to address at many levels but there will already be positive practices for you to build upon. You can prioritise 'hotspots' where things do not seem to be going smoothly and bring your colleagues with you in a shared vision.

# Further reading

Brooks, R (2020) *The Trauma and Attachment-Aware Classroom.* London and Philadelphia, PA: Jessica Kingsley.

- This book offers strategies for children displaying the most challenging behaviour, including guidance for 'what to do when you don't know what to do'.

McIntyre, J and Hall, C (2020) Barriers to the Inclusion of Refugee and Asylum-Seeking Children in Schools in England. *Educational Review*, 72(5): 583–600.

- This article applies Bronfenbrenner's ecological systems theory model to a study of headteachers' perspectives on supporting pupils who are asylum seekers or refugees, considering ethical and moral dilemmas.

# References

Bellis, M, Hughes, K, Ford, K, Ramos Rodriguez, G, Sethi, D and Passmore, J (2019) Life Course Health Consequences and Associated Annual Costs of Adverse Childhood Experiences across Europe and North America: A Systematic Review and Meta-Analysis. *The Lancet Public Health*, 4(10): e517–e528.

Bomber, L M (2020) *Know Me to Teach Me: Differentiated Discipline for Those Recovering from Adverse Childhood Experiences.* London: Worth Publishing.

Bronfenbrenner, U (1979) *The Ecology of Human Development: Experiments by Nature and Design.* Boston, MA: Harvard University Press.

Department for Education (DfE) (2022a) Children Looked After in England. [online] Available at: https://explore-education-statistics.service.gov.uk/find-statistics/children-looked-after-in-england-including-adoptions/2022 (accessed 24 April 2023).

Department for Education (DfE) (2022b) *Keeping Children Safe in Education*. [online] Available at: https://assets.publishing.service.gov.uk/government/uploads/system/uploads/attachment_data/file/1101454/Keeping_children_safe_in_education_2022.pdf (accessed 24 April 2023).

Early Intervention Foundation (EIF) (2020) Adverse Childhood Experiences: What We Know, What We Don't Know, and What Should Happen Next. [online] Available at: www.eif.org.uk/files/image/reports/aces-key-messages.jpg (accessed 24 April 2023).

Equality Act 2010. [online] Available at: www.legislation.gov.uk/ukpga/2010/15/contents (accessed 14 June 2023).

Estyn (2020) *Knowing Your Children – Supporting Pupils with Adverse Childhood Experiences (ACES).* [online] Available at: www.estyn.gov.wales/system/files/2022-01/Knowing%2520your%2520 children%2520%2520supporting%2520pupils%2520with%2520adverse%2520 childhood%2520experiences_0.pdf (accessed 24 April 2023).

Goding, N, Hartwell, B and Kreppner, J (2022) 'Everyone Has the Ability Actually to Do Well in Education. It's Just the Support Mechanisms That You Give to Them…': A Systematic Literature Review Exploring the Educational Experiences of Children in Care. *Children and Youth Services Review*, 137: 106474.

Joseph Rowntree Foundation (2022) *UK Poverty 2022: The Essential Guide to Understanding Poverty in the UK.* [online] Available at: www.jrf.org.uk/report/uk-poverty-2022 (accessed 24 April 2023).

Lalli, G S (2022) 'In Most Supermarkets Food Does Not Cost £3 Per Day …': The Impact of the School Food Voucher Scheme during COVID-19. *British Educational Research Journal.* [online] Available at: https://bera-journals.onlinelibrary.wiley.com/doi/full/10.1002/berj.3828 (accessed 24 April 2023).

Minahan, J (2019) Trauma-Informed Teaching Strategies. *Educational Leadership*, 77(2): 30–6.

McIntyre, J and Hall, C (2020) Barriers to the Inclusion of Refugee and Asylum-Seeking Children in Schools in England. *Educational Review*, 72(5): 583–600.

Mowat, J G (2019) Exploring the Impact of Social Inequality and Poverty on the Mental Health and Wellbeing and Attainment of Children and Young People in Scotland. *Improving Schools*, 22(3): 204–23.

National Association for Language Development in the Curriculum (NALDIC) (2023) About NALDIC. [online] Available at: https://naldic.org.uk/about-naldic/vision-mission-and-values (accessed 24 April 2023).

National Literacy Trust (2022) *Seeing Yourself in What You Read: Diversity and Children and Young People's Reading in 2022.* [online] Available at: https://cdn.literacytrust.org.uk/media/documents/Diversity_in_children_and_young_peoples_reading_in_2022.pdf (accessed 24 April 2023).

NHS (2022a) Adverse Childhood Experiences (ACEs) and Attachment. [online] Available at: https://mft.nhs.uk/rmch/services/camhs/young-people/adverse-childhood-experiences-aces-and-attachment (accessed 24 April 2023).

NHS (2022b) *Mental Health of Children and Young People in England 2022 – Wave 3 Follow Up to the 2017 Survey.* [online] Available at: http://digital.nhs.uk/pubs/mhcypsurvey2022w3 (accessed 19 July 2023).

O'Regan, F (2020) 'Firm, Fair and Funny': The Skills of a Teacher. [online] Available at: www.fintanoregan.com/firm-fair-and-funny-the-skills-of-a-teacher (accessed 24 April 2023).

Offerman, E C P, Asselman, M W, Bolling, F, Helmond, P, Stams, G-J J M and Lindauer, R J L (2022) Prevalence of Adverse Childhood Experiences in Students with Emotional and Behavioral Disorders in Special Education Schools from a Multi-Informant Perspective. *International Journal of Environmental Research and Public Health*, 19: 3411.

Smith, L (2018) *Adverse Childhood Experiences (ACEs): Interventions in Education.* [online] Available at: www.iriss.org.uk/sites/default/files/2018-04/iriss-esss-outline-adverse-childhood-experiences-2018-4-23.pdf (accessed 24 April 2023).

Strudley-Brown, E and Prowle, A (2022) Understanding and Responding to Adverse Childhood Experiences in Practice. In Richards, H and Malomo, M (eds) *Developing Your Professional Identity: A Guide for Working with Children and Families* (pp 97–112). St Albans: Critical Publishing.

UNICEF (1989) *The UN Convention on the Rights of the Child*. [online] Available at: www.unicef.org.uk/wp-content/uploads/2016/08/unicef-convention-rights-child-uncrc.pdf (accessed 19 July 2023).

Young Minds (2018) *Addressing Adversity and Prioritising Trauma-Informed Care for Children and Young People in England*. London: Blackmore Ltd.

# 8  Working with parents

## PETER HARWOOD AND ZOE STUART

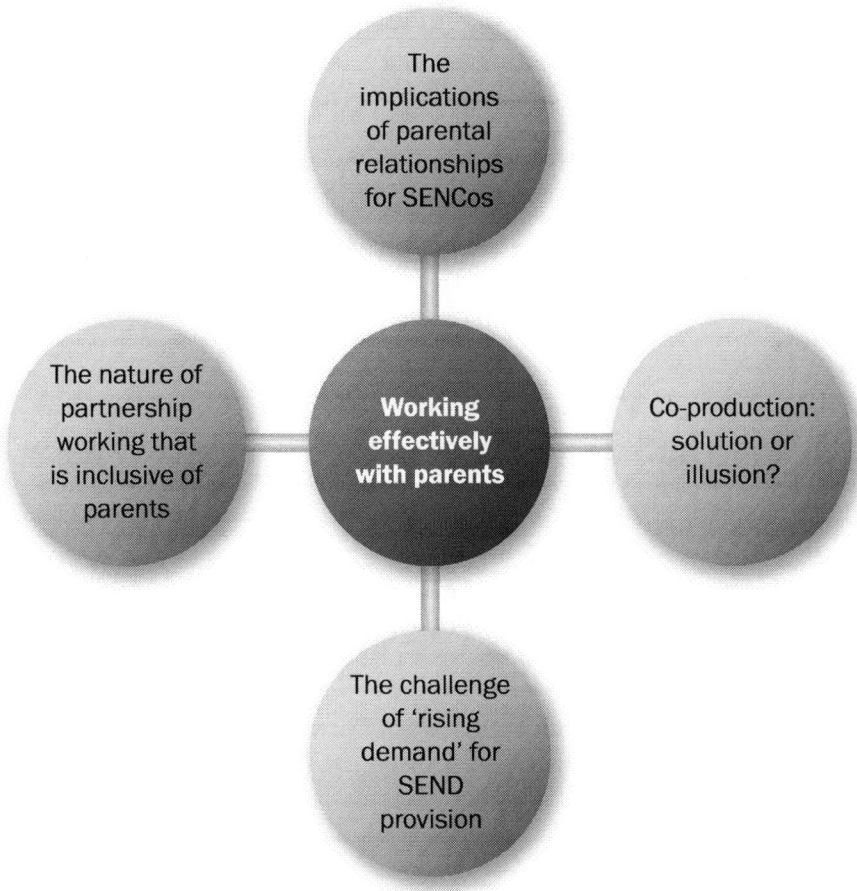

The implications of parental relationships for SENCos

The nature of partnership working that is inclusive of parents

**Working effectively with parents**

Co-production: solution or illusion?

The challenge of 'rising demand' for SEND provision

## Chapter objectives 🎯

This chapter explores the ways in which SENCos might work with parents. The chapter:

- examines the nature of partnership working with parents envisaged by the SEND Code of Practice (CoP) (DfE and DoH, 2015);

- critically engages with current debates about parental partnership, considering the implications for a SENCo;

- considers what further work is needed by schools and SENCos to better understand the wider contextual factors which impact on parents and their ability to be fully involved in the SEND processes for their child;

- offers a range of strategies SENCos could put into practice, as well as case studies of relationship building based around empathy and inclusive communication.

### STARTING POINTS 🏁

- » What are the typical interactions you have with parents and carers?

- » What features do you think make for positive collaboration with parents and carers?

- » Not all parents and carers engage directly with SENCos. What strategies work best for ensuring all parents are engaged with your school or setting?

## Introduction

This chapter explores the ways in which SENCos work with parents and uses the term 'parents' to encompass parents, carers and guardians. The current SEND CoP (DfE and DoH, 2015), called for '*a clearer focus on the views of children, young people and parents in the decision making at individual and strategic levels*' (DfE and DoH, 2015, p 14). This represented a huge cultural shift from the previous code (DfES, 2001) and was broadly welcomed by parents. However, evidence from the recent consultation process suggests a high degree of parental dissatisfaction remains (DfE, 2022). There is a consensus, supported by the House of Commons Education Committee report (House of Commons, 2019), that the current system is not working. Consequently, this chapter does not seek to set out extensive guidance on how best to manage the systems required of the SENCo by the SEND CoP (DfE and DoH, 2015), but is rather concerned with an exploration of the wider factors which impact parents and families, considering how that impact might be understood and suggesting how SENCos can engage more effectively with parents as partners.

## How parents experience the current pressurised SEND system

The UK government committed to involve parents in all aspects of decision making, including how the money provided by their local authority is spent on their child (DfE and DoH, 2015). The government launched a further enquiry into special educational needs and disabilities in

2018 with the express intention of scrutinising Part 3 of the Children and Families Act (2014) in the context of the Act's implementation and the '*human experience of the reforms*' (House of Commons Education Committee, 2019). The certainties are that parents will remain central to the SEND system however it might be reformed or redefined. For a SENCo, then, the relationship with parents will remain key to developing successful and effective provision for children and young people, irrespective of any changes to the details of the SEND CoP (DfE and DoH, 2015).

Existing challenges faced by all those agencies involved in the SEND system are exacerbated by the continuous rise in demand. Since the introduction of legislation to support children and young people with SEND, numbers have grown significantly, and parents report dissatisfaction with their experience of the process even if the nature of that dissatisfaction is contested (Tirraoro, 2019). The numbers are clear and in 2022, 17 per cent of children and young people were registered as being somewhere on the SEND continuum (Gov.uk, 2022). To put it another way, on average **five** children in every class of **30** are identified as having special educational needs.

The numbers of children and young people with SEND are clearly rising and for many families, the SEND system remains in a state of crisis. Parental concerns about the provision are as much if not more of an issue than had been the case prior to changes to legislation in 2014. In its report of the 2019–20 session on special educational needs, the House of Commons Education Committee were explicit in their assessment of the state of the system:

> *The system is not working—yet. There are clear and fundamental problems that need fixing now, not left waiting on the outcome of another review. Apparently random examples of children getting good support are not enough. A reliance on relationships, luck or family circumstance is not enough. Families are in crisis, local authorities are under pressure, schools (and colleges) are struggling. And they cannot wait for the outcome of another review: they have waited patiently for long enough.*
>
> (House of Commons Education Committee, 2019, p 83)

---

### *Critical questions* (?)

» How have parents been incentivised by the current system to seek formal assessment and to consequently increase demand?

» What strategies might local authorities use to disincentivise demand and what are the implications for educational professionals?

---

## The nature of contact between parents and SENCos

SENCos are aware of the daily pressure to manage the SEND processes in their setting. For parents, interaction with the SENCo (often as the face of the institution) is mostly characterised by the need to navigate specific points of transition, demand and stress. This might be on admission, at the time of the transition meetings or through the protracted process of identifying and naming a preferred school. In many cases, failure or inability to implement the changes required in a child or young person's provision results in disruption and a potential crisis that could involve formal exclusion on a fixed or permanent basis or something less formal such as '*grey exclusion*' or '*off rolling*' (Done, Knowler and Armstrong, 2021).

Of course, for many parents and for much of the time, the SENCo is a positive source of information and reassurance. In facilitating inclusive education within the tensions of the SEND processes and the context of a post-pandemic world, SENCos may act primarily as advocates (Clarke and Done, 2021). However, the systemic requirements of the role mean the relationship with parents is conditional. It is subject to the possibility of significant and intense change when, for example, they must adopt a position that might, to the parent, feel defensive or obstructive. This could be because of conflict between the parents' perception of the right action for the child and barriers to implementation. On occasion, it might be because of a clash with wider school policy, for example related to standards or progression. As Done et al (2022) suggest, conflicts such as this are evocative of a paradox of '*good intentions*' (Popkewitz, 2020, p 271). SENCos can, for example, be put in a position of simultaneously promoting the interests of students with SEND while feeling compelled to defend their headteacher's exclusionary actions (Done, Knowler, Warnes and Pickett-Jones, 2021).

For the parent of a child with special educational needs in general and particularly a child or young person who has an education, health and care plan (EHCP), the number of contacts with a setting is significantly greater and much more burdensome than for most parents. Often the cumulative effect of a history of such contact is that parents can have feelings of anxiety, stress and hostility about once again being asked the same questions or having to face the same assumptions about their child. Individual SENCos in a receiving secondary school placement may perceive the parents as unnecessarily confrontational or defensive when they have had no previous relationship with them. For the parents, however, the transition to secondary school is just another point at which they must restate and reargue what they may have been saying about their children since birth. For many parents, the experience of engaging with SEND systems and services throughout their children's educational and care journeys is understood and characterised as a fight or struggle.

This sense of being in a fight with authority is most acutely felt by parents in relation to securing provision for their child or young adult. While in the general population there tends to be certainty about having a school or college place, albeit that this is becoming increasingly contested in some areas, it is widely recognised that for many disabled young people and their families there is frequently a sense of doubt about their future provision. Many refer to the fear of '*falling off the cliff*' (Warwick, 2017, p 48), when faced with moments of transition in general and the move beyond statutory educational and health services into adulthood in particular. The fear is of an absence of provision because of the failure on the part of the placing authority to secure an appropriate placement. The consequence of this for families is daunting, with the prospect of their child or young adult being left with nothing other than intermittent contact with social service support or day services.

The point at which the cliff edge of provision appears for children and young people with SEND leaving compulsory education has undoubtedly been pushed back with the raising of the participation age and the opening of access to legal protections for young people to the age of 25 with an EHCP, but it still exists. The 'new' SEND CoP (DfE and DoH, 2015) was intended to address this dilemma along with what government recognised as other serious flaws in the SEND system. Prior to introduction of the revised code, it was recognised in 2006 that: '*The SEN system is demonstrably no longer fit for purpose and there is a need for the Government to develop a new system that puts the needs of the child at the centre of provision*' (House of Commons Education and Skills Committee, 2006, p 6).

It is notable that so soon after the introduction of legislation in 2015 to address these flaws, the government engaged in another major review of SEND legislation in what they described as a '*response to the widespread recognition that the system is failing to deliver for children, young people, and their families*' (DfE, 2022, p 1).

---

### Critical questions ?

»   What are the implications for educational professionals of a 'state of crisis' in SEND provision?

»   What strategies have you found for establishing trust with parents and how does this help to address issues associated with a sense of crisis in the system?

---

## Understanding the parental perspective

Given the likelihood of frequent legislative change in the face of persistent parental concern about the system, and the role of parents in shaping choices for young people, it seems appropriate for SENCos and others to re-examine some questions of parental voice. Many parents feel worn down and hostile towards 'the system' before they encounter a school SENCo, and that can be an immediate barrier to positive collaborative relationships. It is, however, increasingly recognised that parents of a disabled child are the experts regarding their own child and that they can provide professionals with valuable information, perspective and guidance in developing education and support plans (Kruithof, Olsman, Nieuwenhuijse and Willems, 2020). It is therefore vital that the SENCo, as often the primary contact, offers space for the parent to become an expert co-productive partner. To do this, it is important that barriers to active and purposeful engagement with parents are identified and addressed.

Schools, colleges and other settings tend to be oriented towards the ordinary range of familial expectation. Achievement and attainment are often prioritised in the ways in which they relate to parents and families. For many families of children with SEND, the parameters, expectations and priorities are simply different.

## CASE STUDY ☺

### Anna, the parent of a child with SEND

**'Quite often my only contact with school was when he was in trouble.'**

Anna often feels frustrated: she wants to concentrate on the things her son can do and the progress he is making but feels everything is negative. She is often called when things go wrong at school and feels under pressure to have a solution. She works hard to try and 'pick apart' what has happened during the day and often this leads to a 'battle' with the school over ensuring his EHCP is met. *'Everything changed'* for her son during the transition to secondary school. The movement around the school and multiple staff in contact with her son means *'it just can't be as flexible anymore'*; contact with the school has become more infrequent and difficult. It isn't that they don't care: secondary schools are just always so busy and have so many children to take care of. Sometimes she feels judged, under pressure and lonely. She doesn't feel able to relate to other parents and, without a network of other parents as support, feels left out.

Family quality of life is an outcome indicator for measuring overall family satisfaction for children with disabilities (Werner et al, 2009). It suggests that while all family life can of course be stressful, for families of children with special needs stress is measurably greater. The role parents play in the education and personal development of a child with SEND can often be more central and vital than for parents in general. It is crucial for SENCos to recognise the level of impact that stress can have on families' quality of life. However, it is also important to see beyond the manifestations of this stress and to recognise the contribution and insight that parents and families can offer. Parents are a valuable resource and literature suggests that parents of children with profound intellectual and multiple disabilities, for example, have *'unique and crucial knowledge of their child'* (Kruithof, Willems, van Etten-Jamaludin and Olsman, 2020).

## The co-production illusion

There have been significant attempts to ensure parents of children and young people with SEND are included as active and central participants in planning for their provision. This is of course written into the SEND CoP (DfE and DoH, 2015), but it has also been evident in wider social policy. Through the New Labour years (1997–2010) and into the coalition era (2010–15), there was a policy focus on person-centred planning, a concept originally developed in healthcare which spread into the wider social care and education fields. Person-centred planning was described as an empowering philosophy that shifted power from professionals to service users (DoH, 2010). Person-centred planning is evident throughout the SEND CoP (DfE and DoH, 2015), and the Lamb Enquiry (2009) strongly suggested that one solution to the then perceived failings of the system was to have a greater emphasis on parents as partners with distinct expertise in a person-centred system.

Despite the focus on person-centredness throughout various reforms, lack of parental confidence has been an ongoing feature of the SEND system since its formulation, and confidence remains low, as evidenced by the review process (DfE, 2022). Nevertheless, the SEND CoP (DfE and DoH, 2015) explicitly states that education, health and social care partners are required to consult with and respond to the views of parents, children and young people to make improvements to services.

## CASE STUDY ☺

### Rita, the parent of a child with SEND

*I was made to feel like I should be grateful for all these people who had my son's best interest at heart but there was a power imbalance. They used codes and words which I just didn't get and I felt so under pressure to pretend I knew what they were talking about. I felt angry because some of these people had never even met my son. How could they be part of a process to decide what's best for him?*

The process of an EHCP has been difficult for Rita to navigate. She has spent many hours researching legislation and using parental advice forums online to try and understand the EHCP process. She wants to advocate for her son but finds this challenging when the process is overly formal. She has only ever had contact with the SENCo before and other professionals are not known to her. Despite being 15, Rita's son was not invited to the meeting, and she feels she is responsible for ensuring his voice is heard. The SENCo has asked for pupil voice to be recorded through a statement he has written, but Rita doesn't feel this accurately represents his views.

For some families, the practicality of consultation means that often it is a tick-box exercise in which the families are at best passive participants. In many cases, paperwork is late or hurried and parents struggle with the sequencing and flow of the processes which are dependent upon many different agencies contributing against a short, statutory and consequently pressurised timeline (Harwood, forthcoming). Co-production is explicitly recommended in the SEND CoP (DfE and DoH, 2015) and is seen to be an important part of the EHCP process. However, many parent groups have long been sceptical about the extent to which collaboration and indeed co-production happens (Tirraoro, 2013).

Co-production demands equal and meaningful partnership between professionals and parents, but research by Boddison and Soan (2022) has found this often isn't the case.

*Currently co-production is an illusion. In fact, it could be posited that the current EHC needs assessment process unwittingly encourages inharmonious, unproductive, and disruptive relationships between parents and educational professionals...*

(Boddison and Soan, 2022, p 102)

---

### Critical questions ❓

»   How do parents of pupils with SEND access your setting?

»   Is regular, routine contact built into the systems for offering feedback and information about their children or young people?

»   Do your colleagues accept parents as partners and is there a sense of co-production when working with parents and families in relation to EHCPs?

---

## Lessons from practice

Many recent studies have identified that to effectively support the education of pupils with SEND, sufficient time needs to be allocated for the SENCos to carry out the full range of their duties (Esposito and Carroll, 2019). This includes time for the valuable formal and informal interaction with parents that builds good relations. An important feature of good practice is to see parents as a resource and as experts in their own children. This of course is not without challenge and SENCos need to be supported to develop the skills to manage these relationships. The support for SENCo training and development is a particular issue in this regard (Pearson, 2008). Lamb (2009) recognised the need for intervention because of the impact that poor relationships could have. He acknowledged that some individual parents' concerns were liable to build up through a sequence of frustrations about provision and that *'as the system stands, it often creates "warrior" parents at odds with the school and feeling they have to fight for what should be their children's by right, engendering conflict in place of trust'* (Lamb, 2009, p2)

While it is difficult to acknowledge and accommodate such feelings, it is possible to build or build back trust. SENCos need to be seen to include parents as equal partners, to establish frequent, honest and open communication and to demonstrate that they, as representatives of the school, are equally committed to working with parents for positive outcomes for their children and young people. Simple strategies such as maintaining contact through home–school journals and providing parents with a secure route to get information in and out of the school, college or setting can be hugely impactful in creating an atmosphere of trust and co-operation. Parents are quick to identify reluctance, scepticism or opposition in relation to a child or young person's placement and the importance of the tone of communication should not be underestimated (Harwood, forthcoming). Parents often report problems around basic communication, such as having to repeat information to different professionals (Lake and Billingsley, 2000; Holland and Pell, 2017) so the SENCo should ensure that, wherever possible, information is properly transferred and interpreted before they ask parents to just tell them again about their child.

## CASE STUDY ☺

*Indra, the parent of a young adult with SEND*

**'I have fought for my daughter for so long I think I have forgotten who I am.'**

Indra has been unable to work since her daughter was born: she found there were too many meetings and hospital appointments. Finding a school setting had been a real challenge and Indra felt the school environment just didn't suit her daughter. Despite a change of setting in Year 9, her daughter was often unable to attend school due to anxiety. At the end of Year 11, Indra attended a co-production meeting, which was *'a game changer'*. Her daughter was allowed to discuss what she needed and her plans for adult life. After a discussion with the case officer and SENCo, a package was agreed where Indra's daughter can attend college, which includes an education and skills study programme, independent living skills and work experience. Independent travel training and a transport package was also agreed. Indra now feels confident her daughter has the right support in place and her daughter's attendance is much improved. Seeing her daughter happy and thriving at college, Indra is now able to return to work, as well as looking at a college course for her own development.

The importance of an empathy-based approach in developing positive home–school relationships is now well understood. Schools and parents do not always work well together and the reasons for this are complex and multifaceted. Empathy plays a significant role in the building of trust to pave the way for a real team approach when supporting families who have children with additional needs (Bootman, 2021). Just as the expertise of other professionals is acknowledged as a positive benefit in a collaborative process, so too parental expertise should be drawn on to inform and support better outcomes for children and young people – although not all parents have the privilege of being well informed. SENCos should be cautious about what has been described as the pernicious narrative of the sharp-elbowed middle classes (Tirraoro, 2019). This trope of pushy middle-class parents using the law to get the provision they want and thus driving demand is common in the press, and there is a danger that it is a narrative that drives policy. However, despite an increased understanding of SEND systems for some parents, parental involvement in the EHCP process has remained at a low level. It was reported by a parliamentary committee that parents were either not involved in EHCP production or that their involvement was problematic (House of Commons Education Committee, 2019).

The SENCo can play a major role in facilitating and supporting parental engagement in SEND processes. Having a good relationship with a child or young person and their family prior to any process beginning positively supports the family's involvement in the process (Redwood, 2015). Equally, knowing the child's needs and the family's background beforehand has been found to support collaborative involvement (Adams et al, 2018). Families can feel there is a power hierarchy through the SEND system and that education professionals hold the dominant position (Ahad et al, 2022). The way the SENCo presents and shares information can support parents in feeling a valued part of transparent and inclusive processes.

## Chapter summary 📝

This chapter concludes by suggesting that for the SENCo the relationship with parents should be considered a priority and that time and resources invested in developing good parental relationships are likely to result in better collaborative and co-productive processes. Trust between parents and the SENCo is necessary for the emotional well-being of all concerned (Solvason and Proctor, 2021) and is likely to help SENCos to recognise the vulnerability of parents, and to advocate for a more empathetic approach from the setting. Hallett (2022) suggests that the role of the SENCo is to acquire practical wisdom, which Cowan argues requires '*inclusiveness, foresight, and decisiveness*' (Cowan, 2017, p 6). In building trust with parents and working collaboratively, SENCos need to be '*brave enough to expose the silences, inconsistencies, contradictions and incompleteness relative to their grounding assumptions*' (Skrtic, 1991, p 151).

Any change to the system is likely to enhance the centrality of parental involvement, and SENCos should be encouraged by the ongoing recognition of the role which parents should and could play in developing SEND provision for their children and young people. Despite the concern explored in the chapter about the '*co-production illusion*' (Boddison and Soan, 2022), SENCos should seek to further develop the structures and forums they have in their settings to encourage and enable full parental participation in SEND processes in general and particularly in the EHCP process.

## Further reading 📚

Fricker, E, Moon, S and Vodden, T (2023) *Can't Not Won't: A Story about a Child Who Couldn't Go to School.* London: Jessica Kingsley Publishers.

• This book follows a family through the early days of school avoidance, the process of accessing support and the challenges of dealing with health, social and educational systems.

Mavir, H (2023) *Your Child Is Not Broken: Parent Your Neurodivergent Child without Losing Your Marbles.* London: Bluebird/Pan MacMillan.

Tutt, R (2011) *Partnership Working to Support Special Educational Needs and Disabilities.* London: Sage.

• Each of these texts offer parental perspectives and provide further guidance and advice on partnership working that is inclusive of parents.

## References 📚

Adams, L, Tindle, A, Basran, S, Dobie, S, Thomson, D, Robinson, D and Codina, G (2018) *Education, Health, and Care Plans: A Qualitative Investigation into Service User Experiences of the Planning Process.* Department for Education. [online] Available at: https://assets.publishing.service. gov.uk/government/uploads/system/uploads/attachment_data/file/695100/Education_ Health_and_Care_plans_-_a_qualitative_investigation.pdf (accessed 15 April 2023).

Ahad, A, Thompson, A M and Hall, K E (2022) Identifying Service Users' Experience of the Education, Health and Care Plan Process: A Systematic Literature Review. *Review of Education*, 10(1). [online]

Available at: https://bera-journals.onlinelibrary.wiley.com/doi/full/10.1002/rev3.3333 (accessed 20 March 2023).

Boddison, A and Soan, S (2022) The Coproduction Illusion: Considering the Relative Success Rates and Efficiency Rates of Securing an Education, Health and Care Plan When Requested by Families or Education Professionals. *Journal of Research in Special Educational Needs*, 22(2): 91–104.

Bootman, J (2021) SENDCAST. [online] Available at: www.thesendcast.com/follow-the-empathy-road (accessed 19 July 2023).

Children and Families Act 2014. [online] Available at: www.legislation.gov.uk/ukpga/2014/6/contents/enacted (accessed 19 July 2023).

Clarke, A L and Done, E J (2021) Balancing Pressures for SENCos as Managers, Leaders, and Advocates in the Emerging Context of the Covid-19 Pandemic. *British Journal of Special Education*, 48(2): 157–74.

Cowan, M A (2017) Inclusiveness, Foresight, and Decisiveness: The Practical Wisdom of Barrier Crossing Leaders. *New England Journal of Public Policy*, 29(1): 1–10. [online] Available at: https://web-p-ebscohost-com.ezproxy.wlv.ac.uk/ehost/pdfviewer/pdfviewer?vid=0&sid=44d603ed-4436-41dc-bf88-c22f514aef81%40redis (accessed 23 April 2023).

Department for Education (DfE) (2022) *SEND Review: Right Support, Right Place, Right Time*. HM Government Green Paper. [online] Available at: https://assets.publishing.service.gov.uk/government/uploads/system/uploads/attachment_data/file/1063620/SEND_review_right_support_right_place_right_time_accessible.pdf (accessed 19 July 2023).

Department for Education (DfE) and Department of Health (DoH) (2015) *Special Educational Needs and Disability Code of Practice: 0 to 25 Years* [online] Available at: https://assets.publishing.service.gov.uk/government/uploads/system/uploads/attachment_data/file/398815/SEND_Code_of_Practice_January_2015.pdf (accessed 22 May 2023).

Department for Education and Skills (DfES) (2001) *Special Educational Needs Code of Practice*. [online] Available at: https://assets.publishing.service.gov.uk/government/uploads/system/uploads/attachment_data/file/273877/special_educational_needs_code_of_practice.pdf (accessed 18 April 2023).

Department of Health (DoH) (2010) *Personalisation through Person-Centred Planning*. [online] Available at: www.choiceforum.org/docs/pcpplan.pdf (accessed 20 April 2023).

Done, E J, Knowler, H and Armstrong, D (2021) 'Grey' Exclusions Matter: Mapping Illegal Exclusionary Practices and the Implications for Children with Disabilities in England and Australia. *Journal of Research in Special Educational Needs*, 21(S1): 36–44.

Done, E J, Knowler, H, Warnes, E and Pickett-Jones, B (2021) Think Piece on Parents, 'Off Rolling' and Wavelength Methodology: Issues for SENCos. *Support for Learning*, 36(1): 69–82.

Done, E J, Knowler, H, Richards, H and Brewster, S (2022) Advocacy Leadership and the Deprofessionalising of the Special Educational Needs Co-ordinator Role. *British Journal of Special Education*. [online] https://doi.org/10.1111/1467-8578.12449

Esposito, R and Carroll, C (2019) Special Educational Needs Coordinators' Practice in England 40 Years on from the Warnock Report. *Frontiers in Education*, 4.

Gov.uk (2022) *Education, Health and Care Plans: England 2022*. [online] Available at: www.gov.uk/government/statistics/education-health-and-care-plans-england-2022 (accessed 9 July 2023).

Hallett, F (2022) Can SENCOs Do Their Job in a Bubble? The Impact of Covid-19 on the Ways in Which We Conceptualise Provision for Learners with Special Educational Needs. *Oxford Review of Education*, 48(1): 1–13.

Harwood, P (forthcoming) *Stories of Learning in Parenting Young Adults with Learning Difficulties through the Transition Process from Statutory Provision to Adulthood*. Unpublished Doctorate in Education thesis, University of Wolverhampton.

Holland, J and Pell, G (2017) Parental Perceptions of the 2014 SEND Legislation. *Pastoral Care in Education*, 35(4): 293–311.

House of Commons Education Committee (2019) *Special Educational Needs and Disabilities. First Report of Session 2019*. [online] Available at: https://publications.parliament.uk/pa/cm201919/cmselect/cmeduc/20/20.pdf (accessed 9 July 2023).

House of Commons Education and Skills Committee (2006) *Special Educational Needs: Third Report of Sessions 2005–06*, Vol 1. [online] Available at: https://publications.parliament.uk/pa/cm200506/cmselect/cmeduski/478/478i.pdf (accessed 13 April 2023).

Kruithof, K, Olsman, E, Nieuwenhuijse, A and Willems, D A (2020) 'I Hope I'll Outlive Him': A Qualitative Study of Parents' Concerns about Being Outlived by Their Child with Profound Intellectual and Multiple Disabilities. *Journal of Intellectual & Developmental Disability*, 47(2): 107–17.

Kruithof, K, Willems, D, van Etten-Jamaludin, F and Olsman, E B (2020) Parents' Knowledge of Their Child with Profound Intellectual and Multiple Disabilities: An Interpretative Synthesis. *Journal of Applied Research in Intellectual Disabilities*, 33(6): 1141–50.

Lake, J F and Billingsley, B S (2000) An Analysis of Factors That Contribute to Parent–School Conflict in Special Education. *Remedial and Special Education*, 21(4): 240–51.

Lamb, B (2009) *Lamb Inquiry: Special Educational Needs and Parental Confidence: Report to the Secretary of State on the Lamb Inquiry Review of SEN and Disability Information*. Department for Children, Schools and Families (DCSF). [online] Available at: https://dera.ioe.ac.uk/9042/1/Lamb%20Inquiry%20Review%20of%20SEN%20and%20Disability%20Information.pdf (accessed 20 April 2023).

Pearson, S (2008) Deafened by Silence or by the Sound of Footsteps? An Investigation of the Recruitment, Induction, and Retention of Special Educational Needs Coordinators (SENCOS) in England. *Journal of Research in Special Educational Needs*, 8(2): 96–110.

Popkewitz, T S (2020) The Paradoxes of Practical Research: The Good Intentions of Inclusion That Exclude and Abject. *European Educational Research Journal*, 19(4): 271–88.

Redwood, M (2015) *Insider Perspectives of Education, Health, and Care Plans*. Doctoral thesis. [online] Available at: https://ore.exeter.ac.uk/repository/handle/10871/18459 (accessed 19 July 2023).

Skrtic, T M (1991) The Special Education Paradox: Equity as the Way to Excellence. *Harvard Educational Review*, 61(2): 148–206.

Solvason, C and Proctor, S (2021) 'You Have to Find the Right Words to Be Honest': Nurturing Relationships between Teachers and Parents of Children with Special Educational Needs. *Support for Learning*, 36(3): 470–85.

Tirraoro, T (2013) Is Parental Co-production Just Smoke and Mirrors? *Special Needs Jungle*, 24 July. [online] Available at: www.specialneedsjungle.com/is-parental-co-production-just-smoke-and-mirrors (accessed 10 April 2023).

Tirraoro, T (2019) SEND Inquiry Takedown: Parents vs DfE. *Special Needs Jungle*, 19 May. [online] Available at: www.specialneedsjungle.com/send-inquiry-takedown-parents-vs-dfe (accessed 19 July 2023).

Warwick, H (2017) Growing Pains. *Community Practitioner: The Journal of the Community Practitioners' and Health Visitors' Association*, 90(11): 48–9.

Werner, S, Edwards, M, Baum, N, Brown, I, Brown, R and Isaacs, B (2009) Family Quality of Life among Families with a Member Who Has an Intellectual Disability. *Journal of Intellectual Disability Research*, 53(6): 501–11.

# 9 Working with other professionals

**STEPHANIE BREWSTER**

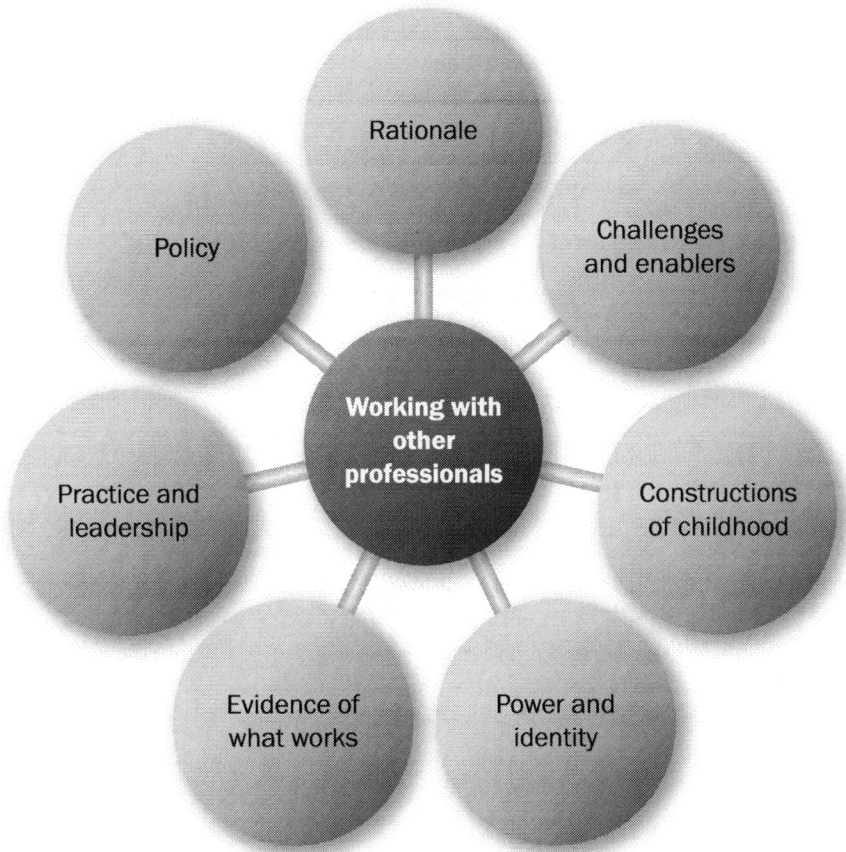

## Chapter objectives 🎯

This chapter explores how professionals can work together to improve outcomes for children and young people with SEND. The chapter:

*   considers the rationale for working with others and reviews how this is reflected in policy;

*   examines the complexities, challenges and enablers of multi-professional working;

*   critiques common constructions of childhood and need;

*   reflects on issues of professional power and identity;

*   critically discusses evidence of effectiveness of working collaboratively;

*   considers implications for practice and practitioner well-being;

*   refers the reader to resources such as toolkits and case studies to support development of their practice.

---

### STARTING POINTS 🏁

»   What other professionals do you work with?

»   To what extent do you view yourself as a member of a team?

»   What outcomes do you aim to achieve through this approach?

»   What risks might arise from not working effectively with others?

---

## Introduction

The importance of developing effective working relationships with other professionals who share your concern for individual children and young people is beyond question. You may already be working with others within and outside your school or setting, often with professionals outside of education – in health, social care, youth services, children's centres and so on. The plethora of literature published in recent decades about how different professional groups can and should work together is indicative of both of its importance but also its complexity, and its apparent resistance to easy solutions to the challenges it presents. Of course, working in partnership with children, young people and families is also important (see Chapter 8) and arguably is driven by similar values, such as respect and service, and a willingness to listen deeply and learn continuously. Such values align with the ethos of inclusivity and person-centredness which can serve to unite diverse professional perspectives.

This chapter aims to stimulate reflection on one's own values and experiences of working with other professionals, both in terms of coming together to meet the needs of particular children and young people and developing longer-term strategic partnerships. Clarity of practitioners' own values supports such relationships and underpins well-being, providing the confidence and courage to question and challenge SEND practice.

# Why work with other professionals?

## Rationale

This holistic approach to child welfare and development encompasses both collaborating across professional role boundaries and working with other agencies, and is particularly salient for SEND. SEND does not exist in isolation from social, cultural and economic factors affecting children and young people and families, who may also be engaging with a range of other agencies such as the police, refuge services, social services, drug counselling and housing. Add to this the health services that may be required to address medical conditions, and the result can be a bewildering and extensive array of professionals and agencies whose work may lack co-ordination and continuity.

And this brings us to a significant difficulty. While the rationale for working with other professionals may be clear, the many terms used to describe it (sometimes used interchangeably, sometimes not) can result in a lack of shared understanding about how exactly practitioners hope to work together. Soan (2012, p 93), for example, lists three prefixes which can be applied to the levels of **agency**, **discipline** and **professional**:

- **multi** = more than one, working with a child but not necessarily working together;
- **inter** = working in parallel but with greater collaboration;
- **trans** = working across professional boundaries; this represents a significant shift in ethos towards greater child-centredness, in which services fit round the needs of the child, rather than the child having to fit the service provided.

Frost's continuum (2005, cited in Soan, 2012) adds further nuance.

- **Co-operation:** agencies share information but work independently.
- **Collaboration:** services are planned together but may not share goals.
- **Co-ordination:** services plan and work together, taking account of each other's aims and expectations.
- **Merger/integration:** different services become amalgamated.

In fact, none of the many configurations of working together can guarantee the best outcomes for children, and the lack of conceptual clarity is indicative of the real-world complexity of the ways in which services for children and young people are arranged.

## Policy and political climate

The expectation that professionals and services work in partnership is explicit in national policy. A 'national vision' of working in a holistic and 'joined-up' way with children with SEND dates back to the 1970s (Soan, 2012); indeed, one of Hellawell's (2019) 'key SEND policy moments' is the 1978 Warnock Report, ever since which partnership working has been a major focus within policy. Subsequent 'key moments', the Children and Families Act 2014 and the SEND Code of Practice (CoP): 0 to 25 years (DfE and DoH, 2015) made it a statutory requirement for education, health and social services to work together to identify and provide services for children and young people with SEND. Collaboration is therefore expected in the commissioning and designing of services, and also for the provision of support to individual children and young people; education, health and care plans (EHCPs) are one route through which to achieve this. This legal document is used for those with more significant or complex needs, for whom multi-agency processes will be most common.

More recently still, the Improvement Plan for SEND and Alternative Provision (DfE, 2023) set out government intentions to create partnerships at both local and regional level. Phase Three of the Plan will '*seek to introduce primary legislation… to put partnerships on a statutory footing and mandate collaborative working*' (DfE, 2023, p 32). In addition, the creation of multi-agency panels to bring together all stakeholders in the EHCP process would appear to be a response to previous concerns that there was little guidance on how to achieve good collaboration (Rose and Norwich, 2014). We are yet to see to what extent the Plan is implemented, and what consequences it will have for practitioners, children and young people with SEND and their families, although SENCos will continue to fulfil '*a crucial intermediary role between external agencies, schools and families*' (Ofsted, 2021: no page).

---

### Critical questions (?)

»   Solvason and Winwood (2022, p 106) state that multi-professional working '*is not about structure and procedure, it is about feeling listened to, feeling valued and respected; success is not found in systems, but in the dynamics of personal relationships*'. Do you agree?

»   To what extent do you think effective collaboration can be brought about through top-down measures such as legislation and policy, as compared to individual commitment to effective team working and child-centred practice?

---

Whatever the latest policy development brings, it is set within a wider ongoing policy context and economic climate. The SEND workforce will be familiar with the demands brought about by budget cuts, changes to local authority funding for SEND, a growing school population with increasingly complex needs (Hellawell 2019) and – especially since the Covid-19 lockdown measures from 2020 onwards – increases in social and mental health needs.

Although policy may be clear and explicit in its expectation that services work in partnership, 'policy layers' can pull professionals in different directions (Hellawell 2019). Hellawell's (2019) discussion of the 2015 SEND CoP (DfE and DoH, 2015) urges us not to read the policy as simply an instruction manual, but as the basis for negotiation around the multiple values, dilemmas and tensions, contradictions and challenges, ambiguities and conflicts within SEND policy, in relation to professional practice generally and partnership working specifically. One such tension, much rehearsed in the literature, relates to the standards agenda, by which schools are required to improve their academic results, at the same time as which they are exhorted to include children who need high levels of support, creating what many perceive as the opposing forces of competition and collaboration.

Thompson (2017) discusses how the current political and philosophical climate of neoliberalism challenges public services and the equality and social justice they aim to achieve. Within such policy regimes, increasing managerialism and performativity (Hellawell 2019) have a deprofessionalising effect, such that bureaucracy, productivity and output are emphasised at the expense of sensitive, autonomous and skilled professional judgement and co-operation that are responsive to the complexity of the situations with which we deal. This has tended to undermine professional identities and made it harder to value ourselves and other professionals with whom we wish to establish effective multi-professional relationships (Thompson, 2017).

## Challenges and enablers

There is considerable consensus about what conditions support effective working across professional boundaries, and about how these conditions can be challenging to achieve. Rose and Norwich (2014) propose an inter-disciplinary framework of collaborative working to analyse the relationships between factors affecting multi-agency and inter-professional collaboration. The framework considers the social-psychological motivational processes in operation, and situates these processes within a set of nested social contexts (see Figure 9.1).

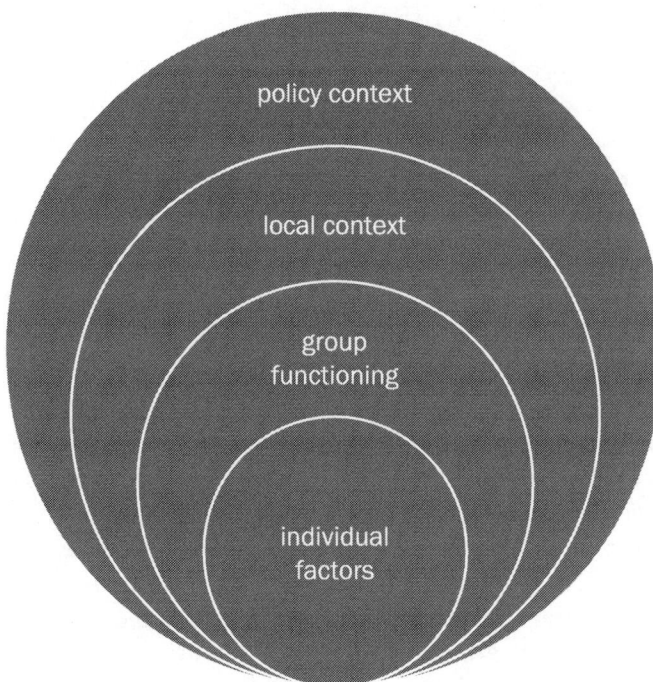

policy context

local context

group functioning

individual factors

**Figure 9.1** *A contextual framework of collaboration*
(Adapted from Rose and Norwich, 2014, p 64, Figure 1)

- The outermost **policy context** refers to the prevailing political ethos and policy discussed above and includes professional codes of practice and regulations.

- The **local context** entails the roles and responsibilities of specific professions, leadership and management structures, lines of accountability, resourcing, and concepts and knowledge that may be common to agencies or may differ.

- The level of **group functioning** encompasses roles and responsibilities within teams, and the joint activities and collaborative relationships that exist there.

- At the centre lie **individual factors** such as professional expertise, perceived status, personal skills and experiences of collaboration.

The motivational processes for individuals engaged in collaboration entail joint commitment to common goals (Rose and Norwich, 2014). There is much literature exploring the more practical challenges and enablers of working collaboratively, and these arise through interaction between the contexts identified above. Two recurring themes in the literature are the exchange and management of information (for example, Hellawell, 2019) in relation to confidentiality and safeguarding concerns, and secondly, communication (for example, Solvason and Winwood, 2022). Walker (2018) warns of the risk of failing to establish shared understanding when profession-specific jargon is used; this can sometimes be a way to boost confidence or assert power and authority. This is not just a superficial issue of terminology but more deeply of differing discourses maintained by different groups (see below).

## Aspirations versus actualities

The simplicity and common sense of multi-professional collaboration as an aspiration belies the challenges it presents, and raises questions about at what level of bureaucracy and administration responsibility is held for making it work. Inter-agency working brings together those working under different lines of management, pay scales and conditions of employment, codes of practice, career paths, funding streams, and so on (Stone and Foley, 2014). Different agencies will be subject to different measures of success and may be aiming for different outcomes for children and young people (Stone and Foley, 2014). Unless such differences are recognised, demands or attempts to simply get on with multi-agency work will breed anxiety, defensiveness and mistrust, and it is then far from likely that children and young people and their families will have positive experiences.

Research published by Ofsted (2021) reported that while ambitions for strong collaborative working were evident among education, health and care professionals, '*the experiences of families did not always match these ambitions*' (no page). Effective collaborative practice was found to often be patchy; access to specialist services was often inconsistent; and families experienced delays and waiting lists for assessment, advice and intervention. Families found the bureaucracy frustrating and sometimes felt the need to pay for services themselves to plug the gaps. This could add a further level of challenge for SENCos, who already have little time available to build relationships and networks with external partners.

## Constructions of childhood and needs

It was noted above that different agencies may have different aims and routinely use different language. The discourses used by professions both reflect and reinforce the ways in which children and their needs are constructed. Such discourses are central to how professionals work together (Anning, 2010). For example, a child's special educational needs can be understood as primarily arising from a diagnosed condition or alternatively as a function of family and social dynamics and the education system (as illustrated by Walker, 2018). Thus, tensions can arise between agencies whose practices and philosophy differ in their alignment with either the medical or social model of disability. But as Anning (2010) points out, there are many more sophisticated models and discourses, and a practitioner may hold multiple explanatory frameworks that can be complex, overlapping and complementary. This is not just a matter of language (Hellawell, 2019): it influences what each discipline sees as the main priority for the child, as well as how it can be achieved. Communication difficulties aside (Solvason and Winwood, 2022), this diversity of explanatory models is something to be celebrated: negotiation around dilemmas of practice, requiring flexibility and responsiveness, can bring about team cohesion and the development of individual professional identities, such that personal beliefs and values become reconciled with those which are dominant in the team within which one is practising (Anning, 2010) (see Chapter 2).

## Person-centredness

Arguably, foremost among the values and commitments that should be demonstrated by both practitioners and the services they work for is person-centredness (see Chapter 8). This provides, according to Thompson (2021), a *'focal point'* for effective multi-professional co-operation, since it creates a *'unifying force that channels efforts in the direction of the individuals' needs and interests'* (Thompson, 2021, p 182). The power of this unifying force is that it encompasses pupil-, child-, parent- and family- centredness. Viewing the child as being at the centre of a web of factors within the wider environment (family, school, community, society) lies at the heart of Bronfenbrenner's (1979) ecological systems theory of child development (see Chapter 7). This model reminds us that all aspects of a child's life are connected and interact with each other and therefore each practitioner has a valid perspective and valuable contribution to make. No single perspective is definitive or has all the answers, and the varied array of contributions must be co-ordinated if they are to be fully effective and efficiently deployed.

## Professional identities and power

The SEND workforce is diverse, consisting of many 'professional' roles such as teachers, health visitors, social workers and psychologists, with varying qualifications, professional bodies, skills and status. It is generally agreed that professional practice entails specialist knowledge, scope for autonomy, accountability, adherence to ethical standards, membership of a professional body, and a high level of education required for exercising independent judgement and skill (Stone and Foley, 2014). We also expect those in volunteer or assistant roles to behave in a 'professional' manner, even though they may not fit a traditional model of 'a professional'. Thompson (2017) suggests that it is important to recognise professional boundaries, although these may not be clear cut and may shift and evolve. With incomplete insight into others' roles, it can be hard to establish shared understanding and goals (Thompson, 2017).

We saw above how each discipline is based on a distinctive yet often implicit combination of theory and knowledge; but certain types of knowledge, and certain roles, are more highly valued than others. Solvason and Winwood's (2022) research revealed how clinical professionals (who may draw heavily on medical models of disability) and those with formal qualifications were perceived as holding a position at the top of a hierarchy within multi-professional teams. Roles traditionally based on the gradual accrual of professional knowledge and experience are relatively undervalued, compared to disciplines based on an explicit body of scientific evidence. For this reason, we have seen the gradual professionalisation of many roles, as they have sought greater recognition through formal qualifications and accreditation (Stone and Foley, 2014). The National Award for SENCos that became mandatory in 2009 reflects this trend, although more recently there are indications (eg DfE, 2023) of a reversal, that is, the de-professionalisation of teaching (Done et al, 2022).

Power dynamics and status have implications for professional relationships and identities (Ekins, 2015) in the multidisciplinary context. Individuals may vie for control and become defensive when confronted with challenges to their status and identity (Solvason and Winwood, 2022). Power and identity are also considerations regarding the families of children and young people, who paradoxically may hold a negative view of the high-status 'experts' who do not know the individual very well (Ekins, 2015); in contrast, practitioners who work with children and young people daily such as teaching assistants may hold the least influence and status. Parents whose cultural capital is not recognised or valued by the practitioners they encounter – those without the knowledge, qualifications, skills and access to resources to match that of the professionals – may struggle to voice their perspectives and effectively advocate for their children. Practitioners aiming to develop more equal and empowering relationships with families (for example, by avoiding specialist jargon), may thereby encounter a tension with their desire to assert professional credibility (Stone and Foley, 2014).

## Participation and learning

Becoming a member of a team involves the transformation of professional identities (Rose and Norwich, 2014) as we learn new knowledge, roles and activities (see Chapter 2). This process can be uncomfortable and destabilising (Anning, 2010, p 61) but also exciting. Wenger's theory of communities of practice (1998) frames learning as a process of social participation: engaging in actions and interactions in pursuit of a joint enterprise, through which our identities are constructed. Thus, formal and informal activities such as meetings, discussions and joint visits act as collaborative learning environments (Davis, 2013) through which practitioners learn both *about* each other and *with* each other (Gasper, 2010), discovering what is distinctive to the professionals involved, what is complementary between them, and where there are tensions and conflicts. This may not, according to Davis (2013), always lead to consensus; rather, critically considering different options (Richards, 2022) has the potential to produce more diverse solutions. Richards claims that the quality of relationships is central to person-centred, multi-professional practice, and that these relationships develop through engaging with others' knowledge and skills. Such willingness to learn also encompasses listening to the voices of children and young people and their families, whose experiences have much to teach us within a relationship of mutual respect.

---

### *Critical questions* (?)

» How would you describe your professional identity? In what ways are your values and culture distinct, and which are shared with others with whom you work?

» What can you do to mitigate problems arising from status in your working relationships?

---

# Is working in partnership 'effective'?

Working in collaboration with other professionals is rarely questioned as anything other than effective, but does the available evidence justify this assumption? The answer to this question depends on what outcomes you are seeking: whether for children and young people and families, or for professionals, and whether you are interested in the *process* of collaboration or on *outcomes*. Frost (2014) indicates that there is strong evidence of improved professional processes when practitioners learn new skills, share information, feel more effective and reduce duplication of effort through collaboration. But in terms of the ultimate aim of working together, Hellawell (2019) is less positive: '*While collaborative practice is seen as the definitive form of contemporary professionalism, there is little evidence this this measurably benefits users or professional services*' (Hellawell, 2019, p 114). However, there are also other less direct advantages, such as a workforce that feels more effective, families that feel more respected, and early intervention that prevents future crises (such as a child's exclusion from school) (Frost, 2014). We clearly need more robust research evidence but must also take care to avoid the risk of collaboration becoming a distracting end in itself (Soan, 2012).

---

### *Implications for the SENCo role, identity and practice*

#### Role of the SENCo

Arguably, working with other professionals is one of the core functions of the complex and varied SENCo role. This is explicitly recognised in the National Award for SENCo learning outcomes (NCTL, 2014), which refer to liaising with professionals within and outside of the school setting, being a key point of contact with external agencies, and taking a leadership role in co-ordinating such partnerships. The SENCo role is also important in building relationships between school and family, through mediating and

$\longrightarrow$

sense-making, and '*helping parents/carers engage with external practitioners*' (Ofsted, 2021). Positive relationships with SENCos improve parental satisfaction and raise parents' confidence that their views will be taken into consideration in the planning and review of provision.

SENCos feel their responsibility to achieve these aims keenly, often finding that accountability for making professional partnerships work falls to them by default (Ackers, 2021) rather than being shared. Fair division of workload and responsibility is often a concern (Solvason and Winwood, 2022) and the relative lack of involvement of health and care professionals in the EHCP process is a challenge frequently cited by SENCos (Boesley and Crane, 2018). Working with others, including such tasks as arranging multi-professional meetings, takes a considerable amount of SENCo time, and can leave little left for strategic leadership (Ackers, 2021).

### Leadership

Working strategically with senior colleagues is central to the leadership and co-ordination function of the SENCo role; this surpasses acting as intermediary between agencies, schools and families (Ofsted, 2021), important though that is. Gasper (2010, p xviii) describes the quality of leadership as a '*critical ingredient*' in successful partnership working, which challenges traditional hierarchical models of leadership and potentially destabilises pre-existing power relationships. Gasper (2010, p xviii) argues for '*Non-judgmental and open approaches where dialogue, reflection and discussion help shape policy and practice and where contributions from all are encouraged and everyone is valued*'. Such a model can conflict with the 'top-down pressures' exerted through government priorities such as national targets around education, health and social issues (Gasper, 2010). As Thompson (2017) suggests, leadership must inspire and motivate others, in line with our own professional values, not simply enforce compliance with bureaucracy and reinforce the managerialism so prevalent today.

### SENCo well-being

The Teacher Wellbeing Index (Savill-Smith and Scanlan, 2022) draws attention to chronic and worsening teacher retention and recruitment, with over half the teachers surveyed considering leaving their job or the sector, for reasons to do with workload and stress and not feeling valued. Organisational and team culture affects well-being – whether positively or negatively – in any sector, and senior leaders may be particularly vulnerable to poor mental health, exhaustion, burnout and stress (Savill-Smith and Scanlan, 2022). Hellawell (2019) argues that this can be conceived as a result of 'responsibilisation', a neoliberal ideology through which individual professionals (rather than systemic failure) are held personally responsible for educational outcomes, their own actions and even their own well-being. This results in self-doubt and anxiety. Add to this the threats to professional identity and fear of change potentially arising from working with others, which can undermine confidence.

However, professional networking could be argued to have a mitigating effect on isolation and low morale. Risk taking, flexibility and a willingness to work in different ways, breaking down rigid thinking and professional boundaries can all be achieved with the support of others, leading to greater job satisfaction, confidence and personal development. Since educational success and pupil well-being are inextricably linked to staff well-being, if the latter is poor, then the former are at risk.

# Chapter summary

Looking to the future, the sector will undoubtedly see increasing use of technology to facilitate timely networking, communication and information exchange between professionals. Indeed, the Department for Education (2023) have stated their intention to digitise the EHCP process to improve the experience of both families and professionals. This is against a backdrop of increasing social and economic pressure across the public sector, requiring greater efficiency and effectiveness of services. Evidence of poor well-being and retention in the education workforce adds urgency to the need to get team working right. Only if there is a positive culture in which diverse practitioners feel valued and can work effectively together will the best educational outcomes and well-being for children and young people with SEND be achieved.

# Further reading

Frearson, A (n d) *Partnership Self-Assessment Toolkit: A Practical Guide to Creating and Maintaining Successful Partnerships*. Leeds Health Action Zone. [online] Available at: www.iapo.org.uk/sites/default/files/current/resources/LHAZ_Partnership_selfassessment_toolkit.pdf (accessed 19 July 2023).

• Provides a basic overview of best practice in partnership working and a useful checklist to help identify strengths and weaknesses.

Hellawell, B (2019) *Understanding and Challenging the SEND Code of Practice*. London: Sage.

• This critique of the 2015 CoP includes a chapter on multi-agency working and inter-professional collaboration and provides case studies throughout the book elucidating the complexities of working with other professionals.

# References

Ackers, H (2021) Multi-professional Meetings: SENCos' Reflections on the Empty Chairs at the Table. In Beaton, M C, Codina, G N and Wharton J C (eds) *Leading on Inclusion: The Role of the SENCo* (pp 143–51). London: Routledge.

Anning, A (2010) *Developing Multi-professional Teamwork for Integrated Children's Services: Research, Policy and Practice*. 2nd ed. Maidenhead: Open University Press.

Boesley, L and Crane, L (2018) 'Forget the Health and Care and Just Call Them Education Plans': SENCOs' Perspectives on Education, Health and Care Plans. *Journal of Research in Special Educational Needs*, 18(1): 36–47.

Bronfenbrenner, U (1979) *The Ecology of Human Development: Experiments by Nature and Design.* Boston, MA: Harvard University Press.

Davis, J M (2013) Supporting Creativity, Inclusion and Collaborative Multi-professional Learning. *Improving Schools*, 16(1): 5–20.

Department for Education (DfE) (2023) *Special Educational Needs and Disabilities (SEND) and Alternative Provision (AP) Improvement Plan: Right Support, Right Place, Right Time.* [online] Available at: https://assets.publishing.service.gov.uk/government/uploads/system/uploads/attachment_data/file/1139561/SEND_and_alternative_provision_improvement_plan.pdf (accessed 19 July 2023).

Department for Education (DfE) and Department of Health (DoH) (2015) *Special Educational Needs and Disability Code of Practice: 0 to 25 Years.* [online] Available at: https://assets.publishing.service.gov.uk/government/uploads/system/uploads/attachment_data/file/398815/SEND_Code_of_Practice_January_2015.pdf (accessed 8 June 2023).

Done, E J, Knowler, H, Richards, H and Brewster, S (2022) Advocacy Leadership and the Deprofessionalising of the Special Educational Needs Coordinator Role. *British Journal of Special Education.* https://doi.org/10.1111/1467-8578.12449

Ekins, A (2015) *The Changing Face of Special Educational Needs: Impact and Implications for SENCos, Teachers and Their Schools.* 2nd ed. London: Routledge.

Frost, N (2014) Interagency Working with Children and Families: What Works and What Makes a Difference? In Foley, P and Rixon, A (eds) *Changing Children's Services: Working and Learning Together.* 2nd ed (pp 143–82). Bristol and Milton Keynes: Policy Press and The Open University.

Gasper, M (2010) *Multi-agency Working in the Early Years: Challenges and Opportunities.* London: Sage.

Hellawell, B (2019) *Understanding and Challenging the SEND Code of Practice.* London: Sage.

National College for Teaching and Leadership (2014) *National Award for SEN Co-ordination: Learning Outcomes.* [online] Available at: https://assets.publishing.service.gov.uk/government/uploads/system/uploads/attachment_data/file/1163082/nasc-learning-outcomes-final.pdf (accessed 19 July 2023).

Ofsted (2021) Research and Analysis: Supporting SEND. [online] Available at: www.gov.uk/government/publications/supporting-send/supporting-send (accessed 19 July 2023).

Richards, H (2022) Developing Your Identity, Agency and Voice. In Richards, H and Malomo, M (eds) *Developing Your Professional Identity: A Guide for Working with Children and Families* (pp 7–20). St Albans: Critical Publishing.

Rose, J and Norwich, B (2014) Collective Commitment and Collective Efficacy: A Theoretical Model for Understanding the Motivational Dynamics of Dilemma Resolution in Inter-professional Work. *Cambridge Journal of Education*, 44(1): 59–74.

Savill-Smith, C and Scanlan, D (2022) *The Teacher Wellbeing Index.* Education Support. [online] Available at: www.educationsupport.org.uk/media/zoga2r13/teacher-wellbeing-index-2022.pdf (accessed 19 July 2023).

Soan, S (2012) Multiprofessional Working: The Way Forward? In Cornwall, J and Graham-Matheson, L (eds) *Leading on Inclusion: Dilemmas, Debates and New Perspectives* (pp 87–96). London: Routledge.

Solvason, C and Winwood, J (2022) Exploring Drivers and Barriers: Working in Multiprofessional Teams to Support Children and Families. *School Community Journal*, 32(1): 105–26.

Stone, B and Foley, P (2014) Towards Integrated Working. In Foley, P and Rixon, A (eds) *Changing Children's Services: Working and Learning Together* (pp 49–92). Bristol and Milton Keynes: Policy Press and The Open University.

Thompson, N (2017) *Theorizing Practice: A Guide for the People Professions*. 2nd ed. London: Macmillan Education.

Thompson, N (2021) *People Skills*. 5th ed. London: Red Globe Press.

Walker, G (2018) *Working Together for Children: A Critical Introduction to Multi-agency Working*. 2nd ed. London: Bloomsbury Academic.

Wenger, E (1998) *Communities of Practice: Learning, Meaning and Identity*. New York: Cambridge University Press.

# 10 Critical reflection in professional practice

## HAZEL RICHARDS AND ALICJA LEGARSKA

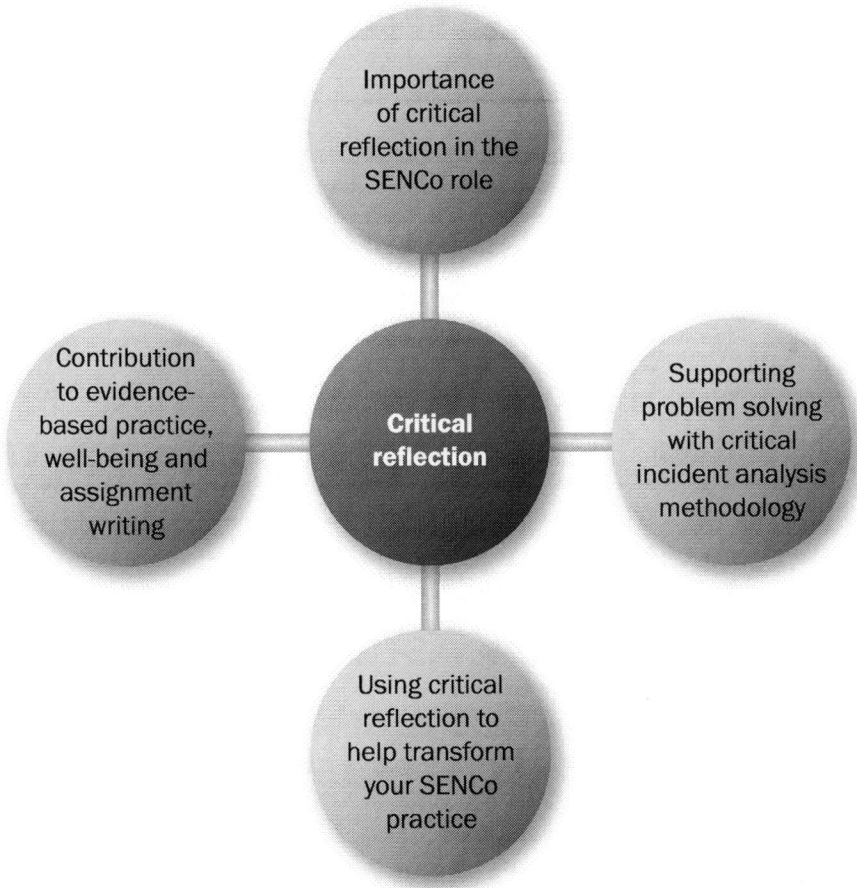

Importance of critical reflection in the SENCo role

Contribution to evidence-based practice, well-being and assignment writing

Critical reflection

Supporting problem solving with critical incident analysis methodology

Using critical reflection to help transform your SENCo practice

# Chapter objectives 🎯

This chapter explores the important contribution critical reflection makes to SENCo practice. The chapter:

* explores and illustrates the importance of critical reflection;

* explains and illustrates critical incident analysis methodology;

* considers how critical reflection can help transform practice;

* proposes how critical reflection can contribute to evidence-based practice, well-being and assignment writing.

---

## STARTING POINTS 🏁

» When and how do you use critical reflection at work?

» What benefits and challenges do you think critical reflection has in professional practice?

» Might undertaking critical reflection be helpful in other areas of your life? If so, what are they?

---

# Introduction

The SENCo role is multifaceted, requiring practitioners to weigh up and respond to multiple intersecting issues, such as rate of progress, range of physical, emotional and cognitive needs, resources, staff skills, support of parents and families, school leadership and catchment area. This means contextualisation and judgements are invariably required. This chapter therefore explores critical reflection, which involves deeper engagement with different perspectives and knowledge sources, as a tool with the potential to transform and empower (Hanson and Appleby, 2015) both individuals and professional communities. Using critical incident analysis methodology (Tripp, 1998), we demonstrate the power of reflection to transform practice and support assignment writing for postgraduate SENCo study as well as the development of evidence-based practices (see Chapter 12). We offer examples of reflective writing and show how to move writing from simply describing practice to critically reflecting on practice (Moon, 2013). The chapter also considers how critical reflection can be used to reflect on and support one's own well-being, essential to consider when workloads are demanding, and ethical and moral dilemmas are raised.

# Theory and literature on critical reflection

Critical reflection questions and challenges assumptions held in the constructs and narratives we possess, and which guide our actions. It involves thinking about and learning from evidence and experience and using this knowledge to inform our responses. It goes '*beyond the acceptance of established frameworks (the "what" of practice), to question and consider underpinning issues and perspectives (the "why" of practice)'* in order to *'emerge with a personal position informed by theory and experience (the "how" of personal professionalism)'* (Hanson and Appleby, 2015, p 38). It therefore enables us to move beyond mere compliance and competency to advocacy and innovation.

Brookfield (2009) defines critical reflection as the deliberate attempt to uncover, then investigate and challenge assumptions, dominant ideologies and hierarchical power dynamics. The policy and practice infrastructures we must operate within contain conflicting values, interests and assumptions. Awareness and understanding of these enable practitioners to progress beyond merely complying with statutory inspection and administrative regimes or being *'implicated in the very structures they are trying to change'* (Ellsworth, 1992, p 101). Certainly, heightened awareness and understanding of conflicting demands and dilemmas can help us deal with complex issues (Shapira-Lishchinsky, 2011). Critical reflection enables this by exploring the 'why' and 'how' of practice, while still implementing the 'what' of specific requirements (Callan, 2015). Regarded as the central process in transformative learning, it involves intentionally reflecting on experiences.

## Critical incident analysis methodology

Tripp (2012) states that part of professional practice involves being able to explain and justify actions through knowledgeable and rigorous academic analysis, though in actuality few teachers are taught or required to do so. Tripp (2012, p 13) goes on to argue that we need to do something other than *'merely reflect on our practice'* if we are to change or view it differently. Critical incident analysis allows us to recall and explain events, but also to understand and gain control over our current and future practice and routines (Tripp, 1998). A critical incident is any event or experience that is significant, and which may be out of the range of normal. Such events can be sufficiently disturbing to threaten to overwhelm a person's coping capacity, and analysing the factors which help or hinder a critical issue, experience or activity helps us to define, understand, learn from and change it. Viergever (2019) suggests five steps are involved.

1. Describing the issue, experience or activity.

2. Defining the nature of the critical incident, including its relevance to and effect on the people and practice involved.

3. Collecting information about influences participants perceive to have helped or hindered the critical incident.

4. Analysing the data for themes to identify areas that have practical utility in relation to the issue, experience or activity.

5. Interpreting and reporting the findings, including evaluation of limitations and biases.

Tripp (2012) suggests we should also:

- consider plus and minus points, alternative possibilities and choices, and other points of view;

- ask ourselves a series of 'Why?' questions;

- identify the dilemmas present in the critical incident;

- critique the personal theories, beliefs and ideologies which regulate our behaviour and responses. Although they legitimatise what we do or is done to us by others, they can be irrational.

Reflection at these deeper levels develops our confidence to challenge situations by equipping us to ask '*considered questions and look beyond our immediate role*' (Trodd and Chivers, 2011, p 11). This aligns with '*transformational learning*', which involves thinking systematically and deeply to enable individuals to progress into another way of perceiving (Kegan and Lahey, 2009, p 310). Critical reflection combines an emotional experience with a cognitive one, often in that order (Carroll, 2010), helping individual practitioners to probe a troubling issue, experience or activity. Chris' case study provides an example of how this occurs in practice.

## CASE STUDY ☉

### Chris, assistant SENCo with English as an additional language (EAL) responsibility

*I recently took part in a permanent exclusion meeting (PEX) involving a parent, governors, members of the local council, multi-academy trust leads and the school senior leadership team. I was asked to attend due to the language barrier of an excluded child and his parent.*

*During the break, the assistant headteacher spoke to me about the school's EAL provision for the pupil. The assistant headteacher suggested that should I be asked a question regarding the EAL support given to the student, I should respond with positive feedback and explain how well the EAL department supported the student. I explained that this pupil was never in school due to the high number of suspension days he had: he did not attend many sessions with the EAL team. The assistant headteacher did not like my response, stating 'we can't really say this to the panel'. I replied: 'I will just tell them the truth'. Before the end of the break, the assistant headteacher returned from speaking with the headteacher and told me that for the purpose of this meeting I was only required to translate. I was therefore manipulated into what I was allowed to say, which made me unsure how to react during the rest of the meeting.*

*While in the meeting, I reflected in action (Knowles et al, 2007), deciding quickly whether to follow the headteacher's 'orders' and keep quiet for the benefit of the school or to follow my moral instinct, support the parent and go against the school's orders. The latter could potentially affect my future career at the school and make my job a lot more difficult. For this reason, I followed the assistant headteacher's instruction over revealing the truth to the child and parent.*

*Analysing this incident, I could claim that the power of the organisation was silencing me – stopping me from expressing the truth and making me complicit in illegal exclusionary practices. Foucault (1997) identifies a relationship between 'the power, truth and a subject' (p 47). Triangulation of these factors underpins my view on being silenced during the PEX meeting: the power being the headteacher's request and the truth being what I wanted to present to the subject, the parent. Done et al (2021) highlight the reality of 'silencing the voices of parents' (p 71) within exclusionary practices, and how this results in failure to be heard. In this critical incident, silences and silencing were certainly present – many, including the child, the parent and myself, were silenced during the meeting, which, in my opinion, led to an illegal exclusion.*

*This critical incident highlights the conflicts inherent in the SENCo role. As a leadership position, it carries the understanding that practice serves the best interests of the school, but SENCos must also work in the best interests of the child. Sometimes these two factors are not aligned. While acknowledging parental suffering and recognising the right of all children to mainstream education, this incident demonstrates how SENCos can experience conflict between their commitment to inclusion and their headteacher's decision making, and challenges to advocating for social justice. I have learned there are powerful reasons why a SENCo may not speak up.*

### Critical questions (?)

» How was power exercised?

» How did this influence the outcome for the student?

» What alternative possibilities and choices might have been available?

» What do you think could help Chris access and apply these?

» If Chris had known the process and the outcome of the meeting, how might this have influenced his input and decision making?

While this critical incident tells us much about the underpinning issues and perspectives (the 'why' of practice), Chris is left pondering how to use the knowledge gained to shape his future practice. Dialogue can help identify the learner's *'edge of meaning'* (Taylor, 2009, pp 9–10), described as a transitional [liminal] zone of knowing and meaning making (Bolton, 2018). It is here, in this liminal zone, that we identify the edges or limitations of our knowing and responses and where we begin to stretch these limits (Bolton, 2018). Certainly, generative dialogue (with ourselves and others) *'puts us within a much bigger domain asking bigger questions. What is the purpose of this, why am I doing it, how is it connected to other aspects of life? [which] pulls us inside again to help us see the poverty of our systemic thinking'* (Carroll, 2010, pp 10–11), before moving us outwards again to reconnect, with increased awareness and ways of thinking and responding to the bigger picture.

---

### Implications for the SENCo role, identity and practice

» Achieving a socially just inclusive education system means identifying and responding to conflicting priorities.

» SENCos must address dilemmas and be prepared to make sometimes difficult choices if they are to deliver robust inclusive practice and better outcomes for all pupils.

» Good communication and collaborations between SENCos and school staff enable SENCos to build holistic knowledge of the child and their circumstances. Reflecting critically on the influences present enables priorities to be identified, contributing to support that works in the best interests of the child.

---

Holding ground between the two potentially opposing responsibilities held by SENCos is challenging. As leaders supporting the school vision and advocates for the most vulnerable children, SENCos must continually navigate the middle ground between the two parties. Critical reflection can enable SENCos to identify and weigh up the important components (Yost et al, 2000).

# Spotlight on new developments

It is difficult to imagine what the SENCo's role will be in the upcoming years given the pressure on finances in schools, changes to SENCo training (see Chapter 2), and personal pressures around employment and security, as well as potential changes in government. Therefore, schools and their SENCos should go beyond Department for Education and Ofsted guidelines, critically reflecting on their approaches to inclusion for all vulnerable pupils.

The Department for Education White Paper (2022a, p 16) proposes that by 2030 '*every child will be taught by an excellent teacher trained in the best-evidenced teaching method to help (each) child reach their full potential*'. This policy document also identifies a commitment to training, with the intention of helping all teachers and leaders to support all pupils to succeed, including those identified with SEND (p 17). However, the White Paper (DfE, 2022a) is situated in a context where reviewing and evaluating the progress of pupils with SEND has been found to be the least developed aspect of schools' SEND support (DfE, 2021).

In this context, consultation around the SEND Review: Right Support, Right Place, Right Time (DfE, 2022b) identified the need for schools to change their cultures and practices to be more inclusive and better at identifying and supporting needs, and to improve workforce training (Nasen, 2022). However, professional workforce development is a significant barrier to implementing the reforms and progressing support, with teacher training and development not always equipping education staff with the skills required to support pupils with SEND.

While the SEND and Alternative Provision (AP) Improvement Plan (DfE, 2023) states ways it will develop the workforce (p 52), whether the critical thinking and reflection developed in Master's-level learning (credit level descriptors, Seec, 2016) will be possible in a new National Professional Qualification (NPQ) – to be the mandatory training for SENCos going forward – remains to be seen. This is a pertinent question given the range of evidence and contextual factors SENCos must consider in their role of identifying, developing and rigorously evaluating effective practice in teaching pupils with SEND. Master's-level learning requires students to, for example:

- develop critical responses to existing theoretical discourses, methodologies or practices and suggest new concepts or approaches;

- incorporate a critical ethical dimension to their practice, managing the implications of ethical dilemmas;

- undertake analysis of complex, incomplete or contradictory evidence/data and recognise and argue for alternative approaches (Seec, 2016).

In contrast, it could be argued that the NPQ will not be sufficiently deep and extensive to equip SENCos *'to offer research-based challenges to existing school policies or practices'* (Done et al, 2022, p 2), which has implications for SENCo competency, compliance and advocacy.

---

### 📏 *Implications for the SENCo role, identity and practice*

» Future SENCos may be less able to develop critical responses to existing theoretical discourses, methodologies or practices or to suggest new conceptualisations or approaches.

» Lack of or limited critical reflection skills will prevent new SENCos from undertaking analysis of complex evidence for deeper professional reflection and solution creation.

» What would be valued more? The data and the exam results to show 'successes' or the critical thinking and reflective practice that can be utilised to support all pupils to reach their full potential?

---

## Significance for policy and practice: possibilities and further tensions

### How critical reflection supports evidence-based practice

Evidence-based practice is a key component of the DfE White Paper (2022a) and the need to evaluate the effectiveness of current teaching pedagogies, while concurrently building the capacity and skills of staff to meet diverse needs, is recognised (Peterson, 2017;

DfE, 2022b). Exploring not just 'what works' but also interrogating 'how' and 'why' is necessary and a powerful factor in teacher engagement and agency (Biesta, 2017). Access to these deeper meanings requires SENCos and their colleagues to combine evidence from academic research, practitioner enquiry (such as lesson study or action research) and other school-level data with practitioner observations, reflection and discussions (see Chapter 12).

Reflection is also central to evidence-based practice, with Mintz et al (2021) exploring how research learning communities allow participants to deeply engage in mutual reflection and learning. This results in increased confidence in leading change and developing policy and practice in settings. However, time pressures mean that not only do teachers have limited time to engage in critical reflection, but also that only a subset of teachers can engage at any given time (Greany and Maxwell, 2017; Brown and Poortman, 2018). This means those involved must disseminate and discuss their findings with colleagues if the practice is truly to have an impact on whole-school provision.

---

### Critical questions (?)

» How do you use critical reflection in your practice currently?

» What possibilities do you see for research learning communities in your setting?

» What tensions might arise (see, for example Figure 2.1 in Chapter 2) and how could you ameliorate these?

---

## How critical reflection supports well-being

SENCo well-being is deservedly gaining more attention. The role involves considerable workloads, to be met within tight timescales and resources. The emotional aspects of the work can be unseen, unrecognised and undervalued, and in some instances SENCos prioritise the children and families they work for over their own work–life balance, with attendant risks for well-being, resilience and retention (Richards, 2022).

Socrates highlighted the need to prioritise self-care, and the leading role of self-knowledge in this. Disciplines whose central role involves caring access clinical supervision to support well-being and practice. This is not yet standard practice for SENCos. However, SENCos need to intentionally invest in self-care if they are to be resilient and effective SEND leaders. Devi and Bowers (2022) identify three components that support well-being: people, purpose and place (see Figure 10.1).

Gobin (2019, p 5) states the caring for our well-being involves *'taking a serious look in the mirror'* since we need to understand ourselves and our needs as well as the issues concerned before we begin to seek and identify solutions. Each section of Figure 10.1 therefore identifies internal and external areas that Devi and Bowers (2022) suggest are important to reflect on since they contribute to SENCo well-being.

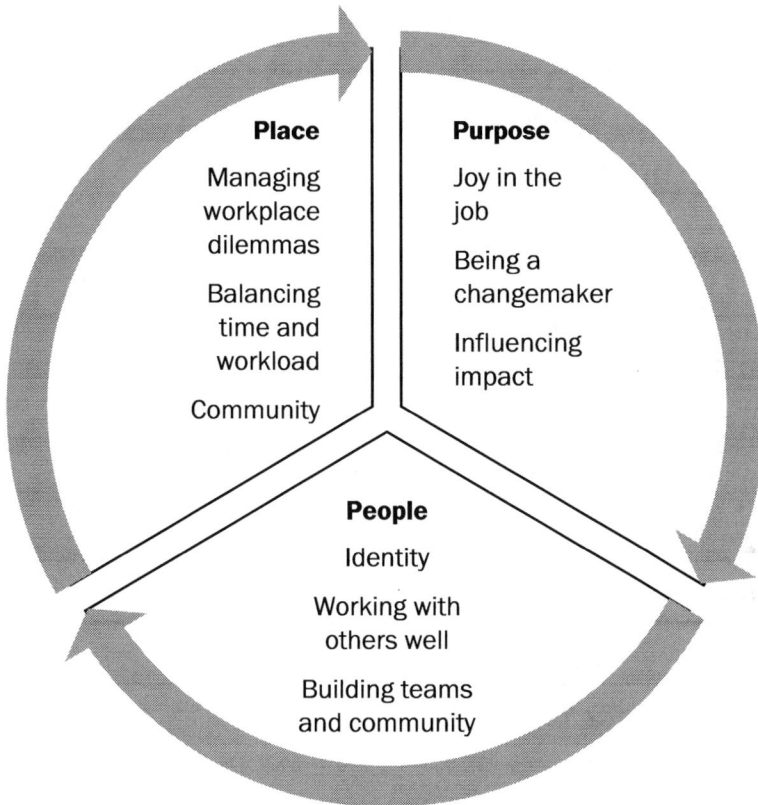

**Figure 10.1** *Summary of Devi and Bowers's (2022) well-being themes*

---

### *Critical questions* ❓

» When and how do you think about your well-being?

» When do you have time to stop and to reflect: *'Am I okay?'*, *'How am I doing?'*.

» How will you apply the learning you have gained from this section to your own well-being?

---

## How critical reflection supports academic writing

Critical analysis is required within Masters'-level learning and academic assignment writing (Tripp, 1998) and evidence-based practice (Moon, 2013). A deep as opposed to surface approach to learning (Moon, 2013) results in *'a qualitative change in a person's way of seeing, experiencing, understanding, [and] conceptualising something in the real world'* (Ramsden, 1988, p 271). This requires us to move beyond description to identifying and understanding influences and their import, and then to work with these meanings, linking them to other ideas to transform learning through the evaluation and restructuring of thinking

(Moon, 2018). Table 10.1 contains sections of reflective writing that illustrate the difference between surface and deep learning, as well as an example of critical incident analysis:

**Table 10.1** *Reflective writing (academic) and critical incident examples*

| Academic reflective writing examples | Level of reflection/impact on learning |
|---|---|
| 1. *'I have both learnt and improved my knowledge within communication, specifically of sign language. A skill I have improved further is research and where to find the correct sources.'* | A surface approach that describes experience and states that learning has occurred, though specific detail about what has been learned and how it will influence future study and practice is limited. |
| 2. *'A learner's ability to assess/evaluate their own work is an important skill that contributes to higher-level learning (Moon, 2013, 2018). Receiving feedback from my peers and lecturer gave me a different perspective and reflecting on this enabled me to see what worked well and what needed changing. As a result, I made several amendments to my assignment, including engaging the audience more, since "communication involves interaction".'* (Thompson, 2018, p 31) | Critically reflects on feedback and self-awareness, identifying strengths and areas to make progress in. Theory and literature substantiate the points. |
| **Critical incident analysis example** | |
| 3. *'I admit I devoted minimal preparation time to my formative presentation since as an experienced practitioner I was confident I could wing it. However, my tutor feedback left me questioning my desire to continue. During a tutorial to view the recording and discuss my feelings, I realised my content was in fact opinionated and lacking in academic sources. My tutor explored the reasons for my change in attitude and achievement, including my study habits. I was upset, but her support enabled me to identify some key changes I could make, and I now feel much happier about the route forward.'* | Here a student describes one specific incident in depth, giving a detailed account of what took place and their reactions to this. A liminal space was entered. Viewing the video recording and discussing the feelings involved resulted in deep personal reflection, which enabled the student to shift from one phase to another, resulting in evident changes in understanding and approach. |

Table 10.1 provides examples of critical thinking, with row 2 harnessing theory to deepen understanding and row 3 demonstrating how engaging with the affect (feelings and emotions involved) can help us to define, understand, learn from and change further. Challenging yourself through critical questioning can also unlock a deeper level of thinking to increase quality in reflective writing (Moon, 2018) as questions act as prompts, progressing us beyond description to critical writing. Yost et al (2000) suggest that we can develop our critical analysis writing skills by writing down critical incidents that may have occurred at work, home or elsewhere, in the form of journal. Such writing allows us to document the critical

incident (see Viergever's (2019) five stages, above), with our reading then enabling links between practice and theory to be made. However, this takes time and commitment, without which opportunities to explore and discover new alternatives may be limited. Worryingly, NPQs will involve less theoretical engagement, critique and deep questioning than Masters'-level SENCo training, which has implications that extend beyond critical thinking and writing to practice.

---

### Critical questions (?)

» How can SENCos best be supported to develop their critical reflection skills?

» How do we measure the level of critical reflection acquired and its effect on practice?

---

### Implications for the SENCo role, identity and practice

» There is a significant rise in new SENCos leaving the profession due to lack of support from senior leadership teams and local authorities.

» Lack of opportunities to construct new knowledge will impact on the reflective practice of teaching.

» The challenge to move from the descriptive level to a higher level of reflection will remain or even increase.

---

# Chapter summary

Schools are led by either values/ideas or data/abstract processes and '*contextualisation and judgements are invariably required*' (Done et al, 2016, p 293). Critical reflection makes a vital contribution to this. Crucially:

• Yost et al (2000) argue that early career teachers' theory of knowledge and world views can be narrow due to limited exposure to literature and critical analysis. In contrast, the theoretical guidance and constructive support offered in Masters'-level study develops critical thinking and, consequently, reflective practice;

• critical incident analysis and reflective practice can support the development of higher levels of thinking. Writing reflective journals can enable you to reach deeper critical understandings as well as support your own well-being;

• these analytical and reflective strategies allow us to go beyond 'what' is happening to explore the 'how' and 'why' – knowledge which can both inform and challenge solutions, situations, people and systems.

# Further reading 📖

Devi, A and Bowers J (2023) *Journeying to the Heart of SENCO Wellbeing: A Guide to Enable and Empower SEND Leaders*. London: Routledge.

- This book uses reflection and activities to consolidate learning and help SENCos to develop their own bespoke well-being toolkit.

Richards, H and Malomo, M (2022) Empowering Reflective Practice. In Richards, H and Malomo, M (eds) *Developing Your Professional Identity: A Guide for Working with Children and Families* (pp 21–37). St Albans: Critical Publishing.

- This chapter explores theory and new debates around reflective practice, proposing that it is a powerful way to build confidence and empower your practice.

Tripp, D (2012) *Critical Incidents in Teaching: Developing Professional Judgement*. Classic edition. Abingdon: Routledge.

- This book explores different strategies and gives advice and examples on how to use critical incidents within teaching to develop professional practice.

# References 📚

Biesta, G (2017) *The Rediscovery of Teaching*. London: Taylor & Francis.

Bolton, G (2018) *Reflective Practice, Writing and Professional Development*. 5th ed. London: Sage.

Brookfield, S (2009) The Concept of Critical Reflection: Promises and Contradictions. *European Journal of Social Work*, 12(3): 293–304.

Brown, C and Poortman, C (2018) Introduction. In Brown, C and Poortman, C (eds) *Networks for Learning: Effective Collaboration for Teacher, School and System Improvement* (pp 1–9). London: Routledge.

Callan, S (2015) The Ethical Practitioner with Children and Families. In Reed, M and Walker, R (eds) *A Critical Companion to Early Childhood* (pp 36–47). London: Sage.

Carroll, M (2010) Supervision: Critical Reflection for Transformational Learning (Part 2). *The Clinical Supervisor*, 29(1): 1–19.

Department for Education (DfE) (2021) *Special Educational Needs (SEN) Support: Findings from a Qualitative Study*. [online] Available at: www.gov.uk/government/publications/special-educational-needs-sen-support-findings-from-a-qualitative-study (accessed 22 May 2023).

Department for Education (DfE) (2022a) *Opportunity for All: Strong Schools with Great Teachers for Your Child*. [online] Available at: https://assets.publishing.service.gov.uk/government/uploads/system/uploads/attachment_data/file/1063602/Opportunity_for_all_strong_schools_with_great_teachers_for_your_child__print_version_.pdf (accessed 22 May 2023).

Department for Education (DfE) (2022b) *SEND Review: Right Support, Right Place, Right Time*. [online] Available at: https://assets.publishing.service.gov.uk/government/uploads/system/uploads/attachment_data/file/1063620/SEND_review_right_support_right_place_right_time_accessible.pdf (accessed 22 May 2023).

Department for Education (DfE) (2023) *Special Educational Needs and Disabilities (SEND) and Alternative Provision (AP) Improvement Plan: Right Support, Right Place, Right Time*. [online]

Available at: https://assets.publishing.service.gov.uk/government/uploads/system/uploads/attachment_data/file/1139561/SEND_and_alternative_provision_improvement_plan.pdf (accessed 22 May 2023).

Devi, A and Bowers, J (2023) *Journeying to the Heart of SENCO Wellbeing: A Guide to Enable and Empower SEND Leaders*. London: Routledge.

Done, E J, Knowler, H, Warnes, E and Pickett-Jones, B (2021) Think Piece on Parents 'Off Rolling' and Wavelength Methodology: Issues for SENCos. *Support for Learning*, 36(1): 69–82.

Done, E L, Knowler, H, Richards, H and Brewster, S (2022) Advocacy Leadership and the Deprofessionalising of the Special Educational Needs Co-ordinator Role. *British Journal of Special Education*. https://doi.org/10.1111/1467-8578.12449

Done, L, Murphy, M and Watt, M (2016) Change Management and the SENCo Role: Developing Key Performance Indicators in the Strategic Development of Inclusivity. *Support for Learning*, 31(4): 281–95.

Ellsworth, E (1992) Why Doesn't This Feel Empowering? Working through the Repressive Myths of Critical Pedagogy. In Luke, C and Gore, J (eds) *Feminisms and Critical Pedagogy* (pp 90–119). London: Routledge.

Foucault, M (1997) What Is Critique? In Lotringer, S and Hochroth, L (eds) *The Politics of Truth* (pp 23–83). New York: Semiotext(e).

Gobin, L (2019) *The Self-Care Prescription: Powerful Solutions to Manage Stress, Reduce Anxiety and Increase Well-being*. Emeryville, CA: Althea Press.

Greany, T and Maxwell, B (2017) Evidence-Informed Innovation in Schools: Aligning Collaborative Research and Development with High Quality Professional Learning for Teachers. *International Journal of Innovation in Education*, 4(2–3): 147–70.

Hanson, K and Appleby, K (2015) Reflective Practice. In Reed, M and Walker, R (eds) *A Critical Companion to Early Childhood* (pp 24–35). London: Sage.

Kegan, R and Lahey, L L (2009) *Immunity to Change: How to Overcome It and Unlock the Potential in Yourself and Your Organization*. Boston, MA: Harvard Business Press.

Knowles, Z, Gilbourne, D, Tomplinson, V and Anderson, A G (2007) Reflections on the Application of Reflective Practice for Supervision in Applied Sport Psychology. *The Sport Psychologist*, 21(1): 109–22.

Mintz, J, Seleznyov, S, Peacey, N, Brown, C and White, S (2021) Evidence Informed Practice for Autism, Special Educational Need and Disability in Schools: Expanding the Scope of the Research Learning Community Model of Professional Development. *Support for Learning*, 36(2): 159–82.

Moon, J A (2013) *Reflection in Learning and Professional Development: Theory and Practice*. Abingdon: Routledge.

Moon, J (2018) *Reflective Writing – Some Initial Guidance for Students*. [online] Available at: https://efs.weblogs.anu.edu.au/files/2018/01/Moon-on-Reflective-Writing.pdf (accessed 22 May 2023).

National Association for Special Educational Needs (Nasen) (2022) *Nasen Responds to the SEND and Alternative Provision Green Paper*. [online] Available at: www.nasen.org.uk/news/sendgreenpaper (accessed 22 May 2023).

Ofsted (2021) *Research and Analysis: Supporting SEND*. [online] Available at: www.gov.uk/government/publications/supporting-send/supporting-send (accessed 22 May 2023).

Peterson, L (2017) A National Perspective on the Training of SENCos. In Hallet, F and Hallet, G (eds) *Transforming the Role of the SENCo: Achieving the National Award for SEN Coordination* (pp 15–27). London: Open University Press.

Ramsden, P (ed) (1988) *Improving Learning: New Perspectives*. San Francisco: Jossey-Bass.

Richards, H (2022) 'It Was Tough Making Sure It Happened': SENCo Experience of the Reality and Risk of Education and Health Care Plan Implementation. *Educational Review*. https://doi.org/10.1080/00131911.2022.2033703

South East England Consortium (Seec) (2016) *Credit Level Descriptors for Higher Education – 2016*. [online] Available at: www.seec.org.uk/wp-content/uploads/2016/07/SEEC-descriptors-2016.pdf (accessed 22 May 2023).

Shapira-Lishchinsky, O (2011) Teachers' Critical Incidents: Ethical Dilemmas in Teaching Practice. *Teaching and Teacher Education*, 27(3): 648–56.

Taylor, E (2009) Fostering Transformative Learning. In Mezirow, J and Taylor, E (eds) *Transformative Learning in Practice: Insights from Community, Workplace, and Higher Education* (pp 3–17). San Francisco: Jossey-Bass.

Thompson, N (2018) *Effective Communication: A Guide for the People Professions*. London: Macmillan Education UK.

Tripp, D (1998) Critical Incidents in Action Inquiry. In Shacklock, G and Smyth, J (eds) *Being Reflexive in Critical Educational and Social Research* (pp 36–49). Social Research and Educational Studies Series, 18. London: Routledge Falmer.

Tripp, D (2012) *Critical Incidents in Teaching: Developing Professional Judgement*. Classic edition. Abingdon: Routledge.

Trodd, L and Chivers, L (2011) *Inter-professional Working in Practice*. Maidenhead: Open University Press.

Viergever R F (2019) The Critical Incident Technique: Method or Methodology? *Qualitative Health Research*, 29(7): 1065–79.

Yost, D S, Sentner, S M and Forlenza-Bailey, A (2000) An Examination of the Construct of Critical Reflection: Implications for Teacher Education Programming in the 21st Century. *Journal of Teacher Education*, 51(1): 39–49.

# 11 SENCos using data to support inclusive practice

**LAURA HOWIESON, KITTY HUTHWAITE AND HELEN KNOWLER**

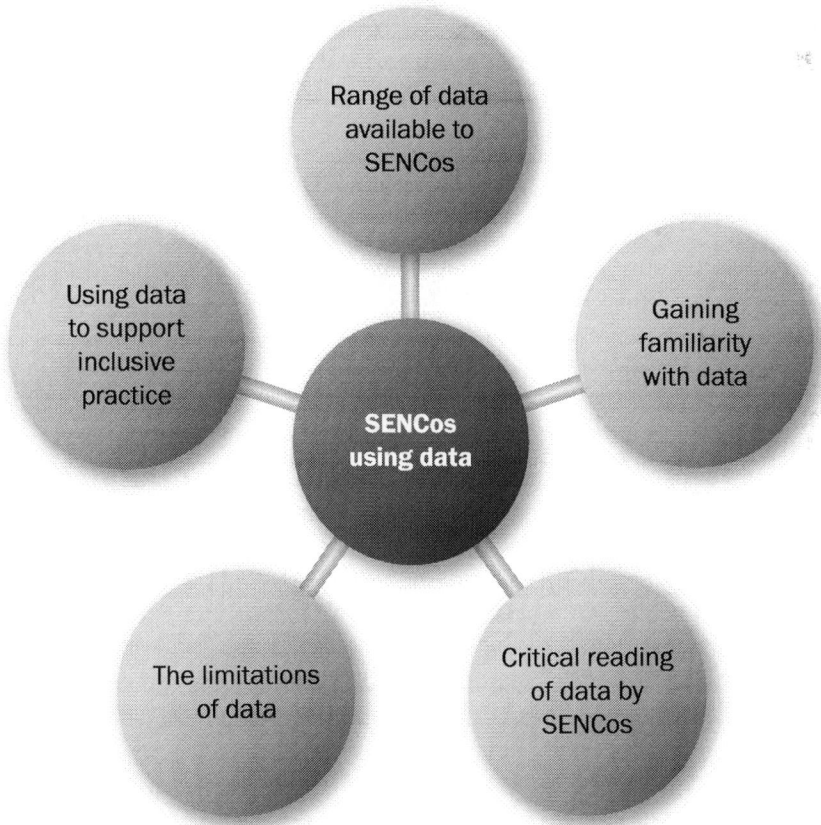

# Chapter objectives 🎯

This chapter explores the ways that SENCos can work with data to support effective interventions, effective communication with staff and parents/families on pupil progress and to report to governors. We argue that this engagement with data plays a vital role in 'data literacy' (Henderson and Corry, 2021), and that this literacy can support the use of critical reflection (see Chapter 10), evidence-based practice (see Chapter 12) and working with parents and other professionals (see Chapters 8 and 9). The chapter:

- explores the different kinds of data that SENCos access and use in their work;

- reflects on the affordances and limitations of the use of data by SENCos, considering the importance of credible and robust analysis and reporting of data;

- considers the ways that SENCos can utilise data to enhance support for children and young people and their families and to give a rich and detailed representation of their social, emotional and educational progress.

---

### STARTING POINTS 🏁

» What kinds of data do you regularly see and use in your current role?

» Who else has access to this data? How is this data shared and 'read'?

» What are your current data literacy skills? Do you need further development or support around this?

---

# Introduction

In this chapter, we explore the ways that SENCos can engage with the wide range of data they have access to in their schools and encourage thinking about how this engagement with data can support inclusive practices. Schools are incredibly data-rich contexts and SENCos have a key role in managing this data to demonstrate the impact of interventions, support and quality outcomes for all learners. However, working with diverse data sets in efficient and ethical ways is a key challenge for anyone new to the role. We reflect on the importance of learning to work with data and to explore the claims that can be made in relation to attainment and achievement. We use a case study example to highlight how interpreting data in the 'wrong' way can be harmful for children and their families, and waste time and resources for your school – while skillful data handling can support effective mobilisation of support and inclusive reporting of progress to parents and families.

It is not the aim of the chapter to explain specific tools or offer tips on data analysis – this would be training and development that you can access elsewhere; indeed, this is arguably an ongoing and long-term endeavour which SENCos would be planning as part of wider professional development. However, we argue that knowing and understanding how to collect data, and how to analyse it and then report findings in accessible ways, can lead to reflective and ethical data-informed decision making. In turn, this can ensure that your reporting of the data is not only accurate, but that it does not cause unintentional harm for pupils and their families by perpetuating stereotypes or discrimination. Following Henderson and Corry's (2021) research on educators' understandings of 'data literacy', we aim to demonstrate some of the critical and reflective questions a SENCo might ask themselves as they work with data collated with a specific tool. In this chapter, data literacy is seen as vital for SENCos for effectively managing and supporting students: data literacy empowers SENCos to make informed decisions, advocate for students and implement evidence-based practices.

# What is data literacy and why does it matter for SENCos?

Data literacy is described by Gummer and Mandinach (2015, p 2, cited in Henderson and Corry, 2021, p 232) as *'the ability to transform information into actionable instructional knowledge and practices by collecting, analyzing, and interpreting all types of data'*. However, this straightforward explanation belies the requirement for SENCos to engage in ongoing professional development, training and critical reflection on their own ability to transform the data they have access to into tangible outcomes for pupils in their settings.

We understand data literacy as the ability to understand, interpret and effectively use data to inform practices and decision making as a SENCo. It involves the knowledge, skills and attitudes necessary to critically analyse and make sense of educational data, such as student performance data, assessment results, attendance records and other relevant information. Henderson and Corry (2021) argue that data literacy is therefore strongly related to professional development models that emphasise the capacity to access, evaluate, interpret and utilise educational data effectively and ethically to enhance support and interventions for pupils with SEND. It encompasses the understanding of data sources, data types and data collection methods, as well as the ability to analyse and visualise data, draw valid inferences, identify trends or patterns and make data-driven decisions. Data-literate SENCos are competent in selecting appropriate data tools and technologies, and communicating data insights to various stakeholders, including students, colleagues and parents. Crucially, data literacy involves a critical mindset, which encourages SENCos to question, reflect upon and continuously improve their leadership approaches based on evidence derived from data analysis (see also Chapter 12 of this book). We think data literacy entails the elements as outlined in Mandinach and Gummer's (2016) paper, as summarised in Table 11.1.

*Table 11.1* *Elements of data literacy for SENCos developed from Mandinach and Gummer (2016)*

| **Understanding data sources** | Familiarity with various sources of data available and understanding of the purpose, limitations and validity of different data sources to make accurate interpretations. |
|---|---|
| **Data collection and analysis** | Proficiency in collecting, organising and analysing data related to SEND. Identifying trends, patterns and outliers in the data to inform decision making. $\longrightarrow$ |

**Table 11.1** *(Cont.)*

| Interpreting data | Understanding statistical concepts and data visualisation techniques. Ability to identify strengths, weaknesses and areas for improvement based on data analysis. |
|---|---|
| Data-informed decision making | Basing decisions on the data available and developing evidence-based strategies to support students. SENCos can therefore ensure that their actions are targeted and responsive to the needs of individual students. |
| Collaborating with stakeholders | Sharing data insights, explaining progress and involving others in the decision-making process, fostering a collaborative approach to supporting students. |
| Data protection and privacy | Ensuring data confidentiality and security, which is essential to maintain trust and protect the privacy of pupils and their families. |
| Continuous professional development | Continuous learning and professional development are necessary for SENCos to stay up to date on research and best practices in data analysis and interpretation. |

By developing data literacy skills, SENCos can optimise their support for pupils and enhance their ability to make informed decisions, track progress and advocate for necessary resources to meet the diverse needs of pupils.

---

### *Critical questions* (?)

» What kinds of data do you regularly see and use in your current role?

» Who else has access to this data? How is this data shared and 'read'?

» What are your current data literacy skills? Do you need further development or support around this?

---

# Types of data in schools

According to provision mapping guidance on the popular TES website, '*If you don't know what to do with the data you're collecting, you probably don't need it*' (TES, 2019). It is often claimed that schools are 'data rich', meaning that they generate, collate, analyse and hold data about learners as they progress through a specific age phase or setting. There is a huge variation in the kinds of data generated from a wide range of data collection activities and other sources such as baseline assessments, snapshot assessments at specific points in time and dynamic assessment across a year or school phase (eg Key Stage 2). In this chapter, we are not making judgements or suggestions about the kinds of assessment tools used in schools specifically, but it is important to note that critically reflecting on the ways that data is used once collected is a crucial skill. Although not an exhaustive list, it is acknowledged that schools increasingly have access to rich and varied types of data on which they can draw, such as:

- prior attainment data showing levels and grades achieved in national tests and examinations;

- teacher assessment data, for example periodic assessment for pupils with SEND working below the expected standard;

- national and local data showing proportions of pupils making age-expected progress;

- comparative data indicating how groups in mainstream schools are progressing compared with other schools;

- other pupil- and school-level estimates, such as from the Fischer Family Trust;

- other data likely to impact on pupil outcomes, such as attendance, exclusions, pupil and parent perception surveys, behaviour monitoring, book samples (everyday work), tests/mock exams and involvement in extracurricular events;

- research evidence, such as that published by the Education Endowment Foundation (2021), about studies into the effect of different interventions on groups of pupils, including those with SEND.

We would also encourage SENCos to consider less well-used approaches to data collection in their evidence gathering; this might not relate to learning per se, but it can tell you a great deal about engagement and participation in school life. For example, data around the amount of time spent in 'time out' or 'toilet breaks' can be important for offering a wider picture of pupils' experiences of the school community beyond the classroom. Other sources of important information can come from colleagues in the wider community, and listening to experiences from other people such as teaching assistants, mealtime assistants and visiting staff can be invaluable when thinking about the experience, for example, of pupils identified as having social, emotional and mental health needs.

---

## ⎍ *Implications for the SENCo role, identity and practice*

Below we suggest some questions to help you develop your familiarity with your setting's data for SEND, and to help you start thinking about how you could use it. Find out about the following:

» what percentage of the learners are identified as having SEND in your setting?

» how does your setting's data compare to national data and to other schools (above average/below average)?

» is the percentage of learners identified with SEND increasing or decreasing? Why?

→

> » have you analysed this according to areas of need?
>
> » what is the attendance of children and young people with SEND? How does this relate to behaviour data and exclusion data?
>
> » Consider sharing this up-to-date analysis with your team in a staff meeting or development day. Would you share this with parents?

## Building data literacy skills: developing your data collection strategy

In additional to understanding the range of data that you have at your disposal, you also need to think about how and when you will collect, analyse and report the data to your colleagues and to parent and families. For example:

- when will you collect data? Can it align with other forms of whole-school data collection so that you are not repeating data collection or proliferating data that will not be used?

- Are you a part of whole-school observation schedules and if not how can observation of learners on your SEND register be included?

- When and how will you analyse the data you collect? When will you assess interventions in your setting and how will you communicate your results? How will you include teaching assistants in this process?

- When will you update key baseline data (for example, reading ages)? This aspect has some important implications for encouraging colleagues to be supportive of SEND data collection.

- If you are a setting that does examinations, will you have the data needed for examination access arrangements, or do you need to schedule assessments or book someone to do them? When do examination access arrangements have to be completed? When do you need to apply for modified papers?

These activities have potentially important implications for your workload, so it would be worth considering if others can help you. This could be an opportunity to do whole-school skills development so that others can be involved in analysis and reporting.

You should also use a range of tools to gain a secure view about the progress of children with SEND. The following questions may be useful:

- what are the views of children with SEND about their progress and how will you find these out?

- What are the views of staff and external professionals about their progress?

- What do observations from lessons indicate about progress?

- What does the scrutiny of the child's work across the curriculum indicate about their progress?

## Inclusive practice and reporting your data analysis

The effective use of data helps to support the development of a strategic approach to the management of SEND, as well as informing teaching and learning at the classroom level. The analysis of SEND pupil-level data provides a deeper understanding of the performance of individuals and groups of SEND pupils over time and helps inform the choice of interventions needed to ensure SEND pupils make progress; this includes the progression of those SEND pupils with significant learning difficulties and/or disabilities. Developing your data literacy skills will also help you to gain a better understanding of the impact of different types of interventions and provision on SEND pupils' progress. Analysing your data should enable you to contribute evidence to the school's self-evaluation on how well pupils with SEND are progressing, the impact of intervention programmes on a child's outcomes and on value for money. As a SENCo, you will be able to evaluate progress towards meeting goals set in pupil passports or education, health and care plans as well as to make informed decisions about the deployment of resources. Another important element will be your ability to evaluate the support and interventions provided by external agencies, including the impact of any extended school activities. In terms of 'big picture' analysis, effective handling of the data will help to identify trends over time in your setting and across your Trust (if relevant) as well as identifying any gaps in existing provision and any SEND pupils who may be underachieving.

## Data literacy in practice

In the case study below, Lisa explains her thinking about the use of the Cognitive Abilities Test (CAT4) (GL Assessment, n d) in her setting. The website for the tool mentions that it can 'reveal hidden potential', although this wording needs to be a signal for caution about the ability of a test to tell the full story of a pupil's experience in the classroom. Lisa demonstrates reflectivity and criticality in relation to the tool, what it can measure and what it tells her as a SENCo. In this case study, we have denoted in **bold** places where the reflection demonstrates critical data literacy that supports the development of inclusive analysis.

## CASE STUDY ⊕

### Lisa considers: who is disadvantaged by the test?

CAT4 is for children aged six–17 years; in my Trust, schools administer these tests in the September of Years 5 and 7. It is thought that a standardised quantitative data set could be a useful tool when looking at achievement, as well as assisting identification of potential SEND. CAT4 is a multiple-choice test with answers marked on an Optical Mark Recognition (OMR) sheet. Each battery should take less than 45 minutes, meaning a maximum total of three hours to complete. Tests are taken individually, usually in a classroom setting, with instructions read by an adult. **The use of multiple-choice questions (MCQ) is not without controversy,** the main question being one of reliability and validity. If we take **reliability** to

$\longrightarrow$

mean the consistency of the measure and **validity** the extent to which the **scores accurately reflect** the knowledge (Cook and Beckman, 2006), CAT4 should meet both definitions for its data to be considered useful. Some of my **initial reservations** about the use of this tool **related to use of MCQ as there is a risk answers are guessed**: a guess with no understanding of the correct answer. However, Burton (2005) suggests that guessing is part of the system – all entrants are counted on to make some guesses and therefore this is woven into the standardisation of the scores. If Burton is correct, it **may place some children at a disadvantage;** those with autism, for example, may experience a rigidity of thought that could mean an unease with making guesses. This **questions the reliability of any data produced** from CAT4. Burton and Miller (1999) suggest that while negative marking could discourage blind guessing, therefore making MCQ more reliable, **this does not inform our understanding of those pupils who may then be discouraged from making an informed guess**. For example, pupils with difficulties controlling impulsivity may be at a disadvantage as visual attention is given to answers already assumed to be correct (Tsai et al, 2012). They may be less likely to examine other possibilities in any depth, and discount a question that, given free text, they might be able to answer. For data to be valid, **we must be satisfied that CAT4 tests the knowledge that it aims to**. This is difficult as, by GL Assessment's own admission, CAT4 does not test knowledge but the ability to reason (Kerr and Dai, 2020). Testing the **ability to reason is dependent on many contextual variables such as factors associated with culture, gender, and locality**. We should therefore be cautious in interpreting data from pupils from a non-Western culture, a welcome addition to the guidance (Kerr and Dai, 2020). For CAT4 to be seen as reliable and valid, as Florian et al (2004) suggest, **the data should be supplemented with qualitative data, allowing exploration of the pupil behind the numbers**.

## Implications for inclusive practice for SENCos

In Lisa's example, we can reflect on the way that it is generally assumed in her Trust that a score disparity between batteries could indicate a SEND. The implication here is that that reliability and validity are not questioned by colleagues using and interpreting the raw data. Mean scores are also examined for those in the below or very low banding. Those with very low scores are added to the 'monitor' register to track their progress for six months. However, Lisa noted that 'monitoring' should consist of more than just quantitative data collection and analysis, and that little qualitative data had been collected, which was a serious oversight. In looking at other ways that the Trust used the data, she noticed that pupils with very low scores in all but spatial ability were automatically put on the SEND register under moderate learning difficulties. However, no qualitative data was collected for these pupils and so she could not be certain that important contextual issues have not influenced the data analysis. Her reflection led her to conclude that using this data on its own offered no indication that pupils fit the definition of SEND according to the SEND Code of Practice (DfE and DoH, 2015).

Schools should use every opportunity to further the learning of pupils; as Jang and Marshall (2018) point out, feedback is needed from any test for pupils to learn. This poses the question of who is the test for and, if it is not for the pupils, is it ethical for it to be taken? The standardised scores generated from CAT4 should be used with caution and certainly as part of a wider data set about a pupil. The labels that can be associated with the data and assigned to pupils could have a negative effect, which can be seen in the study aptly titled, '*I'll be a nothing*' by Reay and Wiliam (1999), where the effects of testing on children's self-esteem were catastrophic.

---

### *Critical questions* (?)

» Testing can yield data that, while seemingly useful for adults, does not always benefit pupils. Think about how your setting can ensure that any testing you do actually furthers pupil learning, rather than hindering pupils from fulfilling their potential.

» To what extent do you feel that data like that yielded by Lisa's school's use of CAT4 allows all pupils, regardless of any SEND, to show their true capability?

» Another potential issue is that of 'over testing'; does your experience support the assertion of Harlen and Deakin Crick (2003) that this can be detrimental to motivation for learning?

» Given the concerns discussed above about the need to robustly question the reliability and validity of quantitative data, take time to consider how to balance such data with qualitative data from ongoing teacher assessment in ascertaining a pupil's areas of strength and difficulty. How will you broach such discussions with your senior leadership team?

---

All humans are susceptible to unconscious bias, which can influence automatic decision making. The unconscious bias that could be prevalent in the adults who view the data may lead to a lowering of expectations, particularly if non-verbal scores are equated with innate intelligence. There is a danger that the data becomes a self-fulfilling prophecy, even if, as Dee and Gershenson (2017) point out, it is inaccurate. Fiarman (2016) implies that unconscious bias could be counteracted, maybe even eliminated, if discussion and normalisation of the biases are considered commonplace in schools. But, as Dee and Gershenson (2017) suggest, traditional educational policies and classroom interventions will not easily address unconscious bias, and biased data interpretation can be detrimental to pupils' future potential.

## Chapter summary

Strong data literacy helps SENCos to collect and analyse information about a pupil's specific needs and strengths; and data-driven approaches also enable professionals to create individualised support or intervention strategies tailored to each child's unique requirements. We have shown that by analysing data on various interventions and their outcomes, professionals can make better-informed decisions about which approaches are most suitable for each child. While progress monitoring is obviously extremely important, we would also advocate for collaboration among professionals working with a child (see Chapter 9). By sharing your data analysis with fellow educators and other specialists, teams can better understand a pupil's needs and then collaborate effectively to provide consistent support across different environments, such as school, home and therapy settings. While we think it is impossible to make completely objective analyses in complex environments like schools, data literacy supports professionals to avoid biases or assumptions by relying on concrete information rather than subjective judgements from snapshot assessment. Data-driven decision-making processes enhance accountability and ensure that interventions and supports are based on evidence and not on stereotypes or discrimination that limit inclusion for pupils.

Data collected over time can contribute to research and the development of best practices in supporting pupils. While analysing large data sets can help identify trends, patterns and factors that influence outcomes for pupils with SEND, collating accounts of experiences using qualitative methods can be vital in developing deeper understanding of how mechanisms of inclusion and belonging are working within a setting. Data used reflectively and ethically empowers professionals, educators and caregivers by providing insights, guiding decision making and promoting evidence-based practices, all of which contribute to better outcomes for all pupils.

## Further reading

- This mini guide from nasen offers a useful overview of the mapping and monitoring of data for progress and inclusion – you will need to register but the guide is free: https://nasen.org.uk/resources/tracking-progress-and-managing-provision-inclusive-practice

- How are parents and carers involved in their children's learning? This Department for Education guide is also helpful when considering ways to explore 'pupil voice': www.gov.uk/government/publications/listening-toand-involving-children-and-young-people

## References

Burton, R F (2005) Multiple-Choice and True/False Tests: Myths and Misapprehensions. *Assessment and Evaluation in Higher Education*, 30(1): 65–72.

Burton, R F and Miller, D J (1999). Statistical Modelling of Multiple-Choice and True/False Tests: Ways of Considering, and of Reducing, the Uncertainties Attributable to Guessing. *Assessment and Evaluation in Higher Education*, 24(4): 399–411.

Cook, D A and Beckman, T J (2006) Current Concepts in Validity and Reliability for Psychometric Instruments: Theory and Application. *American Journal of Medicine*, 119(2): 166.e7–166.e16.

Dee, T and Gershenson, S (2017) *Unconscious Bias in the Classroom: Evidence and Opportunities*. Stanford Center for Education Policy Analysis. [online] Available at: https://services.google.com/fh/files/misc/unconscious-bias-in-the-classroom-report.pdf (accessed 12 June 2023).

Department for Education (DfE) and Department of Health (DoH) (2015) *Special Educational Needs and Disability Code of Practice: 0 to 25 Years*. [online] Available at: https://assets.publishing. service.gov.uk/government/uploads/system/uploads/attachment_data/file/398815/SEND_ Code_of_Practice_January_2015.pdf (accessed 8 June 2023).

Education Endowment Foundation (2021) Special Educational Needs in Mainstream Schools. [online] Available at: https://educationendowmentfoundation.org.uk/education-evidence/guidance-reports/ send (accessed 12 June 2023).

Fiarman, S E (2016) Unconscious Bias: When Good Intentions Aren't Enough. *Educational Leadership*, 74(3): 10–15. [online] Available at: www.responsiveclassroom.org/wp-content/uploads/2017/10/ Unconscious-Bias_Ed-Leadership.pdf (accessed 12 June 2023).

Fischer Family Trust (n d) [online] Available at: https://fft.org.uk (accessed 14 June 2023).

Florian, L, Rouse, M, Black-Hawkins, K, and Jull, S (2004) What Can National Data Sets Tell Us about Inclusion and Pupil Achievement? *British Journal of Special Education*, 31(3): 115–21.

GL Assessment (n d) Cognitive Abilities Test (CAT). [online] Available at: www.gl-assessment.co.uk/ assessments/cat4 (accessed 8 June 2023).

Harlen, W and Deakin Crick, R (2003) Testing and Motivation for Learning. *Assessment in Education: Principles, Policy and Practice*, 10(2): 169–207.

Henderson, J and Corry, M (2021) Data Literacy Training and Use for Educational Professionals. *Journal of Research in Innovative Teaching & Learning*, 14(2): 232–44.

Jang, Y and Marshall, E (2018) The Effect of Type of Feedback in Multiple-Choice Testing on Long-Term Retention. *The Journal of General Psychology*, 145(2): 107–19.

Kerr, B, and Dai, D Y (2020) *Cognitive Abilities Test: Teacher Guidance*. GL Assessment. [online] Available at: https://support.gl-assessment.co.uk/media/2793/cat4-uk-admin-guide.pdf (accessed 12 June 2023).

Mandinach, E and Gummer, E (2016) What Does It Mean for Teachers to Be Data Literate: Laying Out the Skills, Knowledge, and Dispositions. *Teaching and Teacher Education*, 60: 366–76.

Reay, D and Wiliam, D (1999) 'I'll Be a Nothing': Structure, Agency and the Construction of Identity through Assessment. *British Educational Research Journal*, 25(3): 343–54.

TES (2019) Data Collection Available from TES Provision Mapping. [online] Available at: www. provisionmap.co.uk/data-collection/ (accessed 12 June 2023).

Tsai, M J, Hou, H T, Lai, M L, Liu, W Y and Yang, F Y (2012) Visual Attention for Solving Multiple-Choice Science Problem: An Eye-Tracking Analysis. *Computers and Education*, 58(1): 375–85.

# 12 Improving outcomes through evidence-based practice and practitioner enquiry

**STEPHANIE BREWSTER**

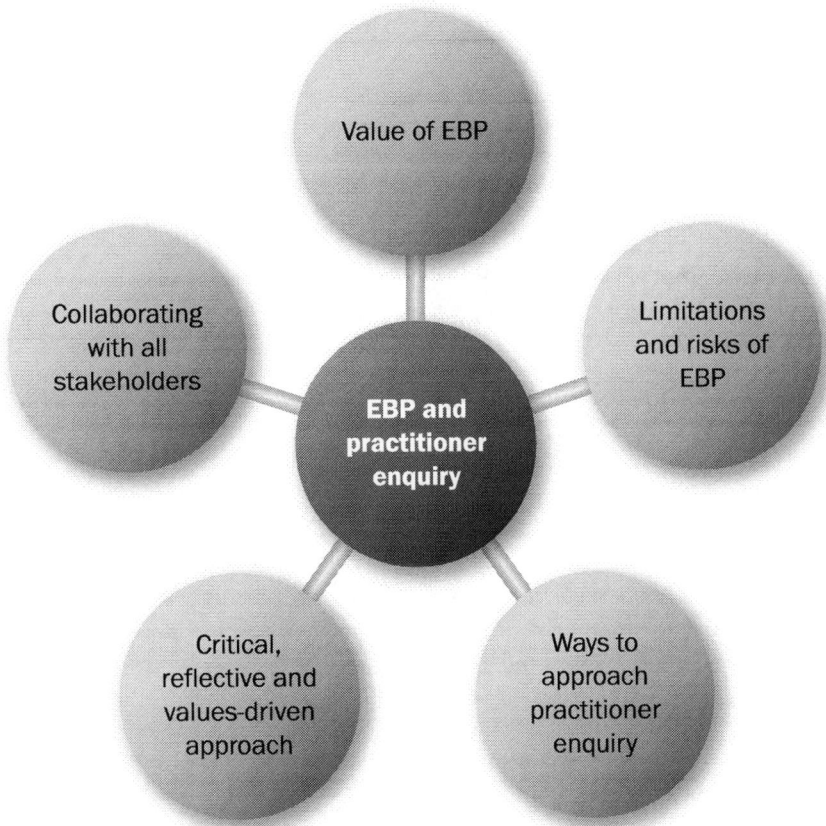

# Chapter objectives 🎯

Evidence takes many forms, deriving from both published sources and from enquiry situated in a practitioner's setting. Learner outcomes can be enhanced by the careful use of such evidence to inform practice. This chapter:

- makes the case for evidence-based practice (EBP) in inclusive education;

- critiques EBP;

- argues for gathering your own evidence through practitioner enquiry or research;

- offers a simple framework for conducting your own investigations through cycles of plan, do, review;

- provides a case study to illustrate the use of Lesson Study (LS) to support practitioner enquiry;

- recommends both EBP and practitioner enquiry to support a critical and reflective orientation to practice;

## STARTING POINTS 🏁

» How confident are you that the interventions used in your setting demonstrate evidence of effectiveness?

» Do you know how to access and make use of such evidence within your own setting? If not, how can you find out?

» What does the word 'research' mean to you?

# Introduction

This chapter conceives of practitioners as learners and aims to act as a catalyst for '*questioning taken-for-granted assumptions in order to enable social progress – a conceptualization of education as a force for actively developing knowledge, rather than passively accepting the current social and political arrangements – the status quo*' (Thompson, 2017, p 50). SENCos, as advocates for inclusive practice, benefit from being both skilled 'consumers' of research and knowledge through evidence-based practice (EBP), and also 'producers' of knowledge through conducting small-scale practitioner enquiry.

Professional practice is continually evolving in response to the changing policy and legal context, societal expectations and our ever-evolving 'knowledge' (Thompson, 2017). SENCos need to appreciate how research evidence and professional judgement can advance the boundaries of their discipline. This is the basis of critically reflective practice (see Chapter 10) which enables us to move beyond assumptions, habits, customs, prejudices, erroneous or out-of-date beliefs, and to develop a deeper understanding of complexity. This understanding necessarily involves listening to and collaborating with children and young people, their families and those who work with them (Armstrong, 2019).

# Evidence-based practice

Evidence-based education is part of the wider movement of EBP that has developed in recent decades, taking inspiration from evidence-based medicine. It goes without question that a patient would want to be offered treatment for which there is good evidence of its effectiveness; so why would a learner not expect similar from their education system? Arguably, persisting with approaches with no evidence of effectiveness is unethical, wasteful and inefficient and risks ineffective decisions being made (DfE, 2017). The obviousness of this position nevertheless obscures some problematic issues to do with the nature of evidence and how it is used (discussed below).

Despite concerns, evidence-based approaches are enshrined within UK education policies, aiming to improve outcomes for learners. In 2022, the UK government confirmed its commitment to educational research and evidence-based educational practice, recognising the need for guidance and support for schools to access and use evidence (DfE, 2022). Likewise, the National Standards for children and young people with SEND proposed by the government in 2023 are to be explicitly evidence based.

Whatever one's views about government agendas around 'driving up standards', there are legitimate concerns (DfE, 2016) about teachers' capacity to access evidence and translate it into practice, and about the evidence bases being patchy, insufficiently robust and not reflective of the priorities of schools (DfE, 2016, p 39). Pegram et al (2022) surveyed the interventions used by schools to address various areas of SEND and found a lack of robust empirical evidence of effectiveness: over two-thirds of interventions had no published evidence, and moderate to high-quality evidence of effectiveness existed for only 11 per cent of interventions being used. Even when presented with summaries of evidence, not all schools used it to make informed decisions. The research found that teachers tend to rely more on anecdotal evidence than external evidence indicating positive impact; and sometimes good-quality relevant evidence may simply not be available. 'Lack of time, underdeveloped research skills, negative attitudes and opinions of evidence' (Pegram et al, 2022, pp 35–6) all acted as barriers. Clearly, despite the SEND Code of Practice (DfE and DoH, 2015) requirement for using 'well-evidenced interventions', this does not always happen.

Texts such as Mitchell's (2020) popular and appealingly titled *What Really Works in Special and Inclusive Education: Using Evidence-Based Teaching Strategies* appear to promise a solution to the need for SENCos to have an up-to-date repertoire of strategies for which evidence exists. This is also recognised in many postgraduate professional programmes of study, such as the National Award for SENCos, learning outcomes for which include the ability to critically evaluate various forms of evidence to inform and improve practice (NCTL, 2014). Such skills can be conceptualised as 'research literacy':

> *the extent to which teachers and school and college leaders are familiar with a range of research methods, with the latest research findings and with the implications of this research for their day-to-day practice, and for education policy and practice more broadly. To be research literate is to 'get' research – to understand why it is important and what might be learnt from it, and to maintain a sense of critical appreciation and healthy scepticism throughout.*
>
> (BERA-RSA, 2014, p 40)

EBP is about creating a culture of enquiry, in which professional decision making is routinely based on evaluation of various sources of evidence (the importance of critical reflection to this is discussed in Chapter 10). Teachers thereby become empowered to make informed and independent decisions, appropriate to the immediate context. Such an approach is especially important when supporting pupils with complex learning needs; Mulholland (n d) likens the process to a detective gathering clues from various sources to solve the mystery of how an individual child learns: *'the more evidence you collect, the better informed you are'* (no page).

---

### Resources to support evidence-based practice

» MESH Guides (www.new.meshguides.org) *'provide teachers and other educators with quick access to summaries of research-based specialist knowledge to support their professional judgement'*.

» Nasen Whole School SEND What Works (www.wholeschoolsend.org.uk/page/what-works) provides resources which have a positive evidence base, *'organised within the Graduated Response to Need Framework'*.

» ResearchEd (https://researched.org.uk) aims *'to bridge the gap between research and practice in education'* and to raise the research literacy of educators.

» The Centre for the Use of Research Evidence in Education www.curee.co.uk translates research findings into materials usable by teachers and policymakers to *'inform and enhance teaching and learning'*.

» The Education Endowment Foundation publishes guidance reports and accessible summaries of educational research: https://educationendowmentfoundation.org.uk/education-evidence. Also, the Toolkit helps you find and use evidence about effectiveness: https://educationendowmentfoundation.org.uk/education-evidence/teaching-learning-toolkit

» The Research Schools Network (https://researchschool.org.uk) is a network of schools that support the use of evidence to improve teaching practice.

---

## Critiques of evidence-based practice

Not only is critical engagement with the evidence essential; critique must also be applied to the concept of EBP itself. There has been growing doubt about the feasibility of evidence-based education for some time despite it retaining significant intuitive appeal for politicians, policymakers, practitioners and researchers (Biesta, 2010). Concerns arise mainly from the distortion of the concept, which has become overly associated with experimental research, especially randomised controlled trials (Dekker and Meeter, 2022). Thus 'scientific', quantitative research is preferred over a more diverse range of research approaches. Findings from such research are not always helpful to teachers, may not reflect their concerns or may not apply to their context; thus, findings may shed no light on *why* an intervention works.

Dekker and Meeter (2022) warn of the oversimplified promises of a 'what works' approach, which risks excluding professional judgement, critical reflection and interrogation of one's own practice (Biesta, 2010). Wang and Lam (2017) claim that EBP frequently lacks cultural responsiveness, and rarely acknowledges how sociocultural factors affect the impact of evidence-based practices. Requirements for fidelity in the implementation of an intervention (ie being carried out in the way in which it is intended) preclude flexibility and responsiveness to the cultural diversity of learners. Adaptation is essential to meet the needs of non-dominant cultural groups: much evidence of effectiveness reflects our culture's conceptualisation of what counts as knowledge, what constitutes effectiveness and for whom (Wang and Lam, 2017).

# Engaging in practitioner enquiry

Conducting educational research as a practitioner is never value neutral. Moore (2019, p xv) sees it as a route for teachers '*to try to turn their commitment to the values and ideals of inclusive education into the actuality of inclusion for children and young people*'. Hallett and Hallett (2012) argue that inclusive practice is always enquiry-led practice, whereby inclusive practitioners routinely and continuously interrogate their own practice with a view to improving teaching and learning for all. These authors call for a thoughtful approach to research that acknowledges the complex ethical considerations that arise when researching 'marginalised learners'. Central to this is power. They question the moral value of creating and researching interventions for learners who have no ownership over them, thereby reinforcing the power dynamics inherent in compulsory education. Professional values such as integrity, open-mindedness, wisdom and courage underpin teacher professionalism and should equally form the basis of your research.

Systematic and reflective programmes of enquiry based on one's own practice and setting (taken alongside other evidence) explicitly aim to bring about change in your setting. The term 'research' might be off-putting to practitioners, but it is helpful to have an inclusive and wide-ranging definition of the term to mean '*any deliberate investigation that is carried out with a view to learning more about a particular educational issue*' (BERA-RSA 2014, p 40).

Engaging in research not only enhances practitioners' research literacy, but also enables you to gather your own empirical evidence in response to the 'particularities' of your own setting and uniqueness of the children and young people you are engaging with (Armstrong, 2019). While some may dismiss small-scale research as anecdotal and not generalisable beyond the specific setting, Richards and Starbuck (2020) assert that the depth of local understanding and relevance achieved through 'insider' perspectives can have real benefits for practice. Indeed, there is increasing recognition of the kind of knowledge accrued through experience, and created and shared with colleagues, children and young people and their families. Teaching is a complex, situated form of professional practice, which draws on professional judgement as well as various forms of evidence (DfE, 2017). It is perhaps rare for published research findings to be applied directly to practice; it is more likely that research literature will inform debates with colleagues, leading to trying out new approaches and evaluating their outcomes. Practitioner enquiry therefore can address some of the limitations of EBP identified above.

There is strong support among commentators in the field for the continued requirement for SENCos to have the ability to use a range of research methods applicable to their professional activities and to '*undertake small-scale practitioner enquiry to identify, develop and rigorously evaluate effective practice in teaching pupils with SEN and/or disabilities*' (NCTL, 2014, p 7) (see Chapter 10). Small-scale research, practical in nature and directly relevant to what is happening (Richards and Starbuck, 2020), helps ensure our interventions have the desired (positive) impact. Richards and Starbuck (2020) explain how research can inform decision making about interventions or strategies at two levels:

- selecting those which have been rigorously tested, and then;
- ascertaining their effectiveness with individual pupils.

BERA-RSA (2014) claim that research literacy and engagement correlate with teaching quality, and therefore student outcomes.

## Undertaking your own investigations

Independent enquiry comes under various labels, including appreciative enquiry, reflexivity, reflection and critical enquiry. Action research (AR) and Lesson Study (LS), two of the most common approaches, are discussed below. Whatever approach is taken, such activity goes beyond the personal; it involves an explicit rationale, an approach that is made clear and can be defended, and findings that will be shared (Cardiff Metropolitan University, 2019). Conducting your own enquiries aligns with the graduated response to SEND (DfE and DoH, 2015), which refers to the Assess, Plan, Do, Review cycle (see Figure 12.1).

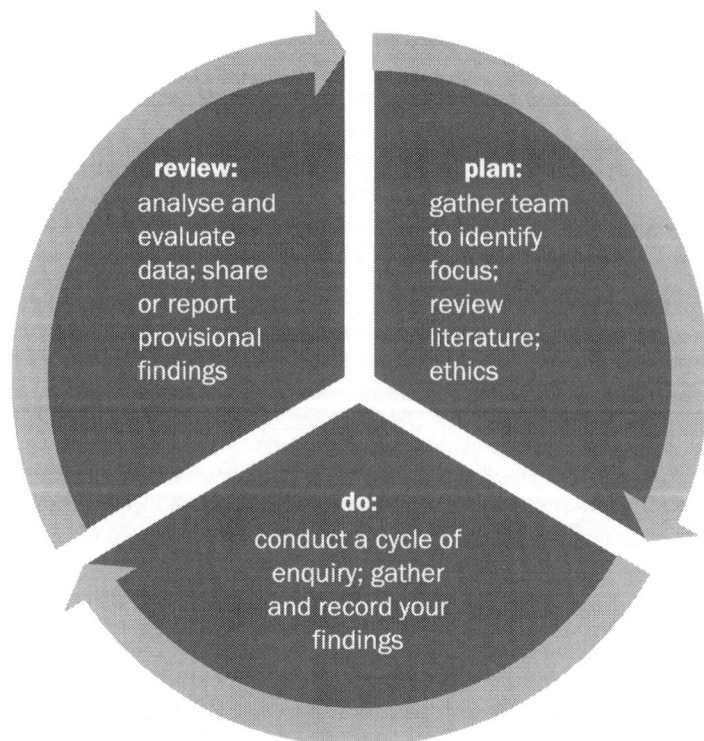

**review:**
analyse and evaluate data; share or report provisional findings

**plan:**
gather team to identify focus; review literature; ethics

**do:**
conduct a cycle of enquiry; gather and record your findings

**Figure 12.1** *A cycle of independent enquiry*

There is no need to strictly adhere to any one approach but having some structure to your investigation can lend considerable credibility to your outcomes. Both AR and LS are 'tried and tested' approaches to small-scale enquiries in an educational context. While LS is specific to evaluating lesson teaching and sharing outcomes within a small team, AR encompasses a broader range of research activities with a view to changing any aspect of practice. Importantly, both lend themselves to incorporating pupil voice as a source of evidence within the enquiry. The true value of an investigation is only realised when your project is seen not as a one-off piece of work, but as ongoing and viewed as integral to the process of becoming inclusive.

---

### *Resources to support practitioner enquiry*

» Brahm Norwich's webpages at Exeter University are aimed specifically at using Lesson Study for special needs and inclusive education: www.lessonstudysend. co.uk/

» Lesson Study guidance booklets and templates can be found at www. lessonstudysend.co.uk/develop-teaching-approaches

» General information on Lesson Study can be found at https://tdtrust.org/ lessonstudy

» National Foundation for Educational Research's collection of 'How to' guides for those conducting their own educational research projects: www.nfer.ac.uk/ how-to-guides-collection

» Nasen (2021) National Award for SEN Co-ordination SENCO Research Posters: https://nasen.org.uk/resources/nasenco-research-posters

---

## Plan your investigation

Your starting point will be a 'real-life' issue or concern. But this must be more than a personal hunch. If identified as a priority in your school improvement or development plan, you are more likely to get support from your leadership team. AR and LS are inherently collaborative from the outset: the agenda should be set by the learning community in a democratic way (Armstrong and Moore, 2004). This should also include children and young people and their families, and recognise the diversity of cultural and family backgrounds (Wang and Lam, 2017).

It is worth recognising at this early stage that you may encounter resistance to your investigation: questioning practices that for some have been their usual way of working for a long time can be profoundly discomforting. Conducting research can cause tensions as policy and practice receive scrutiny and critique. This underlines the importance of enquiry being a collaborative process, supported by leadership, and of a suitably facilitative (rather than defensive) research environment, which acknowledges the insight that research can generate.

## Identify your focus

Think ahead to the kind of impact you hope to achieve. It is often helpful to frame your focus as a question such as:

- What is the impact of X intervention on Y group of learners?
- How do teachers/learners/parents perceive or experience X situation or intervention?
- Why was X intervention more effective for some pupils than others?

## Engage with existing evidence

Your initial area of interest will need to be narrowed, refined or adjusted – and this can take time. You will need to search out locally held, pre-existing data, both quantitative (eg attainment, exclusions, behaviour incidence) and qualitative (eg pupil voice findings, inspection reports) (Dekker and Meeter, 2022). This knowledge enables you to justify your topic and identify the gaps which may need to be filled with your own new empirical data.

Being well informed about your topic entails having a thorough and critical understanding of relevant policy, theory and previous research findings. Original research articles and reports may be somewhat inaccessible to a practitioner readership; 'Resources to support evidence-based practice' above suggests several useful digests of research findings.

At this stage you aim to make explicit the theories, beliefs and values held by all stakeholders, and to consider alternative theoretical perspectives as a source of ideas (Armstrong, 2019).

## Keep your investigation ethical

Most aspects of your investigation will usually be covered by your professional code of conduct, but sometimes additional ethical considerations may be raised. In these cases, you would be well advised to approach this as a matter of 'research ethics'. Gaining ethical approval may be a part of a formal programme of study and require explicit compliance with BERA (2018) guidelines. This entails relatively practical matters pertaining to permission and consent, the right to withdraw, confidentiality, the risk of harm, secure data storage and so on. Additionally, securing fully informed consent from children takes considerable care and time. Hallett and Hallett (2012) go as far as to say that if children cannot be meaningfully enabled to consent to take part in your research, then it should not proceed.

Whatever form your enquiry takes, a key principle is that your investigation brings about no harm to learners, colleagues or other stakeholders; 'harm' is broad and could cover missing out on the benefits available to other learners, embarrassment, upset or additional workload.

---

### Critical questions (?)

» What do your pupils, parents, colleagues and senior leadership team (SLT) see as priorities for investigation?

» How might you realistically go about conducting your enquiry, and what ethical issues might arise?

» Will the outcome of your enquiry reinforce existing practice in ways that continue to disempower learners, or will it empower them, supporting their self-advocacy? In other words, how will your investigation enact your commitment to your professional values?

---

## Conduct your investigation

Your data collection methods must be practical and appropriate to the question(s) you are hoping to answer. LS offers a highly structured approach in which a strategy is implemented and observed, and the learners are asked about their experience; strategies are then adapted through subsequent cycles of enquiry. Methods of collecting data within the broader approach of AR could include questionnaires, observations, notes, interviews, focus groups and informal feedback from pupils, parents and colleagues (see 'Resources to support practitioner enquiry' above and the case study). Documentary evidence may also be available in your setting or area.

## Review your investigation

Reviewing the evidence gathered, your team will reflect on whether the desired outcomes were achieved, and whether your data adequately answers your research questions. Keep an open mind and be prepared for findings you had not anticipated or which might not be popular; findings may be contradictory and far from tidy. Your analysis should summarise your data; interpret it and consider alternative interpretations; and identify patterns and relationships, commonalities and differences. It should be possible to make connections between your new data and published literature. Reflecting on your data then leads to as many further cycles as is useful.

You will decide at what point you are able to make concrete realistic recommendations based on your findings. These might relate to your experience of engaging in your investigation, as well as reporting its content. Given that your aim will be to ultimately improve practice, you need to consider how you will share what you have found in a persuasive and sensitive way. Provided that it is ethically acceptable to do so, you could:

• present anonymous examples of learners' work, or what they said about their experiences;

• use visual methods, eg photos, tables, charts and graphs showing quantitative data;

• write a full report, or a summary to go into a newsletter;

• create a poster or slideshow to present at meetings.

## CASE STUDY ☻

### Using Lesson Study to gather evidence of barriers to learning

Lucy Mayes, SENCo

### Focus

We aimed to identify barriers, address concerns and raise achievement of children identified as having dyscalculic tendencies in a Year 4 maths class.

### Rationale

Our whole-school development plan has prioritised the development of our maths provision for children with SEND. An LS was developed to improve the knowledge of teaching staff and refine strategies to support pupils with dyscalculic tendencies.

A review of the literature indicated that understanding and acceptance of dyscalculia is poor despite affecting 4–7 per cent of children (similar to dyslexia). It can have substantial impacts on educational attainment and subsequent employment outcomes.

### What we did

The two LS case pupils were in the bottom maths set, working below age-related expectations. They were chosen based on their summative test results, observations made by their maths teacher and feedback from parents. Diagnostic assessment suggested that both pupils displayed dyscalculic tendencies.

The introductory conversation with them revealed that both enjoyed maths and felt confident but found it hard. Pupil A mentioned confusing mathematical symbols. Both case pupils relied on what they knew 'off by heart' rather than applying a learnt strategy.

We conducted two LS cycles; during the first, the class teacher used her usual strategies. It was observed that gaps in pupils' knowledge of numbers hindered their learning. Afterwards, when questioned, it was apparent that the pupils did not know how division applied to real life or why they were learning it. In the post-lesson discussion, the team decided that daily starters focused on improving number sense would be beneficial. It would also avoid having to remove the case study pupils for separate interventions. In the second LS cycle, the maths teacher introduced a starter linked to the assessment to build number sense, and gave examples of how division linked to real life.

### Outcomes

Pupil A achieved all the learning objectives and was confident in her approach to learning. The strategies worked and she was able to apply them independently to more complicated word problems in the second LS. Following this, Pupil A was able to evidence her learning and apply it to her own experience of having to share sweets with her brother.

Pupil B did not achieve either learning objective. She appeared nervous and displayed delay tactics. Following the first research lesson, we planned for Pupil B to complete the previous step to help with her understanding; the teacher modelled the method and checked in with her. It highlighted to the team the importance of changing strategy if it didn't work.

### Reflection on the value of LS

The LS supported not only the identified pupils but the whole class. The post-lesson interviews proved particularly useful in refining teaching and learning as teachers are made aware of pupils' perspectives. Through LS, our team were able to gain deeper insight into the teaching and learning process. The teaching assistant felt particularly empowered by the LS process, especially the post-lesson discussions.

There were limitations to this approach such as the time it takes to invest in LS in an already crowded timetable; staff absences and the timing of the LS meant that only two cycles were carried out, impacting the strength of our findings.

Despite LS being a collaborative approach, it can feel like teachers' performance rather than pupil learning is what is being observed and judged and having members of SLT being part of the observation group added pressure. Also, what the children say can feel like a negative reflection on our teaching. If we proceed with LS, perhaps members of the SLT could be observed first.

---

## Critical questions ?

How do you think the process of engaging in the case study project

- » benefitted the learning of the individual pupils?
- » promoted the professional development of those directly involved?
- » contributed to the development of inclusive practice in the setting more widely?

---

## Implications for the SENCo role, identity and practice

- » Senior leadership is influential in creating an organisational culture which facilitates practitioner learning, development and enquiry (Thompson, 2017). Such research-rich environments are important to promote and enhance teachers' research literacy and engagement (BERA-RSA, 2014), which in turn have a positive impact on learner outcomes.

→

> » Teachers who are research literate are empowered to enhance their practice through an ongoing process of reflection and enquiry (BERA-RSA, 2014).
>
> » There is a widespread need for professional development to enhance the research literacy of the SEND workforce, but also engagement in practitioner enquiry is itself a powerfully developmental activity.

## Chapter summary

Practising in an evidence-based way entails deep critical reflection on the nature of knowledge; its many sources can result in complex, possibly contradictory and often incomplete data (see Chapter 11). Among these sources are the use of approaches such as AR and LS to create one's own evidence, which can address issues of relevance to the local context. Conducting practitioner enquiry *'challenges the status quo and... become[s] a vehicle by which power relations are levelled across a school community'* (Hallett and Hallett, 2012, p 114). When such endeavours are *'emancipatory, empowering and ethical'* (Hallett and Hallett, 2012, p 119), professional enquiry enables practitioners to contest top-down policy and practice, and test their own assumptions about pupils' learning. It gives a voice to all stakeholders through collaborative approaches to addressing challenges in the journey towards inclusion for learners with SEND.

## Further reading

Armstrong, F and Tsokova, D (2019) *Action Research for Inclusive Education Participation and Democracy in Teaching and Learning*. London: Routledge.

- This book takes a social constructivist approach to practitioner research in educational contexts, highlighting relationships between theory, research and practice.

Education Endowment Foundation (2021) Special Educational Needs in Mainstream Schools. [online] Available at: https://educationendowmentfoundation.org.uk/education-evidence/guidance-reports/send (accessed 19 July 2023).

- Provides an overview of the best available evidence about teaching pupils with SEND in mainstream schools. Both the full Guidance Report and Summary of Recommendations Poster can be found at the above link.

Norwich, B and Jones, J (eds) (2014) *Lesson Study: Making a Difference to Teaching Pupils with Learning Difficulties*. London: Continuum Publishers.

- The book integrates LS with the principles of inclusion to enhance reflective practice.

## References

Armstrong, F (2019) Social Constructivism and Action Research: Transforming Teaching and Learning through Collaborative Practice. In Armstrong, F and Tsokova, D (eds) *Action Research for Inclusive Education Participation and Democracy in Teaching and Learning* (Chapter 1). London: Routledge.

Armstrong, F and Moore, M (2004) *Action Research for Inclusive Education: Changing Places, Changing Practice, Changing Minds*. London: Routledge Falmer.

BERA (2018) *Ethical Guidelines for Educational Research 2018*. [online] Available at: www.bera.ac.uk/publication/ethical-guidelines-for-educational-research-2018 (accessed 15 April 2023).

BERA-RSA (2014) *Research and the Teaching Profession: Building the Capacity for a Self-improving Education System*. London: BERA. [online] Available at: www.thersa.org/globalassets/pdfs/bera-rsa-research-teaching-profession-full-report-for-web-2.pdf (accessed 15 April 2023).

Biesta, G J J (2010) Why 'What Works' Still Won't Work: From Evidence-Based Education to Value-Based Education. *Studies in Philosophy and Education*, 29(5): 491–503.

Cardiff Metropolitan University (2019) *Undertaking Professional Enquiry: An Introduction for Lead Enquirers*. [online] Available at: https://hwb.gov.wales/api/storage/aeb2810d-f670-4718-87a1-299696ce5156/guide-to-undertaking-professional-enquiry.pdf (accessed 15 April 2023).

Dekker, I and Meeter, M (2022) Evidence-Based Education: Objections and Future Directions. *Frontiers in Education*, 7: 941410.

Department for Education (DfE) (2016) *Educational Excellence Everywhere*. White Paper. London: DfE. [online] Available at: www.gov.uk/government/publications/educational-excellence-everywhere (accessed 15 April 2023).

Department for Education (DfE) (2017) *Evidence-Informed Teaching: An Evaluation of Progress in England. Research Report*. [online] Available at: https://assets.publishing.service.gov.uk/government/uploads/system/uploads/attachment_data/file/625007/Evidence-informed_teaching_-_an_evaluation_of_progress_in_England.pdf (accessed 15 April 2023).

Department for Education (DfE) (2022) *Opportunity for All: Strong Schools with Great Teachers for Your Child*. [online] Available at: https://assets.publishing.service.gov.uk/government/uploads/system/uploads/attachment_data/file/1063602/Opportunity_for_all_strong_schools_with_great_teachers_for_your_child__print_version_.pdf (accessed 15 April 2023).

Department for Education (DfE) and Department of Health (DoH) (2015) *Special Educational Needs and Disability Code of Practice: 0 to 25 Years*. [online] Available at: https://assets.publishing.service.gov.uk/government/uploads/system/uploads/attachment_data/file/398815/SEND_Code_of_Practice_January_2015.pdf (accessed 23 May 2023).

Hallett, F and Hallett, G (2012) Inclusive and Ethical Research. In Cornwall, J and Graham-Matheson, L (Eds) *Leading on Inclusion: Dilemmas, Debates and New Perspectives*. Abingdon: Routledge.

Mitchell, D R (2020) *What Really Works in Special and Inclusive Education: Using Evidence-Based Teaching Strategies*. 3rd ed. London: Routledge.

Moore, M (2019) Foreword. In Armstrong, F and Tsokova, D (eds) *Action Research for Inclusive Education: Participation and Democracy in Teaching and Learning* (pp xv–xvi). London: Routledge.

Mulholland, M (n d) *SEND and the Art of Detection: An Evidence Based Approach to Supporting Learners*. [online] Available at: https://my.chartered.college/early-career-hub/send-and-the-art-of-detection-an-evidence-based-approach-to-supporting-learners (accessed 13 April 2023).

Nasen (2014) *SEN Support and the Graduated Approach: A Quick Guide to Ensuring That Every Child or Young Person Gets the Support They Require to Meet Their Needs*. [online] Available at: https://nasen-prod-asset.s3.eu-west-2.amazonaws.com/s3fs-public/sen_support_press_0.pdf (accessed 15 April 2023).

National College for Teaching and Leadership (NCTL) (2014) National Award for SEN Co-ordination Learning Outcomes. [online] Available at: www.gov.uk/government/publications/national-award-for-sen-co-ordination-learning-outcomes (accessed 15 April 2023).

Pegram, J, Watkins R C, Hoerger M and Hughes, J C (2022) Assessing the Range and Evidence-Base of Interventions in a Cluster of Schools. *Review of Education*, 10(1). https://doi.org/10.1002/rev3.3336

Richards, G and Starbuck, J (eds) (2020) *Effective Interventions and Strategies for Pupils with SEND: Using Evidence-Based Methods for Maximum Impact*. London: Routledge.

Teacher Development Trust (n d) What Is Lesson Study? [online] Available at: https://tdtrust.org/what-is-lesson-study (accessed 15 April 2023).

Thompson, N (2017) *Theorizing Practice: A Guide for the People Professions*. London: Macmillan.

Wang, M and Lam, Y (2017) Evidence-Based Practice in Special Education and Cultural Adaptations: Challenges and Implications for Research. *Research and Practice for Persons with Severe Disabilities*, 42(1): 53–61.

# Conclusion

This book demonstrates the considerable breadth and depth of challenges that SENCos face as they work to support children and young people identified as having SEND. We have framed this challenge as generative and positive when supported by opportunities for professional development and learning. These opportunities can be formal or informal, planned or unplanned, proactive or reactive – but what is common across the chapters is the sense that professional learning plays a vital role in identity formation and well-being. At the core of this professional learning is a critical and reflective conceptualisation of the role of the SENCo (as discussed in Chapter 1): to be an expert does not merely entail accumulating knowledge and knowledge building. Certainly, Chapter 3 and Chapter 5 emphasise the idea that expertise is not to be found in the ability to list everything one knows about every possible area of need in a school setting. Rather, it is the ability to confidently scaffold critical reflection with and for colleagues and offer solutions founded in inclusive pedagogies (Chapter 3) which offers a sustainable route to the solid role identities that Hazel Richards explores in Chapter 2.

Throughout the book we have offered a plethora of examples, activities, ideas, reflections resources and tools for practice. These can be used both to support the professional development of a SENCo at an individual level, and for training activities with colleagues. The tools can scaffold and structure difficult conversations that may be necessary if aspects of school provision are to be developed. We have reflected on the importance of ensuring that time and space is offered for SENCos as part of their role. Curran and Boddison (2021) have demonstrated that workload issues for SENCos often result in the lack of time SENCos have for their own learning. It is reasonable to assume that time for learning would be bumped to the bottom of a 'to do' list if other priorities become too 'urgent'. However, supportive settings protect learning and development time to allow space for transformation and innovation by SENCos and to prioritise their well-being. Chapter 12 has explored the ways that SENCos, if practising in evidence-based and 'research literate' ways, will be able to offer informed critiques of approaches that might not be relevant or suited to their setting. Such a stance offers the ability to 'speak back' to account-ability measures that are punitive or harmful to a school community, as was explored in Chapter 4.

We reflect on three core themes that connect all the chapters in this book, and we would encourage SENCos to consider the ways that these themes impact on their role, both at a day-to-day level but also in terms of their strategic work. The core themes are the following:

- care;
- collaboration;
- challenge.

## Care

This theme relates to the vital role that the SENCo plays in modelling care for pupils and colleagues. It speaks to their responsibilities to centre care in their working practices but also prompts conversations about how we 'see' care happening in practice. Tronto (2013) argues that in organisations (like schools) we should be alert to situations where it is possible for some people not to care about issues of inclusion – Chapter 4 supported reflections on what this might mean for SENCos. In practice, this means SENCos think-ing about care in forming productive and fulfilling relationships, for example in their work with parents and carers and in developing reflective and critical engagement with their work. This could clearly be seen in Chapters 7 and 8, where the authors explored the ways that SENCos consider the lived experiences of children and young people and their fami-lies beyond the school gates. In this way, SENCos are more likely to be working in ways that centre social justice and inclusive practice. Additionally, we think Chapters 3 and 6 prompt reflection on SENCos developing their repertoire of inclusive pedagogies. SENCos, perhaps more than any other role aside from senior leadership, work with a wide range of people and the ability to do this well has a huge bearing on the success (or otherwise) of SEND provision in a setting.

## Collaboration

The chapters in this book have shown that when SENCos work in partnership, they can make a significant impact in their settings. SENCos can help families navigate the complex spe-cial educational needs system by providing them with information about available services, entitlements and rights, as seen in Chapter 8. SENCos act as a bridge between families and the school, facilitating open and effective communication and when working within a social justice framework, rather than an administrative and bureaucratic orientation, they can help families express their concerns, share relevant information about their child's needs and ensure that their voices are heard in decision-making processes. SENCos' collaboration with external agencies, such as local authorities, educational psychologists or healthcare profes-sionals, to ensure that families receive appropriate support and services are unique to the SENCo role, as Chapter 9 has established.

# Challenge

All chapters outline the challenges that the SENCo experiences in their day-to-day work. We have offered tangible tools, for example in Chapters 10, 11 and 12, to think further about how these challenges could be overcome, reframed or confronted. The challenges we have explored are varied but relate to the following areas when developing inclusive provision.

- Meeting diverse needs: SENCos work with a wide range of students with different learning abilities, disabilities and special educational needs. In an inclusive context, this diversity is to be celebrated and SENCos play an important role in this process.

- Balancing the individual needs of each student and providing appropriate support can be a complex task but one where SENCo expertise is vital.

- Legal and policy compliance: SENCos must ensure compliance with laws such as the Education Act or the SEND Code of Practice, as well as with policies and guidance; this can be challenging due to their evolving nature.

- Limited resources: Schools often have limited resources, including funding, staff and specialised equipment. SENCos need to work within these constraints to provide the necessary support to students, which can be a constant challenge in relation to ensuring high-quality outcomes for learners on the SEND register.

- Collaboration and co-ordination: SENCos collaborate with teachers, support staff, parents and external agencies to ensure effective support for pupils. Co-ordinating these efforts, maintaining effective communication and fostering positive relationships can be challenging and professional learning and development will be ongoing.

- Time management: SENCos have multiple responsibilities, including assessments, developing individual education plans (IEPs), monitoring progress and liaising with external professionals. Juggling these tasks within limited timeframes can be demanding. When SENCos are part of senior leadership teams their expertise and scope in the role can be properly recognised and understood so that others do not make excessive (and sometimes inappropriate) demands on a SENCo's time.

- Emotional demands: Supporting students with SEND often involves dealing with emotionally challenging situations. SENCos may need to provide emotional support to students, families and even colleagues, while managing their own emotional well-being. Ensuring that SENCo well-being is a priority will prevent role attrition.

- Changing landscape: The field of special educational needs is constantly evolving, with new research, interventions and best practices emerging. SENCos need to stay updated and adapt their practices accordingly, which requires ongoing and active choices about professional development activities.

In managing these challenges, it can be useful to recognise the difference between areas that are in your control (AOC) and areas beyond your control (ABC) (Covey, 1989) (see Figure C.1).

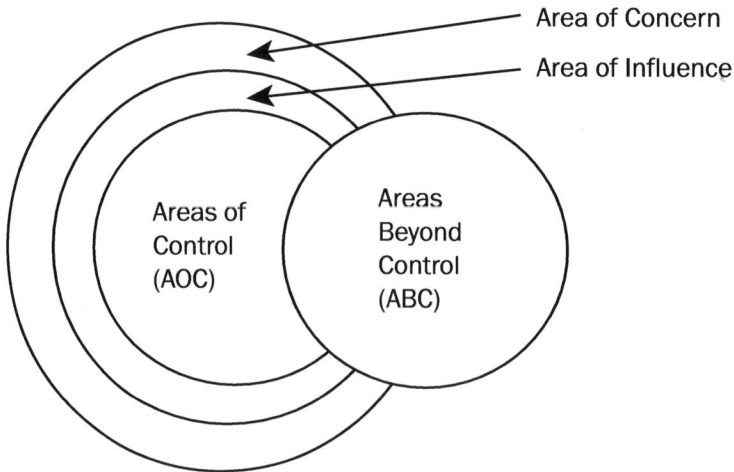

**Figure C.1** *Summary of Covey's (1989) areas of control (AOC), influence and concern, and areas beyond control (ABC)*

This model suggests that whenever you face a conflict or tricky situation, you should work out what areas are in your control and what are ABCs. Focusing on AOCs maximises your impact while identifying ABCs can help preserve your well-being. Covey (1989) distinguishes further between AOCs and areas of influence and concern, with Devi (2023) suggesting:

> If we focus on our area of concern, we reduce our area of influence. If we only focus on our area of control, we never grow. If we stay focused on our area of influence, it increases to meet our area of concern.

> (Devi, 2023, p 113)

We concur that SENCos should identify, be realistic about and grow the areas they can directly influence and change, in order to help progress support for the children and families they work with, and to contribute to their own sense of achievement, well-being and professional or career progression.

## Final thoughts

Our book supports SENCos to ask questions, to reflect on small changes they might make to their daily work and to have conversations with change influencers or impact leaders in their school that will galvanise transformation. We like to imagine a well-worn copy on the desk of SENCos, with highlights, annotations and questions as the book accompanies them through the school year and their continuing career.

Each author has been generous with their time and willingness to engage in the complexities of professional learning and development. Their knowledge and insight come from their research, scholarship and experiences either as a working SENCo, working with SENCos in a leadership position or in their professional development. This means that the resources and tools are rooted in the 'real world' of schools. Even where we have encouraged a critical and theoretical engagement with ideas (for example, in Chapters 5, 10 and 12), it is because the authors believe these elements have a strong role to play in increasing SENCo status and credibility with senior leaders, parents and families, and professionals from other backgrounds.

We want to end by expressing how much we value and respect each one of you – for your diligence and efforts in developing practice to improve outcomes for children and young people with SEND, and their families, in our society. We recognise the commitment of SENCos to removing barriers to learning, advocating for and supporting parents and families as they negotiate the SEND systems, and to showing that an inclusive system where diverse classrooms with learners from all backgrounds can learn and thrive together is possible.

# References

Covey, S R (1989) *The 7 Habits of Highly Effective People: Restoring the Character Ethic.* New York: Simon and Schuster.

Curran, H and Boddison, A (2021) 'It's the Best Job in the World, but One of the Hardest, Loneliest, Most Misunderstood Roles in a School.' Understanding the Complexity of the SENCO Role Post-SEND Reform. *Journal of Research in Special Educational Needs,* 21(1): 39–48

Devi, A (2023) Yielding Influence for Impact. In Devi, A and Bowers, J *Journeying to the Heart of SENCO Wellbeing: A Guide to Enable and Empower SEND Leaders* (pp 100–14). Abingdon: Routledge.

Tronto, J C (2013) *Caring Democracy: Markets, Equality, and Justice.* New York: NYU Press.

# Acronym list

| ACEs | Adverse childhood experiences |
|---|---|
| AP | Alternative provision |
| AR | Action research |
| CPD | Continuing professional development |
| EBP | Evidence-based practice |
| ECCE | Early childhood care and education |
| ECPs | Early childhood practitioners |
| EHCP | Education, health and care plan |
| FE | Further education |
| LS | Lesson Study |
| NPQ | National Professional Qualification |
| PRU | Pupil referral unit |
| SATs | Standardised assessment tests |
| SEN/SEND | Special educational needs / special educational needs and disabilities |
| SENCo | Special educational needs co-ordinator/co-ordination |
| SEND CoP | Special Educational Needs and Disability Code of Practice (2015) |
| SLT | Senior leadership team |
| TA | Teaching assistant |
| TAC | Team Around the Child |

# Index

Note: Page numbers in italics and bold denote figures and tables, respectively.

academic writing, and critical reflections, 141–3, **142**
administrators, support from, 77
adverse childhood experiences (ACEs)
    and Bronfenbrenner model, 95
    critique of, 95–7
    definition of, 94–5
    impact on education, 92–4
    theory and practice, 97–100
advocates, SENCos as, 15–17, 48–9, 55
    challenges in, 50–4
alternative provision (AP) schools, 82–3
areas beyond control (ABC), *176*
areas of control (AOC), *176*

*Bildung*, 28
binaries, 66
Bronfenbrenner's ecological systems model, 93–4, 95
burnout, 55

care, 174
challenges, 26–9, 143, 175
change, adapting to, 175
children needs, construction of, 125
Chris, 136–7
collaboration, 123, *123*, 124, 138, 174, 175, *See also* professionals, working with
collective identity, of SENCo, 22–3
communication skill, 138
Communities of Practice, 126
continuing professional development (CPD), 75
coordination, 175

co-production illusion, 110–12
critical reflections, 170
    and academic writing, 141–3, **142**
    critical incident analysis, 135–7
    developments in, 138–9
    and evidence-based practice, 139–40
    need for, 134
    theory and literature, 134–5
    and well-being, 140–1
critical thinking, 142, **142**
curriculum differentiation, 81

data, 148–9
    and inclusive practice, 153
    types of, 150–2
data literacy
    development of, 152
    elements of, **149**
    meaning and significance of, 149–50
    in practice, 153–4
debates and developments, in SENCo role, 25–6
deputy SENCos, 77
disabled children, 95
disadvantaged children, 95
discourse analyses, 63–4
discourses, 62
diverse needs, managing, 175

early childhood practice, 74–6
ecological systems model (Bronfenbrenner), 93, 93–4, 95
Education and Health Care Plan (EHCP), 13
emotional demands, 175

empathy-based approach, 113
evidence-based practice, 139–40, 161–2
    critiques of, 162–3
    resources for, 162
expecting unexpected behaviours, 99
external model of SENCo status, 22

family quality of life (FQOL), 110
Foucault, M. 127
foundational assumptions, 62–3
further education (FE) practicing, 78–81

Grange, Hannah, 83–4
group functioning, 124

historical development, of SENCo
    role, 10–12

identity, and power, 62
inclusion, 24, 75, 138
    and data, 153
    implications for, 154–5
inclusive pedagogy, 38, 39–41
    all-embracing, 40
    distributed approach in, 39
    mixture of approaches, 40
independent enquiry, 164–5
individual factors, in social context, 124
individual needs, balancing, 175
interaction methods, 99
internal model of SENCo status, 22
international schools, 83–5
interpretivism, 63
intersectionality, 64

Kensett, Kelly, 80
key roles and responsibilities, **11**
knowledge of SENCos, 62–3

leaders, SENCos as, 14–17, 128
    advocate role, 15–17
    specific vs generic, 14–15
legal and policy compliance, 175
local social context, 124
looked after children (LAC), 97

managers, SENCos as, 13
marital relationship breakdowns,
    impact of, 95
marketised education system, operating
    within, 29
Mayes, Lucy, 168–9
Multi-Academy Trusts (MATs), 14

National Professional Qualification
    (NPQ), 139
national standards for SENCos, 11
neoliberalism, impact of, 23, 123
neutrality, 64–5

parents
    communication with, 77
    impact of SEND system on, 106–7
    perspective of, 109–10
    and SENCos, nature of contact
        between, 107–9
parents, working with, 106
    co-production illusion, 110–12
    lessons from practice, 112–13
past, present, and future paradox, 63–4
pedagogy, 36–7, 40–1
    constrains in, 42
    obstacles in, 41–4
    practices, 38
    principles of, 38
    and rights, 38
    scope in, 42–3
    stresses and strains in, 43–4
    values, 38
personal identity of SENCos, 23
person-centredness, 125
policies, and politics, 121–3
possibilities, of SENCos role, 13–14, 28–9
poststructuralism, 66
power, and identity, 62
practical and critical challenges, 26–9
practice, SENCo role in, 12
practitioner enquiry, 163–4
    conducting investigation, 167
    ethics, 166–7
    and existing evidence, 166
    focus, identification of, 166

independent enquiry, 164–5
investigation planning, 165
resources for, 165
reviewing, 167–9
praxis, 66
professional identity of SENCos, 23
professional learning, commitment to, 68
professionalisation, 23
professionals, working with, 120, 127–9
aspirations versus actualities, 124
barriers and enablers, 123–4
children needs, construction of, 125
effectiveness of, 127
identities and powers, 125–6
participation and learning, 126–7
person-centredness, 125
policy and political climate, 121–3
rationale, 121
pupil referral units (PRUs), 82–3
purpose of SENCo, 23–5

Ramsbottom, Sally, 75
resources, limitations of, 175
responsibilisation, 61
rights, and pedagogy, 38
Rose, Phil, 27

scientific paradigm, 62–3
secondary education practice, 76–8
self-care, 140
SENCo identity, 29
across countries, 22
collective, 22–3

personal, 23
professional, 23
SEND and Alternative Provision (AP)
Improvement Plan, 139
SEND Review: Right Support, Right Place,
Right Time, 138
senior leadership, significance of, 169
senior leadership team (SLT), 13, 81
shared understanding, between
professionals, 124
Socrates, 140
speaking up and speaking out, 50–4
special schools practising, 81
specialist subject staff, 77
statutory obligation of schools, 10
strategic leader, SENCo as, 13–14
stresses and strains, 43–4
structuralism, 64–5

Teacher Wellbeing Index, 128
tensions, in SENCo role, 29
terminal examinations, 77
time management, 175
training, 112–13
transformation strategies, 99
trauma, 95
trauma aware approach, 99

values, pedagogical, 38

Warnock Report, significance
of, 10
well-being, 128, 140–1, *141*